HOW TO RECRUIT AND HIRE GREAT SOFTWARE ENGINEERS

BUILDING A CRACK DEVELOPMENT TEAM

Patrick McCuller

Apress·

How to Recruit and Hire Great Software Engineers: Building a Crack Development Team

ISBN-13 (pbk): 978-1-4302-4917-7

ISBN-13 (electronic): 978-1-4302-4918-4

President and Publisher: Paul Manning
Acquisitions Editor: Jeff Olson
Developmental Editor: Robert Hutchinson
Editorial Board: Steve Anglin, Mark Beckner, Ewan Buckingham, Gary Cornell, Louise Corrigan, Morgan Ertel, Jonathan Gennick, Jonathan Hassell, Robert Hutchinson, Michelle Lowman, James Markham, Matthew Moodie, Jeff Olson, Jeffrey Pepper, Douglas Pundick, Ben Renow-Clarke, Dominic Shakeshaft, Gwenan Spearing, Matt Wade, Tom Welsh
Coordinating Editor: Rita Fernando
Copy Editor: Laura Poole
Compositor: SPi Global
Indexer: SPi Global
Cover Designer: Anna Ishchenko

Distributed to the book trade worldwide by Springer-Verlag New York, Inc., 233 Spring Street, 6th Floor, New York, NY 10013. Phone 1-800-SPRINGER, fax 201-348-4505, e-mail orders-ny@springer-sbm.com, or visit www.springeronline.com.

For information on translations, please contact us by e-mail at info@apress.com, or visit www.apress.com.

Apress and friends of ED books may be purchased in bulk for academic, corporate, or promotional use. eBook versions and licenses are also available for most titles. For more information, reference our Special Bulk Sales–eBook Licensing web page at www.apress.com/bulk-sales. To place an order, email your request to support@apress.com

*To Zeno of Elea, who has taught us to question
our assumptions for twenty-four centuries
and counting*

Contents

Foreword

To succeed with software, you need a great team. Not just good—great.

So what does "great" mean? Smart. Focused. Team-oriented, but with a healthy ego and drive. Excellent at both deconstruction and synthesis. A sense of humor. That's just my starting list—yours may be different. No matter what is on your list, you're going to be spending a *lot* of time with these people. Many people spend more time with their coworkers than with their spouses.

Given the stakes involved, you owe it to yourself to get really good at putting teams together. You will succeed either as a team or not at all.

Let's be clear—sometimes you need to trust your gut. If you've been hiring people for a long time, you probably have a bag of tricks for evaluating people. The challenge is for that to not be the end of the game. You may have forgotten why you do the things you do. You may not be able to explain it.

If you are new to hiring, you don't even have that gut feeling to rely on—you're just winging it. Asking senior managers for advice that boils down to "instincts" can be worse than useless.

That's where this book comes in. It breaks down the process of hiring into a structure—something more useful, a full methodology. If you haven't done a lot of hiring, it works as a handbook. If you have done a lot of hiring, it will explain the "why" behind a lot of the little things—and fills in a lot of the kind of gaps that come from ad hoc learning.

There's a great chart in the first chapter. It describes the kinds of challenges you may be having, and you can jump right to the section that discusses solutions. In the book itself, you'll find detailed pipeline diagrams, advice on streamlining the process, interviewing, closing, and more.

Most important, you can start to build a culture around how you hire. You can explain it to your recruiters, your manager, and your team. You can move from a hazy, fuzzy, "wing it" model to one of consistent excellence.

That's how you succeed.

—Will Iverson
Chief Technology Officer
Dynacron Group

About the Author

Patrick McCuller is a software development manager in Seattle, Washington, with eighteen years of engineering and engineering management experience. As an engineer at Microsoft, Sony, and many other companies, and as a development manager at Amazon, Live Nation, and Audience Science, he has conducted hundreds of interviews and made a significant number of extraordinary hires. He has spent countless hours analyzing and engineering the hiring processes, and he loves to interview.

Acknowledgments

The ideas in this book were formed over many years through interaction with many brilliant people—managers, peers, reports, candidates, and friends—so many that I cannot record and acknowledge them all. I hope the great majority will understand when I list just a few of the people whose critical conversation, support, intellectual generosity, and *isshoukenmei* excellence influenced me the most: Mario Adoc, Jonathan Mastin, Ian Bone, Ethan Evans, and Shefali Shukla. In addition, Ian Bone and Will Iverson provided important feedback on an early draft of chapter 7.

This book would not have been possible without Andrew Pasquale, who taught me by example that I am the one who decides what sort of person I will be. Less importantly, but just as well, he also taught me high school calculus. I am grateful for both.

I am indebted to Magdalena Donea for discussing and helping with virtually every topic in this book and for her indefatigable encouragement.

Introduction

This chapter describes the audience and scope of this book and suggests how you can use it to recruit the best software engineers available. It explains the central themes: hiring well is a competitive advantage, treat candidates as well as you treat customers, and take an engineering approach to the recruiting and hiring process. This chapter also provides a troubleshooting table to identify the appropriate chapters for answers to the most common and easily articulated questions.

Who Should Read This Book

This book is intended for technical managers who need to hire software engineers to build core software applications. Technical managers at all levels of hiring experience will benefit from this book—from absolute beginners looking for a place to start to veterans looking for ways to optimize the hiring process. That includes software development managers, directors, chief technology officers (CTOs), and entrepreneurs.

This book is not meant to be a deep analysis of the realm of recruiting. Some topics, such as sourcing candidates, are treated lightly, as hiring managers are less likely to need to drive that process personally. You will, however, learn enough about sourcing to work with and help sourcers and to pinch-hit in that role.

The topics addressed in depth are the most useful to hiring managers, addressing critical points and issues with detail. That includes optimizing the overall process, evaluating résumés, conducting interviews, asking interview questions and interpreting answers, and maximizing the use of allies and partners, such as professional recruiters.

The software engineers who are the subjects of the hiring process described in this book work under many titles:

- Software Engineer
- Software Design Engineer
- Software Development Engineer
- Software Development Engineer in Test
- Principal Engineer
- Programmer
- Lead Engineer
- Java Developer
- UI Developer
- .NET Developer
- Systems Analyst

To a lesser degree, this book will also be helpful when hiring people with the following job titles:

- Operations Engineer
- Support Engineer
- Software Manager
- Information Architect
- General IT staff

How to Use This Book If You're Pressed for Time

The chapters of this book are modular, in the sense that you may read a given chapter in isolation from preceding chapters. After reading this introduction, you may jump to the parts that are specifically relevant to your current recruiting needs. Here's a quick troubleshooting guide.

Not sure what kind of person to hire?	Chapter 1
Process is slow or unwieldy?	Chapter 2
Not finding enough candidates?	Chapter 3
Résumés don't help distinguish good candidates from bad candidates?	Chapter 4
Interviews aren't going well, or not hiring at all?	Chapter 5
Interview questions are mysterious?	Chapter 6
Hiring decisions are difficult or random?	Chapter 7
Candidates don't accept offers?	Chapter 8
New hires don't thrive?	Chapter 9

Content Overview

There are several professions dedicated to aspects of recruiting and entire sciences dedicated to measuring human capability. This book is not a replacement for or even an introduction to these professions and sciences. It is a compendium of the practical knowledge, heuristics, and tips that I have found and observed to be critically useful for managers hiring software engineers.

Chapters 2, 3, and 4 are concerned with defining what sort of engineers you want, evaluating and optimizing the overall process of hiring them, and finding candidates, respectively.

Chapters 5, 6, and 7 drill down into the interview process: reading résumés, running interviews, and creating and asking technical questions.

Chapters 8, 9, and 10 discuss hiring decisions, making offers, and getting newly hired engineers off to a great start.

Legal Disclaimer

Hiring is closely regulated by federal and state law. Although the information I present here is, to the best of my knowledge, both practical and legal in my jurisdiction at the time of writing, I am not a lawyer and I proffer no legal advice in this book. Always consult your company's human resources (HR) department and counsel before making changes to your hiring process.

Analytic versus Intuitive Styles

Everyone has a different style of approach to solving problems. Some rely on intuition; others rely on analysis. Any person usually uses a combination of these methods with one predominating.

The stereotype for engineers and engineering managers is that of a highly analytical person who uses careful reasoning, charts, logic, and mathematics to make decisions. The truth is very different: most people are not analytical most of the time.[1] In my experience, engineers analyze only slightly more than the average person does. That modicum of analysis is usually sufficient, but it's a mistake to assume that there is a careful framework behind each of an engineer's decisions.

It is possible to be quite successful in any number of fields going by intuition and rough estimation. I present analytical tools in this work—such as maintaining and analyzing detailed records of candidates, interviews, and interviewers—but I do not condemn or deprecate decision making by other means. As a professional, you should rely on the tools that you know work. The existence of an efficient tool is not sufficient reason to compel you to learn it and use it. All tools require training and investment, and the more they resemble tools you're familiar with, the easier they will be to master. If you're an intuitive person, some of the tools and methods in this work may seem like overkill to you.

That's all right. This is not an all-or-nothing system. Pick out the parts that are sensible and feasible for you and your situation, and disregard the rest or stash them away for future use. Where there are tools and methods that work most effectively in concert together, I point that out. Adapt the ideas and make them your own. If you can make sensible judgments without a calculus, go right ahead. If you find that the analytical results don't match your experience, needs, or sensibility, do the right thing for you and your business.

As I tell my employees: never suspend your judgment (especially when I ask you to).

The Competitive Advantage

The day-to-day activity of the employees of a company at all levels—from broad strategy set by executives in the C-suite to the commonplace choices and prioritizations made by interns in the mailroom—drives success in the short and long run. Each person contributes to the whole by performing or failing to perform every day.

Productivity compounds. Improvement, optimization, eliminating waste and unnecessary tasks, deftly creating a brilliant customer experience with small and easy touches—all the natural and continuous *kaizen* that occurs by the actions of talented, skilled, and motivated employees—will drive (or in its absence, fail to drive) growth and success.

---

[1]See, for example, Daniel Kahneman, *Thinking, Fast and Slow* (New York: FSG, 2011).

Employees are the lifeblood of the organization—your organization—and your success depends on their success. You set up them up for it with tools, comfortable environments, encouragement, guidance, strong coworkers, and appropriate and strategically important goals, but the raw material of talent and prehoned skills you start with determines *how* they use this and *whether* they achieve today's and tomorrow's goals. As a result, a discrepancy in employee capability between competing companies will drive a widening gap in their productivity and innovation levels, which in turn results in a gap in serving customers and overall competitiveness.

Over the years since the formation of the modern software industry, there have appeared tools such as career websites, knowledgeable headhunters, boutique recruiting firms, résumé repositories, recruiting coordination systems, and some specialized HR roles. General momentum in this area has improved the situation across the industry, and companies willing to invest in tools, process, staffing, and training have benefited even more.

In the big picture of business optimization, the science of effective technical hiring has barely changed. It has not received a fraction of the attention and effort that has gone into logistics, construction process, or development tools, such as languages, compilers, and integrated development environments.

I suspect this is due to a general perception that hiring is driven by luck or intuition, and that the managers who tackle these problems are generally uncomfortable or unfamiliar with the process and working for or with recruiters who are not especially technically minded.

However we got here, there are opportunities to do much better than average. Bring in better talent and more skilled employees and you have built or shored up the foundations of a great and successful business.

A small difference in hiring effectiveness will amplify over time into a substantial competitive advantage. You don't need to have the best recruiting and hiring method in existence, but any improvement you make and any movement above average will benefit you considerably.

Central Ideas

While engineering my own recruiting processes, I found three key ideas that reliably improved each step and decision. These themes, elaborated here, are taking an engineering approach, relying on evidence, and treating candidates as customers.

An Engineering Approach

Recruiting is a process with inputs and outputs and actions in between, so it's within the realm of engineering, and we can treat it as an engineerable subject.

This book is not framed as "Here's my way, which is the right way"—but is instead an examination of the process and its components, highlighting the role of thoughtful, intentional choices. It's your process because you own the outcome. That outcome is extremely important to your success, so it deserves your attention and the application of your hard-won skills, energy, resources, and creativity.

You may have inherited a process (or find yourself inside one), but that process is not everything it can be or must be to drive your success. Instead, think of that process as a prototype and a list of parts. Look at it like an engineer would: figure out how it works, how it doesn't work, and what makes it run quickly and slowly. Take care with what you put into it and how it behaves, and examine the output regularly to make sure it's running the way you want and need it to run.

Every section in this book describes recurrent realities and discusses options for dealing with them and succeeding. It's not a "this-is-my-method-follow-it-and-you-will-be-successful" book because that's not realistic. What I do varies with time and circumstance, and your time and circumstances vary from mine. It would be impertinent to insist on a particular hiring process.

Instead, I am lending you my perspective on the nature and purpose of the general hiring process for software engineers and many of the options you have available while building and tinkering with your own hiring machine. It's an approach that says, "Here are the kinds of parts that fit into this slot, and what's worked for me best has been XYZ—but keep in mind that I don't necessarily know all the parts that fit into your particular slot."

The keys to great engineering are meticulousness and creativity. Attention to detail, and returning your attention to it over time, will drive your ability to find what needs to change. Designing an optimal new process will take all your creativity, and the very best process you can craft will take you past what's in this book and beyond what anyone currently knows how to make.

Evidence-Based Hiring

Effective decisions require data that represent reality. Much of the information we need to make great hiring decisions is hidden in noise: inaccurate résumés, irrelevant personal data, ambiguous answers to interview questions, and so on. The purpose of interviewing is to identify the useful information by separating signal from noise, so we must be diligent and thorough in rooting out the truth.

Paired with the need for good data is a perennial need for effective decision making. All too frequently we lead with intuition and back it up with whatever evidence is at hand. We have many biases that we don't normally detect or even know exist, and our colleagues in the recruiting process have them, too.

Humans have built-in cognitive defects that we can adjust for if we are vigilant and purposeful, understanding and working with our limitations. We are unconsciously prone to anchoring, confirmation bias, framing effects, and all sorts of pitfalls described in chapters 4 through 7.

Candidates as Customers

Long-term success is usually the result of consistently applied strategy and principles. This book takes an engineering approach to the strategy and tactics of hiring; making a sound decision also involves applying behavioral principles rooted in human feelings. The principle I have had the most success with is that candidates are customers.

Thinking of candidates as customers caused a shift in the way I treated them and my overall approach to fine-tuning the recruiting process. Teaching my teams to think of candidates as customers not only elevated the candidates' experience when interviewing with us, it also increased my teams' empathy with the candidates. The interviewers thought more deeply about their own actions and interpreted candidates' behaviors more in the context of potentially working together—and less against an abstract ideal. Allies in the recruiting team appreciated how much easier it was to work with happier candidates, and negotiations became more likely to succeed. It also avoided losing or alienating real customers, and every customer counts.

Employees have tremendous investment in their work, from acquiring a job to putting in daily effort to move products forward, so they typically take job hunting quite seriously. You may remember doing so yourself!

Software engineers know that there's a lot riding on landing the right job. They need to secure suitable compensation, they need an environment to grow their skills and career, they need a job that maintains their interest and stimulates their active and powerful minds, and they need a bit of dependable stability. Too much stress can hurt them; too little can demotivate. Engineers can lose their jobs at any moment through a company's caprice, so they must have a basic sense of trust that the employer is stable, reasonable, and humane.

You can establish that trust with your own behavior. The hiring process has a large number of actions that a candidate can see, so they are exposed to a lot of what your company does—more specifically, what you do—and will draw conclusions about your character.

All people want to work with and for people who respect and care about others—the fundamental hallmarks of good customer service. Treating all candidates with respect and (affordable) deference makes for a smooth and effective process all around. Your players—interviewers, recruiters, and so on—will know the right thing to do most of the time, whether they are trying to follow a well-established procedure book or winging it.

Last, hiring is a human process. You find, evaluate, hire, or pass on folks just like yourself. This critical idea boils down to a simple prescription: *treat candidates as human beings.*

Talent Management

This chapter describes engineer work styles, planning for team and product evolution, and the importance of hiring only the best engineers.

Team Planning

As a development manager, you have goals and deadlines for products and particular customer needs, and that is the day-to-day part of your business. You also have innovation and strategic maneuvering, which drive tomorrow's goals and deadlines. Capable leadership will identify and guide the organization toward shifting goals over time, perhaps rapidly, so your teams should be prepared to meet today's and tomorrow's needs.

Specialists and Generalists

Two categories of tools are required to build software products. First are the tools at hand: the methods and construction tools you use to build software and solutions to meet current goals. I call these *immediate tools*. Second, meta-tools allow you to identify, learn, and when necessary construct the new immediate tools you'll need to solve the next set of goals. I call these *capability tools*.

It is easy to find engineers who have experience and expertise with a limited domain of immediate tools, relatively speaking. Hiring exclusively these engineers may give you the ability to deliver on today's goals, but if these people are not also experts with capability tools, then your products may stagnate over time, and your team may be unable to adapt to meet new goals in a rapidly shifting industry.

Many software engineering teams are expected to be long-lived, creating and redefining a product or product class over time, or moving from one product or goal set to the next and doing it again. Because of these expectations, there is a great need to avoid stagnation. Unfortunately, it is difficult to see at hiring time what the long-term effects of hiring just immediate tools experts will be, as the difference between the team's capability and the team's needs will start small and grow over time, usually slowly enough that the cause of the attenuating effectiveness becomes lost or hard to spot in a sea of other difficulties.

Whenever possible, it is best to hire engineers who are excellent with capability tools, in preference to expertise with immediate tools. Capability tools include the ability to learn, master, and teach:

- New construction methods
- New programming languages
- New techniques
- New platforms
- New software domains, such as embedded systems or cloud services
- New knowledge domains, such as statistical analysis or 3D simulations
- Recognizing the need to innovate
- Innovating and building new tools
- Collaborating with experts in disparate roles and domains

Of course there are and should be specialists, by which I mean people who have put substantial time into mastering a relatively narrow domain of software engineering, such as database design, compiler architecture, or machine learning, as well as people with who are also specialists in nonsoftware domains such as statistics, molecular biology, and the like—whatever applies to your team, products, and customers. Specialist experts seem to be all too rare when you actually need them.

At first, specialists may be rapidly productive on your team, with their command of the particular immediate tools you use right now. However, generalists, with command of general-purpose capability tools, can rapidly acquire new skills, adapt to evolving technology, and build new technologies to keep your products on the cutting edge.

Your engineers must be able to recognize when they need to find new tools, and then use those tools, and repeat as necessary to deliver to every goal and continuously improve your team's overall capability. You must find and hire such engineers.

Capability: Set Your Sights High

In this chapter and elsewhere in this book, I strongly advocate only targeting and hiring the top engineers in the market. You don't need justification to hire top performers, but you might believe you need justification to hire *only* top performers. There are many possible objections to focusing on the top. Here are a few, with my retorts:

- **"I Must Hire Quickly, So Hiring High Is a Luxury."**

    I reply that hiring low would be a luxury—as in, it is something you don't really need. Low-capability engineers will consume your time and energy and you will get less done, maybe a lot less.

- **"I Don't Have the Budget to Hire the Best."**

    I reply that the best cost only marginally more but create substantially more value. The math is simple; what you don't have is the budget to hire low.

- **"Who Will Employ the Bottom 90 Percent?"**

    I reply that someone less clever than you are will hire them.

... and Not Low

You may be tempted or even instructed to hire the first basically competent developers who show up for interviews. This would be an effective strategy only if the great majority of developers were excellent developers. There would still be a capability curve—Bell, Gaussian, Poisson, and so on—but the lower quartile would still be competent, be effective, and help drive your business forward. Today that's far from the case, and the simple reality is that at this time the majority of developers are not at all competent and will actually hurt your business.

Don't hire anyone but the best. You are too likely to accidentally hire below the best anyway, due to a minimal, unavoidable level of error and uncertainly in the hiring process; aim low and you could hire abysmally. Just as a high performer can dominate the output of an otherwise mediocre group of workers, a low performer can sink it. The cost of dealing with the associated problems, the messed-up projects and missed deadlines, eventually firing the low performer, and then replacing him with *another* round of hiring may be such a net negative that you would have been better off not hiring anyone at all.

At times I have been instructed to lower my hiring standards, and for all the listed reasons I refused. That tactic might not be appropriate for your situation, but if you can even hire well *surreptitiously* you will prevent a lot of personal frustration and help your organization, maybe more than it deserves.

Another thing to keep in mind, even for your own career, is that organizations that hire low tend to deteriorate over time. It's tempting and straightforward to think that because they hired *you* they take hiring seriously and only go after the best. But everyone can make mistakes and win by accident.

Absolute Performance

There is a common understanding in the industry that the best software developers are 10:1 as productive as average ones. Sometimes it's said to be 16:1 or more, and it's held occasionally to be the difference between the best and the worst or between the best and the average. That's an impressive set of numbers, but there is good reason to doubt those figures, as the original studies behind them are doubtful in origin and method.

In his self-published book *The Leprechauns of Software Engineering,* Laurent Bossavit describes his efforts to track down and verify the ultimate, fundamental sources of these commonly held axioms. It's not a pretty story, and the ultimate conclusion is that there is no firm basis for believing those ratios.

There is undeniably a substantial productivity difference between engineers in the market, and it is more than a 10% or 50% difference. I think it's much more, but I have no quantitative characterization. I have had the experience of meeting a superstar engineer, who outperformed every other engineer I knew by quite a margin in any dimension you might care to name. Much later, I met another superstar who was as far ahead of the first as that star was ahead of others. And then another. These are exactly the sort of people you want to find (before I do).

Net Capabilities: Using a Talent Portfolio

Every engineer has strengths and weaknesses, but across an entire team you need a certain set of strengths, as well as particular skills and knowledge at the moment and for the foreseeable future. One of the tools I use for recording and planning across a team is building a portfolio.

A portfolio allows you to easily see who and what you have now, for review or reminder or even for eventually briefing a successor. (You should always keep in mind that you will have a successor one day and arm that person for success with a rock-solid team and lots of data they would otherwise have to scrape together over a long time.)

In a portfolio you can keep records of former team members as well, so you can contact them if you need to, though realistically this is not always a possibility. You can collect the job descriptions you've written and filled over time.

To build one, keep résumés on file as you hire and ask for résumés from all of your engineers. Ask your team to make periodic updates to their résumés, perhaps every quarter or so. You might worry that this will bring their attention to finding another job, because after all, that's when people tend to think about and work on their résumés! But if they are happy, relax—this won't make them find another job. Actually, it can refocus them on their current and ongoing success with your team and on making sure they spend time and energy advancing their careers—that is, improving their capabilities and pushing *your* technology and your products forward.

If your organization uses a "capabilities," "competencies," "leadership principles," or another sort of system for articulating desirable traits and behavior, the portfolio helps you track how well your team as a whole fulfills the capabilities, and you can use this information to characterize the strengths you must find in new hires. If your organization doesn't have some sort of behavior evaluation framework, now is a good time to adopt one, if only for your own purposes.

A portfolio is also useful for skill distribution measurement. Teams are vulnerable to member loss, creating a gap in understanding the product or projects and how to work with them. Too few team members with any given knowledge or skill can create a project bottleneck as well. Avoiding those problems is an important aspect of risk management, so a tool that organizes available information on what people know and can do will aid you in recovering from employee loss and lend your team flexibility in task assignments.

Natural Team Life Cycle and Personality Types

Some people like to start new things, and others like to tweak and optimize existing things. These are the general preferences engineers have, too. Individual preferences vary over time, but each engineer tends to have one of two stable core personalities. "Startup engineers" frequently remain startup engineers for a long time: I call them *Creators*. Long-haul systems engineers similarly stick to their pattern: I call them *Optimizers*. Both are critical, but the Creator set is more critical at the outset of a product, and the Optimizer set is more useful toward its sunset.

As you kick off a product, you need a heavy slate of Creator engineers to get things moving. They bring a lot of energy to making new software. This phase frequently needs fast motion and rapid iteration, and many important considerations (classically, I have found, monitors and alarms) are pushed out to the future, rather than built in from the beginning. In such a phase, a Creator will say that although these are important and useful, they don't get code in front of customers, and no one knows what the final product should be exactly, so the team is better off building first and asking questions later.

Whether this is really the right approach is debatable, but it summarizes a common attitude. When the product has been shipped to customers and at least some of the team's energy becomes devoted to keeping the product alive for them—customer support, bug fixes, operations, and so on—then the balance of need shifts to the Optimizers. They have the patience and desire to "do it right": systematically fix bugs, lower operational or support costs, refactor for scalability, and so on. They tend to thrive when there is already a product in place.

Mixes of types work well, and the lesson is that a different mix is better for a different time. The Creators will want and need to build new things: either extending the product in critical ways or on new projects and new products. If you don't have these projects, they may drift away. Find them a home on a sister team if you can! The Optimizers won't always be comfortable starting up a team, but you will need them later.

The natural result of this is that the team that made the product won't be the team that keeps it going year after year and eventually retires it. The camaraderie of the founding team won't keep everyone together forever.

These are generalizations, of course, but I would be quite surprised if you don't recognize your engineers and peers as falling into one or the other of these two categories. I am not sure why any particular engineer becomes a Creator rather than an Optimizer. I suspect it has something to do with a personal desire for or ability to deal with the unknown. During a project lifetime, there's a lot of "unknown" up front and a lot less later.

Balance

All right, you're going to hire high-capability engineers—but who are you looking for specifically? An explicit plan gives you a framework for evaluating candidates against your real needs. You can always hire any given high-capability engineer, but hiring to support a balanced team aims the team toward overall high function.

The criteria I use to understand my team and determine what sort of engineer I most need are leadership, experience, style, and roles. First I chart what I have, then consider the consequence of hiring variants in each category. The ones that make the most sense, best filling gaps and complementing the team, are the ones I list in the empty pages of my talent portfolio and hire for.

Leadership

You should expect leadership traits in every engineer you hire, but some stand out. There are engineers who can be the driving force in getting a team to grow through exemplary work, mentorship, and inspiration. (These are fantastically valuable.)

As a manager, you have to express every aspect of leadership, and you must also drive the team with those aspects that do not emanate from any engineer on the team. Too many of those gaps and you will drive yourself to exhaustion, so it's critical for your health and the team's that you keep your team staffed with leaders.

Leaders also serve a purpose in the recruiting process, as engineers have a pronounced preference to work with strong, leader engineers and will not only respond more favorably to offers but rise to the occasion during interviews and are more likely to get offers in the first place.

Experience

Like many people, I heavily discounted the value of experience until I had some. At this point, I hire the best engineers available, however much experience they have, and I don't worry about hiring developers with more experience than I estimate I strictly need.

The question I ask myself is, "Can I hire less experienced engineers?" The answer depends on the existing makeup of the team. If the great majority of the team—or all of it—is composed of engineers new to their careers, then I am better off focusing my energy on identifying highly capable engineers with more experience, rather than less. The team members are better off as well, because engineers have a tremendous ability to learn from each other, and, in my experience, greater differentials in knowledge and skill generated by experience often drive faster and deeper learning.

Experienced engineers as a rule are more capable, but it's not a direct relationship and it's not universal. While hiring, I focus on demonstrated performance, so it's not very important to me how much time an engineer has put into building their capability to their current level. I care about the performance level and worry about experience only to the extent that I try not to staff my team without any.

Style

Your team needs a variety of perspectives and styles to remain healthy, perform at peak levels, and improve over time. However, the nature of your work may call for differing attitudes and perspectives—what I think of as work styles. Knowing and taking advantage of your team's work styles will help you hire effectively in the first place and keep people interested and engaged over the long run as well.

Though you need a mix of styles, it's sometimes a challenge to make everyone realize that all styles are valuable. Many people mistake stylistic similarity to themselves for competence. That is, if your style is like mine, then you know what you are doing; if not, you're a bozo who shouldn't be trusted. A manager's challenge and duty is to keep all styles alive and well at the same time.

Here are a few styles I have used to characterize my engineers and teams. You will think of more that are better suited to your experience and circumstances.

Cautious Style

Some engineers are naturally patient and careful, or have become so through habit and training. They excel at thinking out and planning projects in meticulous detail. Every aspect will be considered and debated: reliability, security, and long-term maintenance. These engineers are particularly useful on projects involving financial transactions or core, critical systems that are essential to your business, such as databases that are used by many systems. They are risk-averse.

Quick Style

Engineers can be fast and furious builders. They may leap into action, building first and asking questions later. Frequently they are not too concerned about understanding every project detail up front, knowing they can check and correct the course quickly. They are not risk-averse.

Adventurous Style

Exploration and the excitement of newness can be fundamental drivers for some people. The software engineering profession has continued to evolve quickly over the past few decades, and that rapid change combined with its relative novelty (as opposed to insurance or accounting, for example) can be a major draw for such people. They are characterized by bringing in new ideas and trying things out. Usually these are tools and languages—sometimes inventions. They are willing to try a new technique right in the middle of a project: to learn about it and see if it helps. They are not risk-averse.

Perfectionist Style

Perhaps too rare are engineers who insist on a professional standard set at an extremely high level. Usually this is in product and code quality. They insist on testing thoroughly; they write their own unit test frameworks for fun; and they explain to anyone who will listen how they managed to get the project's code coverage up to 99.5 percent. The last 0.5 percent keeps them up at night.

It's All Good

I want to stress that these styles and more are *all good*. Sizing up your engineers and deciding what style you need to search for next to extend and complement your team will give you another tool for making great decisions and great hires.

Broad and Narrow Roles

What constitutes a balanced team depends on your organization, needs, and preferences. As an example, you may need test engineers on your team, or you may have a close collaboration with a team of specialist test engineers so you don't have to hire them onto your team.

Bigger teams usually start specializing certain roles, such as build engineer, tool engineer, or user interface (UI) developer. Arguably, civilization as we know it was brought about by the ability of a steady food source to support the creation of specialist roles at the dawn of agriculture—giving us room to become bricklayers, mathematicians, and so on. So there's a lot to be said for the power of specialization to create useful deep expertise.

However, narrowing the scope of a role too deeply will cause narrowed vision for your team and rob you of flexibility and some growth opportunities. A narrowly defined role limits the market you can recruit from and implicitly preempts your ability to hire great generalists. The likelihood is that your organization can be *more* successful with *less* specialization.

Team Flow

As Heraclitus said, all is change. Even a team that looks the same is changing from day to day. It learns new techniques and new modes of operations, experiments with small and large process changes, and responds to new information and new demands.

A team changes in a more obvious way as people come and go. There is an unavoidable rate of attrition caused by entropy, and you will eventually lose team members, however satisfied they are. The attrition rate is predictable across a large group of people, but under macro circumstances—in the scope of one team—there is probably no truly reliable method of predicting how often people will leave except by extrapolating from recent history.

Still, you know there is a rate. You can guess at it from available information, drawing on team history or the organization's rate. Then you can use that information to predict, broadly, how frequently you will need to hire to keep the team at a steady size. My recommendation is to hire ahead of the rate and stay one engineer "above headcount," but that's not always practical.

It may not always be necessary to replace engineers. If the team is growing in strength and overall capability, but the work level remains steady, you may well be able to handle your workload with fewer staff. That's not the general trend these days for at least two reasons. First, it seems that there is always more to do and you can take advantage of any level of capability available. Second, the accumulated work product of a team can drain its productivity to the point that you need more staff to maintain and extend a product over time.

That second effect is the natural product of the support load that products generate and the accumulation of technical debt. A great overview of how that happens and methods for sidestepping the problem can be found in the paper *Nobody Ever Gets Credit for Fixing Problems that Never Happened* by Nelson P. Repenning and John D. Sterman.[1]

All change is stressful, and losing a team member is traumatic—even one for whom no one had special love. As a manager, you can help the team adjust and stay on course by keeping the big picture in mind: every team is dynamic and changing.

Building a New Team

Creating a team from scratch or from a small core of engineers is a wonderful challenge. The software engineers you should hire will be almost entirely Creator types, not Optimizers. These are the sort of people who make their own startups or build them from scratch with colleagues. Startups are a great place to recruit them as well—at any given time, many startups are leaving the inception phase or failing.

The first couple of hires will form the core culture of the team, so it's especially important to hire the right people. You need engineers who are leaders and great communicators, who inspire new team members with their technical

---

[1]Nelson P. Repenning and John D. Sterman, "Nobody Ever Gets Credit for Fixing Problems that Never Happened: Creating and Sustaining Process Improvement," *California Management Review* (2001), 43, no. 4. Available at http://web.mit.edu/nelsonr/www/Repenning%3DSterman_CMR_su01_.pdf.

acumen and welcome and mentor them. Poor hiring choices would include a dour or pessimistic engineer, who can kill your team and your project from the beginning, or a generally incapable engineer who can set the technical direction of the team going the wrong way, propagating large-scale errors that would be difficult to correct later.

Expanding an Existing Team

Most engineers are hired into standing teams, so that's the focus of this book. However, before you hire you should consider the cost carefully: the process of searching will consume your time and your team's time, and onboarding the new engineer will consume even more time. Short-term productivity loss is inevitable; the new team member will start with a net negative impact on team productivity. The team's social structure will shift and adapt to the new member, and the gelling process takes a setback (or starts anew).

Chapter 9 treats the impact of onboarding and is worth a review before you set out to hire more engineers.

Can You Hire?

Before you embark on a labor-intensive effort to find the right people, you must verify that you can hire them. You need to be able to pay the costs of conducting the search, compensation for the new employee, and various overhead expenses connected with any worker, such as insurance, equipment, and so on.

Chapter 3 discusses the cost of hiring and how you may go about measuring and optimizing it. Accounting for overhead is outside the scope of this book. Here I talk about compensation and your ability to make compelling offers to candidates.

If you find you can't afford to hire, focus your effort on making your existing team more effective.

Budget

Organizations vary greatly in how they allocate headcount and account for staffing costs, at least at the front line. Sometimes you get a number (e.g., three engineers); sometimes you get a set of job levels or classes (one senior engineer, two journeymen engineers); and other times you get a dollar figure ($340,000/year).

Whatever way you account for, fight for, or track the budget for employing engineers, the fundamental recruiting ideas do not change. Start by hiring the very best engineer you can afford, and keep hiring until you run out of money.

Compensation

Your task is to pay developers the right amount, bounded at the bottom by local market conditions and at the top by the danger of creating golden handcuffs.

Expense

Though you and your team can offer them a great many immaterial rewards, such as companionship and training, engineers are also going to want money. On the whole, they are excellent mathematicians and quite astute regarding market conditions, so they frequently want very good compensation. You must be able to afford engineers if you are going to pursue them seriously.

When you find the great engineer you want to hire, because she is great she may well ask for top-of-the-market salary, a sign-on bonus, and other cash rewards. It is perennially tempting to save money by hiring people at lower costs, but that approach in itself has substantial costs.

Paying less than top-of-the-market rates will have several undesirable effects. It will prevent you from hiring highly compensated engineers regardless of their fit, skills, and overall capability. It will tend to direct your hires toward the lower end of the market, which as a general but not universal rule has less capable engineers. It directs you toward less experienced engineers, who, no matter how capable they are, will not bring the hard-won lessons that experienced engineers bring with them. It can make you look and feel like a cheapskate, and it will discourage external recruiters from working with you because there are likely to be more lucrative clients hiring.

Losing a great candidate to a disagreement on compensation is a poor experience for both of you—after all, both you and the candidate went to considerable trouble to find each other, or at least you certainly did. That's unfortunate if the candidate wants an essentially unreasonable amount of money, but losing a candidate to a perfectly reasonable compensation request is heartbreaking.

Price Sends a Signal

You need and demand greatness. Offering high compensation informs candidates in unmistakable terms that you expect great things.[2] You tell candidates with dollars up front that you believe in their competency and the large impact they will have on your customers and your business.

---

[2]Valarie A. Zeithhaml, A. Parasuraman, and Leonard L. Berry, *Delivering Quality Service: Balancing Customer Perceptions and Expectations* (New York: Free Press, 1990).

The Use and Misuse of Golden Handcuffs

Golden handcuffs are levels of compensation high enough to substantially discourage employees from resigning. Companies frequently offer golden handcuffs to key members of teams and companies they buy out, so that the expertise they "bought" doesn't immediately disappear. Frequently these are time-triggered bonuses that mature in months or years.

Another kind of golden handcuff is not explicitly offered but occurs in regular compensation, intentionally and unintentionally. In the intentional case, the idea is that if you pay someone enough money they will not look for or be interested in any offers from competitors and startup opportunities. Unintentional handcuffs are formed when standard compensation packages become worth much more than originally intended. For instance, a stock plan that offers regular, timed stock disbursements may turn into handcuffs if the stock becomes worth much more than anticipated by compensation analysts.

In any of these cases, it becomes painful to leave. Retention of capable employees is a priority to companies because of the many obvious benefits, but sometimes attrition is necessary and good. When an employee is in a situation in which they would be interested in a new job *except for the handcuffs*, this creates a stressful tension. Situations that would otherwise be unbearable and lead to resignation, such as transfer to an inexperienced and irascible manager, don't resolve in the expected outcome. The employee stays on, and stress mounts. If you've seen someone in this position, you know that it is a bit torturous for them. They become unproductive and unhappy, and that unhappiness spreads.

In this case you now have an employee you should replace, because he or she is unproductive and damaging to morale. Firing the person is a lot more expensive and troublesome than if the natural progression of circumstances had led to a cleaner turnover.

I'm not saying you should never use golden handcuffs, and you may well run into the situation unintentionally. What I am saying is that when golden handcuffs are applied, perhaps through no fault of your own, you must be especially vigilant to monitor the employee's stress level and take early action to reduce it or help the employee move on. If you don't, you will be hurting—for paying your employees *too much*. Strange, but true.

Candidate Pipeline

The focus of this chapter is understanding your recruiting process and adapting it to suit your needs. The chapter shows you how to diagram, analyze, and optimize your recruiting system. With this high-level approach, you can improve the rate at which candidates flow through the system, increase the number of candidates you can handle simultaneously, reduce the number of process failures, and improve the customer experience. It identifies specific options and trade-offs for optimizing for different outcomes, such as hiring speed versus quality of hires.

Life Cycle and Pipeline

A *life cycle* is an individual candidate's journey through your recruiting process, including all touch-points and major interactions. The *pipeline* is the flow of all candidates through the system. Not all pipelines are perfectly malleable, but a clear understanding of the process will give you options nonetheless.

The pipeline you have now probably does not exactly fit your needs and goals. To have an optimized process, you'll probably have to build one or craft a new one from existing components.

Pipeline Roles

The pipeline is shaped around the candidates but shepherded by a number of critical roles on the interviewer team. The roles can be filled by different people, or, frequently, some people fill multiple roles. If you are unlucky or especially scrappy, you'll fill all of them yourself, except the candidate role. You're not the candidate—today, anyway.

As you learn and chart the process you have, it's a good idea to explicitly note who is filling these roles and develop a strong working relationship with each person.

Candidate

The candidate may be actively looking for a job, passively looking, not looking but open to moving, not looking and actually quite content, or looking for a future position (such as after graduation). Chapter 4 has more detail on different kinds of candidates and how to treat them differently.

Your best bet is to make sure your process is accessible to and works well for all sorts of candidates, so you don't miss out on great hires.

Sourcer

A sourcer starts with a concept for what sort of engineers are needed and finds candidates who match those needs. Sourcers may employ any method for finding candidates, including but not limited to the sources and suggestions contained in this book, such as searching résumé databases, posting to job boards, sending queries to their networks, and coordinating with external sourcers. The sourcer usually establishes initial contact with candidates.

Scheduler

Scheduling is arranging for phone calls and on-site interviews, sell calls, and the like. This task is frequently shared and often driven by a hiring manager with considerable aid from recruiters. If you're not the scheduler, you can help by preparing interviewer meta-schedules, as described in Chapter 7.

Recruiter

Internal recruiters prepare and present written offers and work with human resources to coordinate legal and policy issues. They are frequently part of HR or a dedicated recruiting organization and usually coordinate the activities of sourcers and schedulers.

External recruiters are contractors or vendors who act as sourcers for hire and are usually paid per placement (see the section "Get Expert Help" later in this chapter).

Hiring Manager

This book is intended for people filling this role, so that is probably you. The hiring manager defines jobs, makes hiring decisions, and makes sure that all other candidate life cycle roles are filled and operating smoothly. They find and fill any process gaps and are the default executor of the other recruiting roles.

Mapping the Pipeline

You need a thorough and accurate understanding of what you have and a way to communicate changes in process and expectations. You can build that understanding by creating and sharing workflow diagrams. That means surveying the actual process by talking with the people involved and doing some drawing, resulting in diagrams like Figure 3-1. In this and subsequent diagrams, a protruding "--o" represents a process exit point, e.g., failing a phone screen.

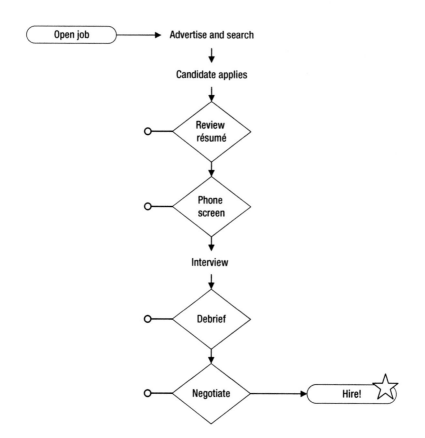

Figure 3-1. An example of a high-level candidate pipeline

I have had the good fortune to work with amazingly dedicated, knowledgeable, and resourceful recruiting professionals. Still, few have had an up-to-date map of their organizations' recruiting systems. Instead, each company and team generally operates by established pattern, habit, undocumented procedure, and lore. Maps of sufficient detail for process surgery are rare.

There are no completely straight, one-directional pipes. You may route a candidate to an earlier point in the pipeline if you determine that he or she needs additional evaluation, or your team determines that the candidate should be referred to a more suitable job.

Pipeline Perspectives

The pipeline has an absolute form, but each person who works with it will have his or her own view. It's instructive to consider your pipeline as it appears from these different angles.

Candidate's Perspective

The one who knows the least about the pipeline is arguably the one most affected by it. Candidates try to grasp how your system works, and the better they understand it, the better their experience will be and the fewer opportunities for misunderstandings. Figure 3-2 has a typical pipeline from a candidate's point of view. Even if this is exactly your process, the candidates will have a better experience if you tell them explicitly what it is.

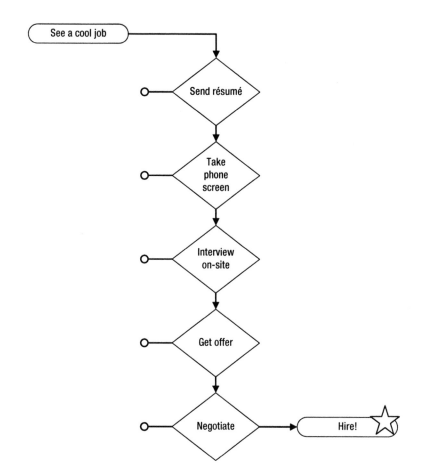

Figure 3-2. A candidate's perspective on their lifecycle in a typical pipeline

Hiring Manager's Perspective

You may find it useful to document and study your own perspective and responsibilities in the pipeline. This will let you find opportunities to streamline and delegate. Figure 3-3 has an example of a possible pipeline from a hiring manager's point of view.

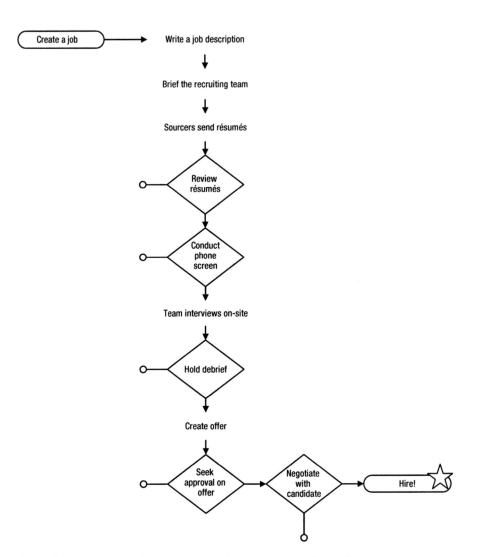

Figure 3-3. An example of a hiring manager's perspective on the pipeline

Other Perspectives

Each member of the recruiting team will have his or her own view of the pipeline, although to conserve space these are not illustrated here.

Time Lapse

Consider how long it would it take your team to hire an ideal candidate. That's a candidate who meets your every expectation and causes no delays—she can take a call at any moment, come in for an interview the minute you ask, and accept an offer on the spot. Could you hire this fantastical candidate in a day? A week? A month?

The moment you identify a potential candidate, the clock starts counting down. You have only so long to hire each candidate, though it's naturally different every time. For some candidates there's little time to waste, whereas for others you have so much time that it hardly matters what you do. Unfortunately, there's no sure way to tell how much time you have, even if a candidate denies any other interviewing activity or says she has multiple offers pending. The only safe assumption is that it's always urgent.

On several occasions I have lost candidates to competitors because I could not move quickly enough. Sometimes the interviews took too long to schedule, sometimes it took too long to present an offer, and sometimes I didn't have time to negotiate before the candidate had to accept a good-enough offer from elsewhere. It's bitterly disappointing, and each time I vow to streamline the process further. There's no way to make a recruiting process consistently quick enough to never lose a candidate to time lapse, but you can minimize losses by keeping a sense of urgency and tightly managing time spent. It may be worth noting that in a more or less direct way, you are competing with me for top developers, and I will be acting swiftly.

To make it clear where time is being spent, annotate a pipeline diagram with calendar time lapses, as shown in Figure 3-4. It's simple to distill the data from documents like candidate books, described in this chapter under "Keeping and Analyzing Records."

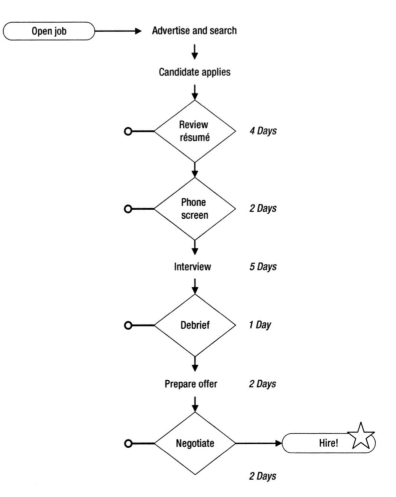

Figure 3-4. Pipeline with mean time to complete each step

It may prove useful to zoom in further on lengthy sections to pinpoint where time is spent. Each micro-step takes appreciable time, such as passing the buck from one person to the next by any means: email, workflow software, shouting across the room, and so on.

Flow Model

Carrying the pipe analogy a little further, you can model the progression of all candidates as a flow through the system. With this perspective, you will see where and how candidates get filtered out of the system and where your bottlenecks lie.

For example, if you have a number of qualified and available on-site interviewers, then that step of the pipe—or, by metaphor, a sluice gate—has a high capacity. However, if you are the only one doing phone screens and you have a lot of other responsibilities, that gate has a low capacity. If phone screening is the bottleneck it would not help the rate of flow to add on-site interviewers, but adding phone screeners would.

Sometimes it's fairly obvious where the bottlenecks are, but in a broader context, on a large recruiting team, or for future planning, building a model can tell you where to concentrate effort to increase candidate flow. Naturally, many candidates will enter the pipe, and a small fraction of them get all the way to the Hire step, so it's sensible to start by allocating more resources to the starting end.

Figure 3-5 indicates the recruiting team's capacity for executing each step with a stack of human figures. To increase throughput in this sample, start by adding resources to the Advertise and search and Interview steps.

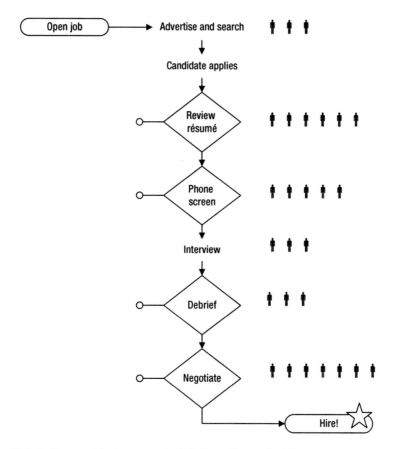

Figure 3-5. A flow model where capacity is indicated by stacked figures

Universal Optimizations

Some recruiting investments will almost always pay off. These practices are so useful that they will aid your recruiting effort whether you are concentrating on increasing the quality and success of your hires, trying to speed up the process and hire well quickly, or trying to reduce the cost of hiring.

In even the most regimented organization, you have some degree of control over how the recruiting process works. You are responsible for the quality of your hires, and people in the recruiting process—HR staff, sourcers, recruiters, and so on—want to staff the company with fantastic hires to make themselves and the business successful. That said, you may want to take a look at the section "Manage Change" later in this chapter for warnings and advice on making changes in the recruiting process.

Candidate as Customer

Candidates will focus their energy and hopes on companies with a reputation for making the application and hiring process easy and enjoyable, so it's essential to establish a great customer relationship immediately.

If your candidate experience is exceptional, they will notice. They will talk. In some cases, they will directly refer others to you.

You will turn down the majority of candidates, so they will do most of the work of spreading your reputation. Therefore, you must treat everyone well, and treat rejected candidates with special care. If at all possible, you want these candidates leaving your process thinking something like:

> *"I didn't make it, but that's a heck of a team and a heck of a company. I want to work there much more than when I applied. Maybe if I study and gain experience I can get in another time. Do I know anyone who might make the cut now—and maybe help get me in later?"*

We've all heard numerous good and bad stories about interviews—mostly bad—and they most certainly shaped our opinion of the responsible employers.

Candidates also report their experiences to other recruiters, who may steer other candidates toward or away from you. Candidates will rate your interviews on websites such as Glassdoor.com. A huge proportion of engineers run blogs or microblogs, and you can expect a mention, rave, or rant out of such vocal people if you impress them or do them wrong. The stories they relate can be good or bad—your choice.

Keep the customer experience firmly in mind as you examine and alter the candidate pipeline in your organization. Consider building and thinking through a candidate perspective model (see Figure 3-3). Think about what sort of information they have available, what they expect from you, and what you and your recruiting team actually tell them. Ask yourself what you would assume if you were the candidate. What would you like to know about how the company views you and treats your application?

A good source of information on the experience you provide is asking or surveying recent hires about their interview process: how it felt, how it could have gone better, anything that stood out (good or bad), and so on. Recently rejected candidates can also give you feedback, although it may be biased. If you are working with external recruiters, they may be willing to pass on comments and complaints from candidates.

Glassdoor.com and similar websites reflect and present your reputation, so it's a good idea to check them from time to time. They are also a source of intelligence on the experience that competitors are giving their customers, which you can use to your advantage by explicitly setting yourself apart.

Remove Pointless Steps and Waste

Dear [Retail Company]: it's unreasonable to ask me four screens of identifying/ account-creating questions just so I can submit one résumé for one job.

Make the application process extremely easy. It probably isn't. To see what's good and bad about it, have a trusted friend apply for the position from "first principles"—say, a job-site posting—and ask them to take notes on the process. Was it always clear what the job was? Was it clear how to apply? Was it easy to apply? How soon did they get a response?

You may want to apply for your own position to see how it works, then optimize away everything that isn't necessary, everything that takes unnecessary time, everything that is broken, and everything that can break. Strip out the junk. Drop the clunky third-party applicant management system and put up an email address, for goodness sake.

Increase Throughput

Evaluating more candidates means you will have more, and the quicker you handle one candidate the sooner you can handle the next. Use flow modeling to find bottlenecks, and scan through the "Optimizing for Speed" section of this chapter to see what you can apply, even if speed is not your primary objective.

Eliminate Barriers

To recruit at speed, you must evaluate candidates frequently. You'll need a lot of them, so you'll need to open up every source and take down barriers.

What I call *barriers* are process elements designed to slow down and stop candidates. When they are most effective, they are a sort of Maxwell's demon for sorting developers by capability, slowing down and stopping lower-capability engineers but letting the rest through. That's a relatively low-cost way to conserve your energy so you can spend it on potential candidates more likely to succeed.

Even well-designed barriers will catch and stop some excellent developers as well, and that's a shame. To increase the number of potential candidates, take down barriers and pay the cost of increased time spent evaluating.

Streamline

Every step in the pipeline has an owner and actions associated with it, and each is vulnerable to the owner being absent, busy, lost, or failing to pass responsibility to the next step owner. In addition, latencies between steps pile up, any step can go awry in some way, and transitions can falter. Getting rid of a step entirely prevents it from causing harm. Similarly, having one person responsible for multiple steps in sequence reduces the number of transitions, thereby reducing latency caused by passing the torch from one person to the next.

Be careful not to streamline away important steps. As an example, one critical step in most pipelines is the debrief, where interviewers meet following an interview to reveal and discuss their findings. For an expert interviewing team, one debrief can be fairly quick, but you should not bypass this step entirely. Instead, you might set steps closer together in time, such as holding an interview debrief on the same day as the interview—and that in particular is a good idea in any event.

Set SLAs

Without expectations for how much time any particular step in a candidate pipeline should take, team members will quite reasonably get around to completing each step whenever they feel like it. Work with your team to set shared expectations on how long each step should maximally take, or service level agreements (SLAs). In its most rigorous form, each step owner commits firmly and the hiring manager formalizes, documents, and enforces the SLAs. Table 3-1 presents a sample SLA formalization of the first part of a candidate pipeline.

Table 3-1. Example of a Service Level Agreement (SLA) for Candidate Evaluation Steps

Step	Maximum Time Lapse	Owner
Forward résumé to hiring manager	4 hours	Sourcer
Review résumé	4 hours	Hiring manager
Schedule phone screen	2 days	Sourcer
Submit phone screen feedback	1 day	Interviewer
Decide whether to proceed to on-site	4 hours	Hiring manager

Help the responsible people keep to the SLAs with habit changes or new tools, and track what's really happening carefully in a candidate book. Set the SLAs for steps you directly own very aggressively, primarily because it's under your direct control, and also as an example.

What's reasonable and what's aggressive will vary with circumstances, and my advice is simply to target far, far less than what it would be if nobody cared much, and far less than whatever you have now. For my own steps in my processes, such as reviewing and returning potential candidates' résumés to recruiters, I commit to turnaround in one business day. Then I target ninety minutes. Ninety minutes is still not quick enough to ensure I have reasonable access to a candidate; I lost one excellent prospect in less time.

Get Expert Help

The standard meaning of "external recruiter" is someone who places people at your company in return for payment. Such recruiters are rewarded for quickly getting expensive candidates hired. Over the long run, they keep relationships with clients like you by sending them great candidates who meet their needs and perform well. But they have an outside view; they can't help you get better at asking interview questions or speed your evaluation process.

An employee or consultant who specializes in getting your process running, training your recruiting staff, interviewing with you and on your behalf, and making your hiring process extremely successful, on the other hand, has quite a bit of motivation to take an inside view and strengthen your team and organization. Perhaps you can find or train such a person.

Train Staff

Hiring great engineers is abnormal; nobody knows automatically how to do it. Unless you are incredibly lucky, it takes plenty of effort and reflection to hire just the right developers—the ones who will succeed and make your business thrive. Since we wisely don't rely on luck, we must apply method and practice to strengthen our skills over time.

Reading this and other books is a great start, but it's unlikely that your entire recruiting team has done that much homework. In addition, even professional recruiters typically do not specialize in hiring software developers, so you may have to build a lot of shared understanding to make your whole team effective. They need to understand, develop, and manage an efficient process; set goals and expectations; and agree on interviewing and evaluation standards. Chapter 6 has details on training your interviewers.

All of this is going to take some initial work and ongoing checkpoints, but it is well worth the investment—or so I think you will conclude after staffing your team with the brightest and most capable developers.

Keep and Analyze Records

The most useful recruiting tool I have ever used is a simple spreadsheet that tracks candidates. I call it my *candidate book*. In it I record candidate names, sources, dates and times they moved through stages of the process, their ultimate evaluations, and specific reasons for moving them forward or rejecting them at each step.

The sheet usually has columns for name, current step owner, role, find date, response date, source, résumé reviewer, review notes, review date, phone screener, screen notes, screen date, interview date, final result, and reason for final result. For space, the sample Table 3-2 is stripped to a few key columns. They are enough for simple analysis.

Table 3-2. Bare-Bones Candidate Book with Dates

Name	Find Date	Screen	Interview	Result	Reason
Amy S.	3/8/2005	—	—	Reject	Experience
Barry T.	3/9/2005	3/10/2005	—	Reject	Design
Claudia U.	3/22/2005	3/24/2005	3/29/2005	Reject	Coding
Daniel V.	4/2/2005	4/6/2005	4/13/2005	Reject	Coding
Eliza W.	4/2/2005	4/7/2005	4/13/2005	Offer/Accept	

With a full record, you can find patterns that let you organize and optimize your time and resource allocation. For example, you may see that you typically reject candidates after on-site interviews for lack of coding ability. In response, you would change your phone screens so you screen more thoroughly for coding ability, which lets you spend less time in expensive, broadly time-consuming on-site interviews.

Charts like Table 3-2 also let you calculate time lapse. In the sample table, the mean time lapse between Find Date and Screen (Date) is three days, and the maximum between them is five days. For my own process, I would try to pull it down to less than two days on average.

Candidate books can also help you discover and optimize flow by showing you the ratio of candidates who arrive at different steps. In the example in Table 3-2, the pipeline is admitting five candidates to four phone screens to three on-site interviews to one hire. If these ratios hold over time, you can predict loosely that bringing in five more candidates will provide you with one more hire.

A candidate book will help you discover latencies that require SLAs. Look at the variance in time lapses for each particular step. Gross or unusual average and maximum times on any given step are ripe for SLAs.

Build the Recruiting Team qua Team

Your recruiting team is a team in the traditional sense. Apply traditional team formation and team-building techniques to speed its development and help it achieve better results.

Spend More Time

Like anything you do, the more you focus on it the quicker and better it will go, and the more you divide your attention, the slower and less predictably awesome the results will be. So, if you need to move recruiting faster, you may have to let some other things go for a while or delegate them to someone you trust.

Hiring well requires colossal time investment. For my purposes, I count on spending a week of personal working time for each hire. When it's not critical that I hire immediately, I spread it over more calendar weeks, though it makes hiring take that much longer. As a result of a combination of pressing and less pressing hiring needs, I have spent the majority of my management career doing some kind of recruiting.

While recruiting takes a lot of a manager's time, it takes about as much time again from everyone else. The engineering team loses time for each phone screen, each on-site interview, and each debrief, as well as in training, preparing, and incidental discussion. Sinking this time into recruiting will take time away from everything else they do, so do it thoughtfully and account for the lost productive time in your project plans.

Spend More Money

A bit of money can buy you better recruiting. Spend it creatively to shore up the weak points of your pipeline, increase the capacity of your recruiting team, and get more out of your advertising efforts by paying for better placement, further placement, or assistance from a recruitment advertisement firm—people who specialize in spending your money on recruiting through advertising. Money can't just fix all your problems, but it opens up your options if you're wise about spending it.

In addition, using more money to increase the compensation you can offer candidates may allow you to reach deeper into the market to more expensive engineers and lower the likelihood of losing candidates during offer negotiation.

Enlist Your Engineers

Software development is understanding, building, and debugging processes. Your engineers hone the skills necessary to do that, and they translate neatly into reengineering workflow processes like recruiting and hiring. Good engineers can understand and alter any system that gets their attention, so focus their attention on recruiting for a bit.

Direct and encourage your development team to think about the recruiting process and they may well take a special interest—they have a stake in making great hires, too—and contribute in ways you never imagined. You hired these brilliant people for a reason, after all.

Optimizing for Quality or Speed

After applying universal optimizations, you may want to further tweak your candidate pipeline by making trade-offs to emphasize higher quality or faster hiring.

Optimizing for Quality

It's likely that the best-paying investment in hiring quality for your team is in the details of the screening, interviewing, and evaluation processes. However, you can also tweak for more quality in the pipeline structure itself.

The structural approach is to add barriers, such as prescreen coding assignments, and to add filtering steps, such as a second and third phone screen or two on-site interviews. I caution against going too far with this; more than two phone screens will introduce large latencies and frustrate candidates. On-sites should happen close to once per candidate, as a high-performing interview team should not need to repeat an interview.

Reject More Candidates

Consider intentionally choking each pipeline step where a candidate can be rejected, such as at résumé review or phone screen. With a candidate book, you can find any low ratios between steps, such as three phone screens to two interviews. Increase the difficulty of passing each stage so the ratio goes higher; for instance, five phone screens to one interview.

It is unavoidable that you will sometimes accidentally reject candidates who would do a fantastic job for your team; those are false negatives. Other candidates that you do hire won't turn out well; those are false positives. Changing the ratios of candidates that pass each step will shift the overall ratio of false negatives to false positives; you will miss out on more candidates that would do well, but you will also fail to hire more candidates that would have done poorly. The total effect is an increase in net hire quality, at the expense of missing some great candidates.

Use caution changing the ratios by passing or rejecting more candidates at résumé review, phone screen, and interviews. The tests at these steps should not randomly throw out some candidates, but must instead be more difficult and more differentiating.

Target Passive Candidates

Passive candidates aren't actively seeking a job right now. They might be interested in a move, at least willing to talk about a new job, or about to reenter the workplace, but they're not looking for you. That's a shame, because many of the best software developers are in one of these positions.

These candidates are harder to get hold of, so it takes more time and effort to get their attention and interest. Reaching them requires tapping networks or drawing their attention with a provocative advertisement. Either approach takes time to plan and execute, but with focus and dedication to hiring super-high-quality developers, you can spare the time.

With passive candidates, plan on doing some wooing. There will be extra steps in the pipeline for these developers, such as getting-to-know-you phone calls and in-person preinterview meetings. With potentially more challenging sells to make, you may need to bring in help. All this costs time and, complicating the problem, once you've started a developer thinking about a move, the clock starts ticking. They may well switch jobs, but if you can't move with some alacrity, they might go to someone else's team.

Build and Act on a Long-Term Plan

Described in detail in Chapter 4, the long-term plan is an especially important technique for boosting net hire quality. By developing a steady flow of excellent candidates, your team will have more options and more exposure to great developers. Execute on the plan both while you're hiring actively and when you're not hiring actively. When you are hiring, you are more likely to hire well, and when you're not hiring, executing a long-term plan allows you to gather a long list of great engineers who will take your call in the future to talk about a job. There are few things more valuable to a development manager than readily available engineering talent.

Optimizing for Speed

I don't advocate reducing the quality of hires under any circumstance, but sometimes you may be pressed to optimize for speed: hiring developers soon and often. Getting faster means making different trade-offs, and because you should generally not be willing to sacrifice quality—that's why you are reading a book about hiring great developers—it means more work for you. It also means more work for your teams.

If you want to measure the success of optimizing for speed, it's natural to look at the calendar time between hires. Whatever you do, there will remain a strong element of apparent randomness in the whole process, as the market and candidates are shuffled by many forces beyond your range of vision. These add up to significant variability in the calendar time between hires; there will be relatively long stretches between hires while you are recruiting, and rapid bursts of hires at other times. It will require several successive hires to have enough data points to measure hiring rate reliably.

Here are some different choices you could make to optimize for speed: delegate, use external recruiters, and target active candidates.

Delegate

Hiring managers tend to pick up any task that someone else isn't doing, so in all likelihood you have a number of responsibilities on your plate. You may spend considerable time finding candidates, reviewing résumés, screening candidates, preparing offers, and so on. Someone has to do it!

It's your responsibility to make sure it's all done to the highest standards, but *you* don't always have to do these things; they just have to be done really well by someone. Training and delegating is a fundamental element of good management, so take advantage of it here. You can work with sourcers to help them find better candidates for your specific roles on their own, teach recruiters and engineers to review résumés, rely on interviewers to conduct phone screens, and so on.

Peer managers are excellent resources. They have exactly the same sort of needs you have, so they are automatically sympathetic, and they are the easiest to brief. You can always return the favor later, or, if you had the time and foresight, you already did some favors.

Organizing the work into shared pools may help remove you as a bottleneck while still keeping you in the loop and allowing you to continue the work when you have the opportunity. For instance, you could send incoming résumés to an email list or central store and have several people signed up to review the résumés as they can. That approach could simultaneously share the load and reduce average turnaround time.

Use External Recruiters

Engaging external recruiters is a classic trade of time for money, bringing you candidates more quickly than you could otherwise accomplish on your own. By using long-standing networks, recruiters can tap parts of the employee market that would take you time to enter and help you find more passive candidates.

Though external recruiting firms can seem expensive (they typically charge a substantial fraction of a new hire's first-year salary), you generally only pay them if they deliver. More important, there is an opportunity cost when you have an open job, such that shortening the time to hire may be worth quite a bit more to your business than a few thousand or few tens of thousands of dollars.

There's no compelling reason to limit your team to working with one recruiter, so consider engaging several recruiters or recruiting firms at once. The incremental cost of briefing and communicating with more recruiters doesn't seem to be very high. I've had no difficulty working with four at a time.

Target Active Candidates

Active candidates are looking for a job now. They have some basic incentive to move; they have an up-to-date résumé, are more likely to interview quickly rather than delay, and, in my experience, are more likely to accept an offer. Because active candidates generally require quite a bit less courting than passive candidates, you save yourself and your team working time that you can spend finding and evaluating more candidates.

Antipattern: Overly Complex Evaluation Models

Keep your evaluation process as streamlined as possible and avoid complications, third parties, approval steps, committees, and "spooky action at a distance"[1] from remote parties. Streamlining will reduce overall recruiting effort and help keep candidates you may want to hire in your pipeline, not wandering off in frustration or to a speedier competitor.

Make the evaluation pipe as close to a short, straight line as you can manage, as in Figure 3-6, and cut the average and maximum time lapse between steps. The more you rely on other players and evaluators beyond the interview team, or evaluate candidates in batches, the more time it will take and the more things can go wrong, slowing you down or just making it impossible to hire any given candidate. Or any candidate at all.

Figure 3-6. A short, straight evaluation pipe

At speed, it's critical to evaluate candidates individually as they enter and pass through the pipeline. Some organizations have adopted a batch evaluation approach, which delays hiring decisions in various ways. For example, a hiring manager may interview several candidates before picking one, if any, for the job. That's batch evaluation, shown in Figure 3-7. I recommend you avoid it.

---

[1]This is how Albert Einstein described quantum particle entanglement in the 1930s. Sometimes dealing with bureaucracy feels like solving problems in quantum mechanics, except that quantum mechanics makes a lot more sense.

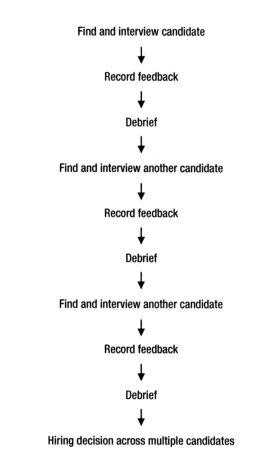

Find and interview candidate

↓

Record feedback

↓

Debrief

↓

Find and interview another candidate

↓

Record feedback

↓

Debrief

↓

Find and interview another candidate

↓

Record feedback

↓

Debrief

↓

Hiring decision across multiple candidates

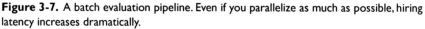

Figure 3-7. A batch evaluation pipeline. Even if you parallelize as much as possible, hiring latency increases dramatically.

The batch approach is a bit appealing because it gives you some perspective across candidates; you have a better broader understanding of what sort of engineers are available and how any given candidate compares to others available right now. It also prevents you from hiring just before a superior candidate appears; you can cherry-pick the best of the batch.

Besides slowing you down, there's an important problem with this method. Once you have identified a candidate that meets your bar, you should try to hire that person immediately. Maybe, in an abstract sense, there's a better hire out there, but you already found a sufficiently awesome candidate. Sufficiently awesome candidates are statistically unlikely (or you would see them more often than not), so you're unlikely to see another one within a reasonable window anyway. If you do keep hiring and find more candidates, hire them, too, of course!

It's possible to take the batch model even further. A recruiting pipeline could be set up to gather interview information about multiple candidates and then periodically review them in batches, then review in batches at multiple steps such as after phone screens and again after on-site interviews. Hiring decisions could be made pretty much entirely by people far away who have never met and will likely never meet the candidate.

There are companies whose recruiting pipelines look more or less like Figure 3-8 and get even more byzantine the closer you look. The effect they are hoping for is to control for and enforce candidate quality no matter who the line manager is. Whether it achieves that goal is open to debate. In effect, there is no local hiring manager, as the responsibility is shuffled away.

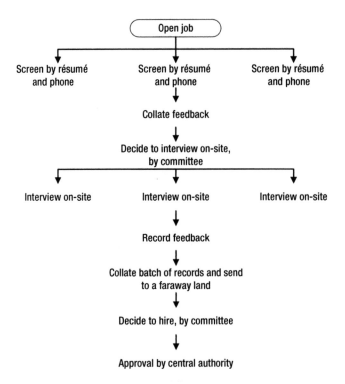

Figure 3-8. Batch evaluation by committee with remote approval

The other effect of batch evaluation is to frustrate and lose many, many candidates. Figure 3-8 is how I would set up a pipeline if I had all the time in the world to recruit candidates and was satisfied with only hiring developers who preferred to be recruited at a glacial pace.

Manage Change

Guiding a team through change is a leader's major responsibility. There are enough suggestions and concepts in this book to change a recruiting process several times over, so you'll have to be judicious about what you try to change and implement and how quickly. You will have to sell the changes to anyone affected and quite possibly proceed in phases.

You have to work within your team's and organization's capacities to absorb and adapt to change. Expect inertia, passive resistance, active resistance,[2] and errors made at every turn. Livelihoods are at stake; in many cases you may have to tackle process changes that others will consider outside your purview. Professional recruiters might consider your meticulous involvement to be impertinence and take offense—particularly if you demonstrate that changing the perspective and process of recruiting makes a critical difference.

The possibility of negative, territorial response makes it especially important to get the key players in your recruiting team on board with experimenting. When you are successful in hiring well, so is your team, and so is your company. Taking the players' motivations into account will not only help you avoid potential roadblocks and political problems, but the players may actively assist and provide new and better insights and methods. Help is available, if you can tap it, however isolated you may feel in your quest to hire only the best engineers in the world.

Other hiring managers in your organization work with the same recruiters, so process changes either affect other managers or your team maintains two processes at once—a daunting task. Those managers may put up a fight against intrusive change. If you get them involved in a recruiting perspective shift, you can create allies and deepen your influence, driving a systemic rethinking of "the way it's done."

A final caveat on introducing process change: many managers judge their employees by strict measurements. For example, a recruiter may be judged by how many résumés she forwards to development managers each quarter. In that case, asking her to send fewer but better résumés goes against her interests. The art of influence is outside the scope of this book, but you can get a great start on working well with others by considering their motivations and reward structures.

---

[2]For fascinating insight into resistance to change in organizations, see Peter G. W. Keen, "Information Systems and Organizational Change," *Communications of the ACM* (January 1981), 24, no. 1.

Fairness

A major theme of this chapter is that the process of hiring should remain malleable, and you have the ability shape and reshape it to meet your needs. As in everything, it is important to shape it fairly.

You should treat candidates for the same role approximately the same way, or you may create grounds for an accusation of unfair evaluations, regardless of your intentions. Protect yourself from both the appearance of and an accidental reality of unfairness by treating candidates broadly the same way, and never specifically calling out particular candidates for different treatment. It won't hurt to document your ahead-of-time decisions to try something new out.

When you make a change, make it across the board, or for a preset block of time, and when you experiment, do so across the board, or apply it randomly and blindly and note the decision ahead of time.

CHAPTER 4

Finding Candidates

You need a steady stream of candidates to make the interview pipeline effective and successful. This chapter provides a framework for organizing and working with sources, sourcers, and recruiters. It also covers basic market analysis and creating effective job descriptions.

The Market

There are only so many engineers available in the world, entering and leaving the workforce every day. The U.S. Bureau of Labor Statistics (BLS) estimated in May 2011 that total number of software engineers employed in the United States was 1,247,030.[1] Including other professional programmers who don't fit the BLS definitions, and adding in estimates for the rest of the world (for which data are unavailable), it's safe to assume that there are several million people you can call software engineers without stretching the term beyond reason.

That's a lot of developers, but it becomes terribly finite when you need to find a great one. As you define your target candidate, you place limitations on the total number of engineers who could fit that description, so the available talent pool diminishes. Therefore, you should define the roles you need with the fewest limitations and as broadly as possible.

---

[1] U.S. Bureau of Labor Statistics Occupational Employment Statistics, May 2011, including occupation categories Computer Programmers (15-1131); Software Developers, Applications (15-1132); and Software Developers, Systems Software (15-1133). www.bls.gov/oes/current/oes_stru.htm.

A typical approach to defining jobs is drawing limitations, such as requiring experience with highly specific technologies, expertise in easily trained skills, a high minimum number of years of experience, a particular class of technical degree, and so on.

If you define jobs with many degrees of freedom, there will be a broad pool of candidates you can reach and select from. Therefore, it's important to examine and carefully weigh each limitation you place on potential candidates. Decide which ones are absolutely mandatory, which are flexible, and which can be cut.

Most traditional developer jobs are defined as "exempt," five-days-a-week-on-site roles. You may be able to redefine and flex your requirements so you can hire part-time employees, job sharers, interns, partial telecommuters, or full telecommuters. The general approach of introducing flexibility makes whole classes of engineering workers available to you, perhaps particularly in the case of the full-time telecommuters. These you might recruit from anywhere in the world. No matter what technology hot spot you live in, being able to hire anyone anywhere expands your talent pool manyfold.

It's possible to accidentally place limitations on the part of the talent pool you can access. If you only hire during certain seasons or times of year, you can only reach the fraction of the market available at that time. That might be a random distribution across all engineers, or at certain times there may be different demographic distributions in the market, such as recent college graduates.

If you tend to hire at the end or beginning of a fiscal year that's shared with other companies, you will have strong competition from others who do the same.

You can express the portion of the candidate market you can reach with a given job definition with fractions. I'll illustrate with an invented scenario to show how a job definition can finely divide the market.

Suppose that your requirements are: computer science (CS) degree, Java experience, J2EE experience, user interface (UI) development experience, and telecommunications industry experience. If there are 2 million professional programmers, 9/10 have CS degrees, 1/2 of them work with Java, 6/10 of those work with J2EE, 1/3 have UI development experience, 1/12 have telecom industry experience, and you want to hire from only the top 10 percent of candidates, then the fraction of the market is 3/4000. That's about 1,500 possible hires.

Defining the Target

You don't always know exactly who you need to hire right away. You need "great," but being more specific will help you attract the most appropriate candidates as well as sort out the ones who will help your business the most.

If you don't have a firm grasp of the sort of developer you want, or you have a tightly constrained set of job requirements in mind, now is an excellent time to consider the definition carefully. Figure out the minimum skill set—which is often less than it would seem—and the personality type you need on team. Chapter 2 has some discussion on general talent management.

Job Descriptions

"Write a job description for your open positions."

When I needed to do this for the first time, I turned to examples to understand what I needed to create. I found some sort of job description once used by a peer manager, or perhaps the company/careers website, checked it for general relevance, made a few corrections and editions, and sent it to the recruiter. Since then I've seen many people do this, and maybe you've done the same.

It is relatively easy, but a motivated hiring manager can do much better. Writing a job description from scratch or using other time-consuming techniques differentiates your job description, so it doesn't become lost in a sea of similarity. The high level of effort means you are forced to think through the role and the capabilities you need.

Purpose

"Job description" is an overloaded term, sometimes used as a technical term for internal accounting and human resources (HR) management. There are relationships between different applications of the word. The document you write for candidates and recruiters should reflect and incorporate the spirit of an HR-oriented definition, but they are not the same thing and should not be used the same way. In every following usage I refer to a candidate-facing document, one that you might post to a website or email to prospective candidates.

Job descriptions exist to qualify, filter, and lure candidates to your roles. If they are evocative, they'll end up widespread and go to odd locations, they will be forwarded without context, and so on. Make them self-contained enough that candidates can decide whether they qualify for the job and whether they want to apply for it—and how to do so—without further research.

The job description is the candidate's entry point to your recruiting process, so it should be as attractive to the right candidates as possible, grabbing a great deal of attention. Expect to spend several hours on each job description and each variant job description, such as software development engineer (SDE) versus software development engineer in test (SDET). This includes research, writing, and gathering and applying feedback. Distributing the resulting job description is likely to take a lot more of your time.

Evolution and Multiple Descriptions

Job descriptions are frequently treated as fire-and-forget exercises. You may be able to gain competitive advantage by periodically revisiting and revising your job descriptions, as well as running multiple job descriptions for the same role simultaneously.

With multiple job descriptions in the marketplace at once, you can increase your exposure to different types of engineers with different personalities, who respond to different job description approaches. This also gives you more room for creativity and experimentation, because you don't have to bet "the whole job" on a single description.

Continuously flooding the marketplace with new job descriptions for the same underlying job is not a good idea, however, as it could appear disingenuous and facilitate an arms race with other hiring managers. If you would prefer not to run and track lots of descriptions, some A/B testing may help you learn what attracts the engineers you want to hire.

Considerations

Aside from being generally alluring, job descriptions have two primary but sometimes opposing objectives: filtering candidates and qualifying candidates. You want to discourage candidates that you are not likely to hire from applying and encourage the candidates you do want. To do that, create a description that speaks to the right kind of person; make the job description itself like the engineer you want. In my experience, the right sort of person is then more likely to respond.

If you are solving new kinds of problems, you need especially creative engineers. To attract them, build a job description that is itself highly—even wildly—creative; it will appeal to the creative individual. If you need a more traditional sort of engineer for your projects (perhaps someone who prefers to maintain and tweak software or work with legacy technologies, who may have a low tolerance for ambiguity), then build a traditional job description—by which I mean roughly similar to other market job descriptions in structure and style.

One approach to writing a job description is to invent an example résumé of the sort of person you want to hire, or borrow one from someone you cannot hire or have already hired. Strip out all the items that don't matter—specific companies and products, for example—until you are left with a quintessential core. It will be very short. Use it as the basis for the job description.

I write job descriptions from scratch every time, without reference to anything I've written before or anything existing, unless I need to produce one in less than an hour (and that is quite rare). It is difficult but liberating: each time a clean slate to fill with only and exactly what I really need. Nothing is carried over by accident.

Use the description to explain the problems you are trying to solve and what new abilities you're giving customers—the best you can within secrecy requirements—and list the methods you expect them to use, but skip the technologies except as example implementation paths. Leave the technologies open because they should be open.

To demonstrate why you should minimize the technology requirements, ask yourself whether you are completely certain what languages and technologies your team will use over the next few years. If you are certain, are you sure you shouldn't be more flexible to keep your team strong and innovative? The business reality is that you need people who can build *types of things* using *classes of techniques,* with judgment and perseverance. If you tell potential candidates what those types and classes are, they can self-select efficiently.

Job descriptions as typically constructed are nearly useless. They are heavy with convention, deadweight, and purposeless verbiage. Keeping the description crystal clear and concise, and avoiding the many pitfalls described later in this chapter, will make your description stand out to exactly the right kind of engineer.

If you take no other advice, at least be scrupulous. Do not make promises you cannot deliver on, even implied promises. If you "work hard, play hard," as the cliché goes, make sure you have concrete examples (in your head, at least) of past and present hard working and hard playing. Doing otherwise is like candidates exaggerating on résumés: common but wrong. That sort of thing sets up a disappointment that can lead to unhappiness, resentment, low productivity, and early termination.

Examples of Job Description Variations

Here are three variant job descriptions for the same job, illustrating different approaches that will attract different engineers. The first is quite standard, the sort of description you might find on any job board. The next is streamlined and rephrased, and the last dispenses with lists and uses a conversational tone.

Original Description, Standard

We are currently looking for talented Software Development Engineers to help build an amazing product. If you are someone who likes to be empowered to own features and thrives well in a high-velocity agile environment, Amazing Amazement is the perfect fit for you.

Responsibilities for this position include architecting, constructing, releasing, and supporting features that enable customers to design their own pizzas. Should have the ability to work directly with the business to determine feature requirements, and will be considered the subject matter expert on assigned features. The ideal candidate must have a mix of technical strength and business acumen. Candidate must be a strong self-starter and should enjoy collaborating with other developers as well as visual designers.

Minimum Qualifications:

- *Minimum 1–2 years professional SDE experience developing commercial web applications.*
- *Proficient with design patterns and object-oriented design.*
- *Strong problem-solving skills, excellent coding/debugging skills, and desire to learn new technologies.*
- *Experience using web-related technologies such as HTML, CSS, and JavaScript is required.*
- *Experience with Linux/Unix is highly desirable.*
- *Experience with Ruby on Rails is preferred.*
- *Experience in SQL programming is preferred.*
- *Excellent organization and interpersonal skills.*
- *BS degree in computer science or related field is required.*

Bonus Points:

- *Open-source project contribution.*
- *Experience making mobile apps.*
- *Experience with HTML5 and CSS3.*
- *Experience with Chef or Puppet.*

Variation: Capability-Based

In this variation, the bullet points are substantially changed. The goal is to clearly describe what you need people to *do* (ability) as opposed to the unimportant things they *did* (experience).

Experience requirements have been eliminated, and the underlying capabilities required have been exposed. Also removed are elements that fail to differentiate between candidates, such as "desire to learn new technologies," and those not actually relevant, such as "open source contribution." Everything that remains is explicit, relevant, and describes the role, and you can test for it in interviews.

Minimum Qualifications:

- *Able to develop commercial web applications with HTML 4 and 5, CSS 2 and 3, JavaScript, and Ruby on Rails.*

- *Able to write select and update SQL queries with somewhat complex table joins.*

- *Able to configure and use deployment management tools, such as Chef and Puppet.*

- *Able to work comfortably in an all-Linux development and deployment environment.*

- *Able to establish clean working relationships across disciplines and sites.*

- *Able to select and create efficient algorithms and data structures based on sound computer science principles and modern software engineering techniques. (This probably requires a CS degree to learn.)*

Bonus:

- *We plan to build mobile applications, so knowledge and development capability in this area will be helpful.*

Variation: Creative, Conversational

This variant tries to describe the experience of working on the team and "put words in your mouth." The better they taste, the better the match and the more likely the right candidates will be motivated to apply. To stand out, it dispenses with having separate "preamble" and "requirements" sections, though it still has a familiar structure.

Your success will be visible, your success will be important to many people, and you will get credit for your success. Your manager cares about you and your career. Your team is positive, energetic, competent, supportive, brilliant, and fun.

This team has many interesting projects; none are easy. Our releases make the news (http://example.com/). Inventiveness and a willingness to explore new business models, new ways of working with other teams and companies, and new ideas are critical to our success. We don't settle for less. We won't.

Early successes have emboldened us; we're increasing our ambitions greatly. As a result, we have a rare opening for a talented software engineer to join us as we move to broader goals. We want someone smart and capable, like us, but also different and unique, like us. You have unusual depth, you like working with people in different roles, and in all likelihood, you like pizza.

Currently we're building our distributed systems on a technology stack including HTML, Ruby on Rails, and a SQL database, spread over Linux boxes with Puppet. Next year it may be different, and certainly more complex. We're thinking of making some mobile apps. But you're flexible about it. You have some experience, maybe a lot, or maybe you're just bursting with talent. Regardless, you know how to keep moving forward, sharing and developing ideas, and you can't help but put your heart into it.

We are the Amazing Amazement team. Who are you?

Alternatives to Job Descriptions

Job descriptions are cultural artifacts we have invented, like money and art. They're not found in the wild, and no law of nature says you have to have one to hire people.

Candidates and recruiters expect a job description, and all the tools and technologies for recruiting that I'm aware of also expect or require a job description. You should fill that cognitive slot with something, but it doesn't have to be with exactly what people are expecting.

For example, human thought seems to be largely based on analogies, patterns, metaphors, and stories.[2] You could tap into our analogical thinking by providing example résumés, saying, "These are the sort of engineers we would like to hire, so if you are like these people, you may fit right in." Or, you might use a narrative to provide the framework they need to know whether they are a good fit: a "day in the life," a real or faux blog entry, and so on.

Innovation is the key to gaining advantages and moving the state of any art forward. Small improvements here and there add up, and when you have a low-risk opportunity to try new things, you should probably take it. By all means, make and distribute traditional job descriptions; then ask yourself what it would really cost you to try something more.

---

[2]See, for example, George Lakoff and Mark Johnson, *Philosophy in the Flesh: The Embodied Mind and its Challenge to Western Philosophy* (New York: Basic Books, 1999); Susan J. Blackmore, *Consciousness: An Introduction*, 1st ed. (New York: Oxford University Press, 2004).

Sell Sheet

It's handy to have a list of reasons why it is awesome to work with you. It should not be over the top or undersell the job, of course—just the reasons you would expect people on the team to give if you spontaneously asked them to say why they enjoyed working there. Doing just that is a great way to start building a sell sheet.

Possible selling points include the team, your management style, opportunities for using and applying new skills, career growth, an evolving industry, interesting problem domains, and technologies you're using, for example.

As with job descriptions, I recommend building the sheet from scratch, then consulting and incorporating any available (and true) written material you can find about the company itself.

Antipatterns and Pitfalls in Job Descriptions

Several common mistakes and misconceptions make job descriptions confusing for potential candidates and ineffective for attracting the best ones.

Alphabet Soup or Jargon Dense

Many managers and recruiters look for applicants through simple keyword searches, and applicant-tracking systems encourage and empower them to do that. Applicants have reacted to this keyword searching by loading their résumés with terms, words, acronyms, and keywords for every technology they have ever seen or heard of, and sometimes they make a few up for good measure.

This situation has resulted in a bit of an arms race, with recruiters searching for more and more different specialized keywords to weed out an increasing number of "false positives" with the résumés they find, and applicants responding by redoubling their keyword use. Many résumés now look like nothing so much as a long list of buzzwords interspersed with semi-grammatical project descriptions.

Managers may helpfully list the kinds of keywords they are going to search on directly in the job description. Listing keywords is partially effective, but tends to build up into a noisy wall of letters and numbers that mean less and less over time. Keeping your job description lean will make it easy for candidates to identify the parts that really matter.

Too Many Requirements

As mentioned earlier, through the magic of statistics, each added requirement substantially reduces the available applicant pool. If you list fewer requirements, each one will seem more important to candidates. Critical requirements, the ones you really care about, will not become diluted and ineffective.

Too Specific

The more specific the requirements you list, the narrower the pool of potential candidates and the fewer candidates will self-select into it. I have observed that engineers have a strong tendency to think "in black and white" about requirements, so many candidates will not submit their résumés if they see that they only match eight out of ten listed requirements.

Unnecessary Experience Requirements

In the end it does not matter to your business whether a candidate has three minutes or three centuries of experience with any given technique or technology. What matters is performance, and experience is only an easily recognized signal that indicates the presence of capability. It's not a noiseless signal by any means.

Job descriptions commonly have a requirement such as this:

6+ years of J2EE application development experience

I doubt that the author of this requirement could articulate what he expects a software engineer to have learned between years five and six of J2EE application development.

A great engineer will learn the vast majority of what they need to know to be truly effective with any technology in substantially less time than this. For something as straightforward as learning a new language in a language type they already know (functional, imperative, etc.), I expect and see proficiency within weeks and mastery in months.

Anything more than two years of required experience is usually overkill, unless you absolutely need a specialist, such as for a Java compiler product. Even then, what you truly need is performance and deep knowledge; years of experience are a proxy signal for those. You may be better off stating that deep mastery is required up front and why ("true mastery required—we're building compilers") and using a very high standard during interviews, than asking for fifteen years of continuous experience.

Unreasonable Requirements

As of this writing, nobody on Earth has five years of experience developing on the Windows Azure platform (because it's only been around for two years or so), but there are job descriptions that list this as an absolute requirement. That sort of incongruity between the requirement and reality sends a signal to engineers that the job description was written by someone who doesn't understand what the words mean. To put it mildly, this is a turn-off. Engineers expect job technical job descriptions to be written by a hiring manager, and few engineers want to work for a nontechnical manager.

Marketing Speak

Highly capable engineers are often interested in the context of a role, including the product, the company, and so on. So it's important to say something about that in a job description—but only enough to attract interest and supply the information and references needed to let an interested prospect continue researching. Everything else is a distraction and may make you look stodgy.

For example, many job descriptions have a thick header describing the company and its position in the industry in marketing speak, a fluffy dialect that is confusing to nonspecialists and anyone who works outside of public relations or industry analysis. Engineers tend to dislike marketing speak, and some seem to be virtually allergic. If such verbiage is even necessary, perhaps due to a company policy, put it in the fine print so potential candidates can quickly recognize and ignore it.

Inattention to Detail

Hiring managers and recruiters normally expect candidates to closely check their résumés for errors and unintended omissions. Résumé readers frequently judge candidates harshly for even small problems, which are considered inattention in some cases (such as spelling errors) or interpreted as fabrication and deception in others (such as erroneous dates of employment).

In my experience as a job candidate, job descriptions typically contain numerous errors: grammatical, spelling, structural, consistency, and so on. I bias my applications against jobs described this way, and I have anecdotal evidence that other candidates do the same.

Great engineers, being meticulous, often pay close attention to details, much closer than average, and errors leap out at them. They may conclude that you are incapable of attention to detail or simply don't care enough about hiring. Attracting these candidates, whom you want, is hard enough as it is without introducing doubt about your capabilities and motivations.

Diagramming

To communicate what you need to recruiters and candidates, you might use a diagram that lays out the structure of your application and where you expect a new hire to contribute first and best. This lets candidates with a basic familiarity with technical architecture readily compare your needs with their previous and future interests, and clarifies what you mean by phrases such as "UI" and "back end," which are otherwise ambiguous.

Figure 4-1 is a simple example diagram for a web application, with areas of general responsibility indicated by circles laid out over architectural elements. The diagram may not match your conceptions and job role definitions, and that is the point. Words are most effective with a precise, shared understanding.

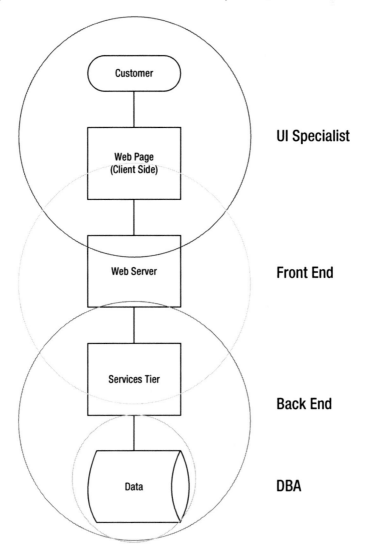

Figure 4-1. Diagram-style explanation of job role responsibilities by reference to architectural elements

Sourcing

With a job description or its equivalent in hand, it's time to tell the masses about your opening. You have a lot of ways to get the word out: career portals, personal referrals, job boards, and more. A number of recruiting specialists work in exactly this space, connecting prospective candidates to employers. This section categorizes candidates, discusses the problems and opportunities in working with internal and external recruiters, and explores some sourcing options.

Candidates

I categorize candidates by their accessibility and whether they are currently looking for a job. Treating them differently gives you better access and lets you act appropriately under varying circumstances.

Active Candidates

Active candidates are looking for a job right now; they are dissatisfied with whatever employment they have or situation they are in, and they are taking action to find a job. These may be engineers who are without a job because they quit one or were laid off, or they may have left the workforce for personal reasons or for education and are ready to return. Other active candidates are employed but in danger of losing their jobs or just want to find something new for any reason: underpaid, underappreciated, bullied, futureless, anything.

These candidates may find you. It's easier to get their attention because they will notice job opportunities. Handily, they are more likely than passive candidates to accept an offer. Unfortunately, thousands of potential employers are competing for them. Your job is one among tens of thousands, so your message must be attention-getting and compelling.

The active candidate pool contains a large number of undesirable candidates. Some have a persistent inability to hold a job, for whatever reason, which returns them to the pool again and again. Lower-skilled developers spend more of their careers between jobs but gain lots of practice interviewing. A history of short, interspersed jobs is one sign of such a candidate.

Passive Candidates

Many potential candidates are sort of looking. They sometimes scan job boards or ask their friends for leads, but if they don't find something really interesting, they are reasonably content to stay in their current arrangement. They are at least as difficult to reach as active candidates, but less likely to accept an offer—you have to present a compelling case, because they feel comparatively little pressure to choose a new job.

Passive candidates tend to be more relaxed about the interview process, which can manifest as an uncaring attitude or a reasonably nonchalant disposition. Sometimes being less nervous makes them interview better. However, interviewers can mistake a bit of appropriate nonchalance for a generally blasé worldview. That can turn off interviewers. After all, if a candidate can't seem to care about getting an awesome new job, what's going to drive them to complete their work and improve themselves?

Open Candidates

These developers are not looking for a job, but they will talk to you about one. Of all candidate categories, this one may provide the richest return on investment. My observation is that they average out as a bit more capable than active job seekers. Maybe it's just because they are usually employed, and not all active candidates can be gainfully employed.

It is difficult and time-consuming to attract people who aren't paying attention. Sourcers and independent recruiters may spend the majority of their time identifying, tracking down, and gaining the interest of this type of candidate. Once you find one, if you act quickly, you have what amounts to right of first refusal on the candidate.

They are tough to hire because they have less at stake; because they weren't looking for a job, they are relatively content and can safely refuse any offer. They are also on average less practiced at interviewing; candidates who are actively looking may have made several interviewing stops before yours and gotten their footing.

When you do get the attention of an open candidate, they may switch to being a passive or active candidate, not just for you but in general. Thinking about their jobs or circumstances and incorporating your apparent interest may drive them into the job market. That means that the offer clock starts ticking immediately, so you need to evaluate such a candidate and make an offer (or not) as quickly as ever.

Closed Candidates

Many software developers are not really interested in talking about getting a new job. Not always, but frequently, these are the most satisfied engineers, with comfortable jobs that meet their needs and dispositions. The most you can do with them is put the idea in their heads that if they ever do want a job, they should start their search with you. It's not an immediate benefit to you, but it sets you up for long-term advantages in hiring, so when you encounter them you should plant that idea. This is the best use of business cards I know of.

Upcoming Candidates

These are people about to enter or reenter the workforce on a schedule. Fresh graduate students, postgraduate students, engineers returning from extended time away from the industry are all interested in securing a job *in the future*. You typically must wait three to twelve months between making an offer and their arrival. Depending on your budget and staffing policies, that might be a hard pill to swallow.

If you are working on a long-term staffing problem, upcoming candidates give you the important advantage of letting you fill future staff positions. In large organizations, a predictable attrition rate means a predictable hiring rate— and that's just for replacement hiring, not expansion.

The better you understand your future needs, the better you can use upcoming candidates. Generally they require the same interviewing effort as any other candidate, but since you can displace the interviewing effort in time, you can better arrange your schedule. Put recruiting-intensive activity in parts of the year when you will have more time or energy to devote to it.

You may also decide that it's acceptable to find a great candidate, make an offer, and wait some months for the developer to arrive. If you are confident that a candidate is going to be a great hire, you can stop further recruiting efforts there. Chapter 3 discusses measuring how long it will take to hire in some given circumstance. If the wait time for a known good candidate is comparable to the elapsed time you expect between hires, then all you are trading off by making an offer and waiting for arrival is that you save yourself some valuable energy.

Career Portals

Career portals are the familiar "/careers" portion of many commercial websites: systems that allow prospective candidates to apply for positions online. Unfortunately, from a prospective candidate's perspective, résumés and applications submitted through application portals enter black holes never or rarely to be seen again.

There are numerous portal software vendors and third-party services. They frequently require visitors to register, fill out many long forms, rephrase and reformat their résumés, and so on. It can be a deeply frustrating customer experience, and I know people who find it humiliating.

If you have a portal, make it as efficient and painless as possible. A job description may be the first point of contact with candidates, but an application system is the first point of interaction with candidates. That experience can form the basis of your relationship. Be sure to use the portal yourself to make sure it works and see how it works.

Job Boards, Mailing Lists, Ads

There are many advantages to hiring through referrals and contacts, but it's also useful to attract talent the old-fashioned way—through advertising. It wasn't too many years ago that technology jobs were advertised in printed newspapers, but sometime between then and now, newspaper ads stopped being cost-effective and stopped reaching the right people.

At the risk of sounding too obvious, put your compelling job description where lots of potential candidates will see it. You shouldn't send any sort of spam, but people are fairly tolerant of very cool job descriptions—and make sure it's very cool.

Google once served its own recruitment ads on results pages for key terms of special interest to them and engineers they might want to hire, such as "Bloom filter." This seems like an ingenious way to use their own capabilities to recruit. Perhaps your team or your organization has a lever it can use to its own advantage.

Use your imagination on how to get it out there. You can send it to for-pay job boards that candidates visit, free boards, mailing lists, social networks, and so on. Here are some ideas to get you started.

Job Boards

Monster (www.monster.com), Dice (www.dice.com), and so on

Careers 2.0 by Stack Overflow (http://careers.stackoverflow.com/)

Craigslist (www.craiglist.org, then choose by city)

Geekwire (www.geekwire.com/jobs)

Networks

Alumni associations for universities

LinkedIn (www.linkedin.com)

Contacts

Professors

Former colleagues

Schoolmates

Specialized and Regional Lists and Associations

National Society of Black Engineers (www.nsbe.org)

Grace Hopper Celebrations (http://anitaborg.org/initiatives/ghc/)

Regional Associations and Conferences

Digital Eve (Seattle; www.digitaleve.org)

Java Users Group (by city)

Meetup.com

Targeted General Advertisement

Google, Bing, LinkedIn ads, etc.

Sponsored Contests (TopCoder, etc.)

Stunts

Billboards

Puzzle contests

Authors, book signings

Acqui-hiring

When all else fails, buy and absorb a company that already employs brilliant engineers, a strategy employed by some large, cash-rich companies such as Google and Microsoft. They commonly discontinue an acquisition's products and close facilities, which highlights the fact that they are simply buying talent, paying sometimes hundreds of thousands of dollars per engineer.

Buying a large, mid-size, or small company may exceed your budget and your pay grade, but from time to time small companies go out of business on their own, and larger companies close branch offices. You may be able to snap up the engineers and intact engineering teams they release into the market.

Referrals

Referrals are all the rage for excellent reasons. People know each other; my observation is that great performers tend to develop strong, lasting relationships with other stars. The network is out there, you just have to tap it.

My consistent experience is that engineers are typically not very good at referring engineers from their networks. However, if they take a special interest they can be marvelously good at it. That's a successful pattern of working with highly capable engineers: get them excited, and then stay out of the way while they overproduce.

For most engineers, networking is not a core skill or interest. The rampant popularity of social networking tools has increased everyone's general awareness of the importance of personal networks, but there's a difference between building or representing a personal network and using that network. Making use of your network requires a modal force, or a skill that you may have to teach and foster.

Some organizations encourage referrals through bonuses and referral drives, motivating employees with cash and competitive instinct. Even so, my observation is that these efforts are not always very effective—again, because engineers just don't know *how* to find referrals.

In addition, engineers are excellent with math, and most referral bonuses are beneath their attention threshold. Cash bonuses must be large enough to get their attention for more than a few minutes—in the same league as professional recruiting fees. When you have that attention, however, and since they are good at math, engineers may devote more of their time than you want. They will figure out that they can double their salaries with a bit of effort. You probably you want your engineers to focus on building products, so you must find a balance or some other means to motivate.

When you get their attention, perhaps by just asking nicely, you may have to help them acquire the skill of tapping networks. Sometimes this requires no more than breaking a few of their assumptions and pointing out a few simple steps, and then lowering the barrier to action. For example, a common assumption is that you will know when people in your network are looking for a job; if you can't think of someone hounding you for a job, then nobody is looking.

Most people aren't looking for work at any given time, so this is no great surprise, but it's not the end of the story. An engineer's contacts might be looking for jobs passively, or they haven't happened to mention it recently, or perhaps they are somewhat distant friends without regular contact. Critically, a developer's network extends far beyond the people they can name if you just ask them whom they know.

One aspect of Granovetter's theory of the strength of weak ties suggests that people tend to find new jobs through weak connections: distant friends, acquaintances, and friends of friends.[3] That's because you're typically either working with your friends already or there are good reasons you aren't. So, to find candidates, you have to reach further out.

There are some ideas and pointers on tapping your own network later in this chapter, which you might use to help coach your team. Any way you approach it, getting strong referrals takes a lot of effort and a lot of your time.

Working with Recruiters

The secret to success in hiring is developing strong relationships and working within motivations. Experienced recruiters have gigantic stores of knowledge of the job market, candidate behavior and psychology, and historical context, so they can be a tremendous asset if you can work with them effectively.

The better you can help recruiters understand your team's needs and your hiring strategy, the better they will operate on your behalf. Arm them with lots of data, give them plenty of access to you and your time, and share your philosophy.

Recruiter Brief

For your benefit and the recruiters', prepare and present a summary of what you want out of your relationship with them, including your needs and expectations and how you expect to participate. Describe the roles you have open, how many, your process, and service level agreements (SLAs). Include or reference job descriptions, example questions, and any other material you have that could help a recruiter find or sell candidates for you.

Absolute clarity will aid you. Tell the recruiter not to bias your evaluation by, for instance, giving candidates inside information and not to share actual questions your team has asked of candidates. Provide recruiters the information and questions you want them to share.

Include the information you use to prepare candidates you find yourself, which gives the recruiters perspective and helps ensure their candidates receive useful preparatory documents.

---

[3]Mark S. Granovetter, "The Strength of Weak Ties," *American Journal of Sociology*, 78, no.6 (1973):1360–1380. http://sociology.stanford.edu/people/mgranovetter/documents/granstrengthweakties.pdf.

Here's an example of a recruiter brief addressing technical questions:

For this position we will ask a couple of coding questions in JavaScript or PHP (candidate's choice). That means solving problems like this one, over the phone: Write a function that takes in a string and returns a string with only the first and last characters. For example, f("abcdefg") would return "ag."

Don't send us answers to this question from candidates; we only need to know that the candidate believes they can solve problems like this for us on demand, during an interview.

We will not use this specific question during interviews, so you are welcome to ask them this and similar questions as a qualification step for your own purposes. It is safe to send to candidates, post on job boards, and so on.

Establishing Relationships

Your goal is for all recruiters you work with to think of you as an outstanding hiring manager who is easy to work with, with whom they can be direct and honest, and who hires only the very best developers.

I strongly recommend you meet all recruiters in person and continue to talk with them regularly. Ask for and share ideas and feedback. As a software development manager, you probably have other duties, but recruiters are recruiting all the time. They build up a lot of experience, so learn as much as you can from them. Like anyone, a given recruiter will have some mistaken ideas, so be receptive but critical.

Strong relationships will last past this job opening and into the future, and you may even find yourself getting a great job in the future through these recruiters. They are the best job networkers in the world.

Recruiters respond to motivation as well as anyone else, and you might as well keep them up to date. Here's a note I sent to a recruiter to let her know that I hired two senior engineers, but not ones she sent:

This week I signed on two senior SDEs. I'd love to hire a bunch more—what can I do to get more awesome candidates from you?

Feedback

Recruiters thrive on feedback. Prepare specific critical feedback for anything they give you—résumés, projections, alternate job descriptions, anything. Send it whether you're pleased or not, whether you interview or not, and whether you hire or not. Directly calling out the most salient differentiating factors will make recruiters more productive for you.

External Recruiters/Headhunters

Most recruiting firms only make money by placing candidates. That motivates them to spend their time on activities and clients that lead to placements, so make yourself a key part of their success. Give them many signals that it is worthwhile to spend a lot of time with you and send you the strongest candidates they find.

External recruiters usually work with numerous hiring managers in different companies. When a recruiter decides where to send a candidate (and whom to sell the candidate on), she considers the likelihood of a successful placement. She looks at cultural fit, the candidate's apparent technical match to your open positions, her estimate of the odds of a successful interview, and her estimate of the odds of a successful hire. In other words, she will send the candidate to the hiring manager most likely to hire. Make it you.

Over time, a recruiter will see you as a source of likely hires only if you hire a relatively high percentage of the candidates she sends you. If you rarely or never hire their candidates, recruiters will stop working with you, either all at once or worse, dropping off little by little. Eventually you'll get nothing or only low-quality candidates and not much attention.

This means you'll need them to send you candidates you are likely to hire; to do that, you need to help them send you candidates that are a close match to your needs. Brief them carefully up front and provide a clear and quick feedback loop. To help the recruiter—and your team, and possibly yourself— best understand what sort of person you need to hire, do more than create and send a job description. Share thoughts, stories, jokes, résumés of team members—anything that exposes the team's makeup, culture, and values.

Cost

Recruiters typically get 20 to 35 percent of a new hire's first-year salary as a finder's fee. A great recruiter puts in tremendous time and energy to find you the kind of candidate you want to hire, so this has always seemed reasonable to me. Keep in mind that recruiters paid this way have the incentive to help the candidate get the highest possible salary because they keep a percentage. Wouldn't you?

Interview Question Leakage

Recruiters may leak questions to candidates, directly or indirectly, accidentally or intentionally. You can keep an eye out for this by looking for a dramatic increase in the number of candidates who ace a previously difficult question. Be explicit to the recruiter that they may not share questions. Interviewed candidates frequently report the exact questions you asked to recruiters, even unprompted, but the recruiter must not share them. Head off that temptation by supplying the recruiter with examples of questions that demonstrate what's important to you but that you never intend to use. Tell them to share those!

Internal Recruiters

Internal recruiters are powerful resources you should take advantage of when they are available. They have motivations that are similar to those of external recruiters, but their motivation is not a finder's fee. Usually an internal recruiter's motivation is set by division policy and, unfortunately, also usually focuses on throughput figures such as the raw number of candidates seen, evaluated, and hired.

Recruiters are usually not directly rewarded (or punished, for that matter) for posthire quality. An internal recruiter wants to work with you to make the numbers happen, so when you are both playing games with numbers, you will work together smashingly.

Measurements of candidate throughput and other numbers can be a signal of ongoing success, but they are not your real goal. You want a high-performing team that drives business value. As a hiring manager, you often have to move in directions that either don't make the numbers go up or sometimes make the numbers go down quite a bit. You may also diverge in your approach and results quite substantially from other managers; for instance, if you insist on hiring at the top of the market while the company, as a rule, does not. In that case, you may well interview many more candidates per hire than otherwise comparable hiring managers.

Learn whether you and a recruiter have different goals by *directly* asking how they are evaluated. You want them to be successful, too—or at least, have great performance evaluations. Take their goals into account and consider how changes you must make and actions you take affect them. You could hinder their careers or help them. Choose the latter whenever you can.

Recruiters are classically busy people, though they sometimes must spend a lot of time dealing with bureaucracy and paperwork, checking databases, and doing far too much data entry. If you're curious how they work, and I hope you are, ask to shadow them for a while.

It's surprising how much busy work recruiters have, but it gives you a great opportunity to help them recruit and win their trust and support. Observe them working and find opportunities to help streamline the process or provide automation. A couple of scripts or browser plug-ins are cheap to make and can go a long way to making life easier for recruiters. It's worked well for me and another manager I worked with, and software engineers seem to enjoy an occasional side project such as building macros and plug-ins.

Contract to Hire

One approach to qualifying candidates is to hire quickly and loosely and then conduct a sort of multimonth on-the-job interview afterward. Essentially you hire on contract instead of permanently and then later make a permanent hiring decision based on sustained performance over time.

There are good reasons to consider this approach. Finding candidates and sorting them into hire and no-hire pools is time-consuming, difficult, and expensive. If you make a mistake, "unhiring" an employee is usually considered expensive, due to the opportunity cost of lost productivity, time investment in intervention attempts, and the overhead of firing.

Contractors are usually thought of as low-cost investments. You don't coach them; if they are not performing, you can tell them to walk, with little consequence other than your inconvenience.

Other factors counterbalance this approach. It does take time to find and qualify contractors; you must go through résumés and conduct at least some sort of interview to have even minimal confidence that contractors will perform. And contractors may cost more than employees in direct pay.

Contractors also tend to have a different mindset and personality profile than career employees. A successful contractor may "hit the ground running" and perform well in the short term but lack the skill set or interest that creates sustained long-term performance. In other words, you may have to terminate them, or they may walk themselves out sooner than you would hope. In that case, the onboarding investment you made bringing the person up to speed will not pay off with a net productivity gain for your team.

When I am hiring, I focus on making employment offers. Hiring and managing contractors have always turned out to be more of a distraction from than a benefit to my long-term goals—but your mileage may vary.

Doing It Yourself

If you are temporarily or permanently without a sourcing specialist or recruiter, you'll have to find candidate résumés yourself. Putting the word out on the street through job boards and networks will bring active and sometimes passive candidates to you. Still, anyone who isn't looking is much less likely to land in front of you, however wonderfully they may fit the role. You'll have search for them, and, as a professional sourcer will tell you, it is neither easy nor quick.

The basic technique is searching—and for the most part, searching the Internet. There are also candidate résumé databanks available, and sites such as Monster.com will let you search them for a fee. Sourcers develop skill in digging through millions of résumés to find the ones they want. Since résumés have gone through a long period of keyword escalation, it is especially difficult to find search methods that produce great results. You are ultimately left with trial and error. There's little risk to error when looking at a page of search results, so try variation after variation until you start to get the results you want.

The wide Internet has many candidates in it: all of them, more or less. Some have put their résumés online, which gives you a ready means of finding them if you can coax your favorite search engine to do so with finely crafted searches. Most have not posted résumés, so ferreting those engineers out requires more time. Without résumés, you can read personal and community blogs, open source projects, forums, and so on to find developers to assess.

Once you have found a résumé for a person you would like to see, reach out to them with a prospective letter. Write a succinct note that states your intention clearly (you want to talk about a job) and exactly what you'd like from them (a call, a résumé, …). Include or refer to a job description and hope for the best, because—however incredibly cool and suitable the potential candidate seems, and even with a first-class opener—about one in ten will take the bait and start talking with you.

Rinse and repeat many times.

Your Network

The existence of social and professional networking services such as Facebook and LinkedIn have greatly aided the process of tapping your network to find strong candidates. However, they don't work automatically, they need to be primed, and it is possible to exhaust your network from time to time.

Priming your network means building it before you need it. It would be a shame to approach friends and colleagues only when you want something from them, so reach out from time to time to find and speak with your contacts well before you need them.

Priming also means keep your individual relationships strong. Online services let you *record* your connections, but it takes ongoing effort to keep them *useful*. Let people know that you are still around and what you're up to now and then, keep track of what they are doing over time, and help out whenever you can. Helping others succeed is a core function of management, so you know how to do it anyway. Assist a wide array of people, and they will remember and help you in return. Something as simple and easy as forwarding an occasional germane article will maintain a relationship for a surprisingly long time.

Another aspect of priming is to make sure your network is itself well connected to the rest of the world. You may have 400 connections, but if all those people only connect with each other, your total reach is limited to just those 400. The best connections for networking purposes are those that have many other connections in the world. They help your reach expand considerably. A good way to expand your network further is to encourage your colleagues to sign up for professional networking services, but the effect is magnified if you can persuade or assist them to reach out to people they know independently from you—people you have no direct connection with.

Tapping Your Network

Once you have a network set up and take care to maintain it over time, it is relatively straightforward to use. Directly contact anyone you personally know that might fit the role and take it from there. For everyone else (probably most of them), write two kinds of messages and stick them together: personal messages and a forwardable message.

Personal messages should be written for as many direct contacts as you can devote time to write to, specially written for each individual. These are your friends and colleagues, so treat them with appropriate respect. Outline the roles you are recruiting for, and ask for referrals. Be specific about your request: you want them to send your inquiry into their network. Make it easy for them by including a message designed for forwarding.

In the forwarded message, be a little less intimate but still personal. You're working within a medium that is most effective with direct, person-to-person communication between people who know each other, so going straight into a totally impersonal job description doesn't quite fit the bill. Speak as if to a friend of a friend.

Attach a job description and a clear, easy way to reach you. The more direct and simple the method the better, such as email sent directly to you. Forms and application websites build up barriers you probably don't need with this channel.

The success of your actions will be counted in resulting hires, but you can measure intermediate signs to guess how widespread your messages are traveling. When I write forwarding messages, I included links to more information that redirect through a redirection service. The service reports to me how the link is used: number of clicks, time of click, general location of the link follower, and so on. Bitly (`bitly.com`) is one such provider.

Tapping Out Your Network

If you tap your network for candidates effectively, you can tap it out. With whatever reach you have, the message that you are hiring will only go out so far and to so many people. Once you've penetrated that far, additional messages won't find more candidates. From there you need to concentrate on expanding and deepening your network, and maybe let it recharge for a little while. People and circumstances need time to change.

Spontaneous Opportunities

I keep an eye out for technology companies announcing reductions in force, early retirement incentives, and office closings. They can be sources of strong candidates who hit the market involuntarily; you might not otherwise have ever had the opportunity to find them. Sometimes companies lay off the less capable people first, but not always. Shutting down a division can indiscriminately terminate employees good and bad and, in addition, smart people sometimes decide it's time to abandon ship before it gets to their turn for layoffs.

Another easy tactic I use is to ask almost everyone I meet if they know great engineers. It's simple, cheap, and sometimes provides leads.

Opening up Your Market

Human brains are far from perfect, so our reasoning is imperfect. We are unduly affected by circumstances both recent and remote in time,[4] our judgment is frequently off-base, and we all have inappropriate biases and prejudices that we can't easily recognize. Identifying, isolating, and accounting for these imperfections will give you a cognitive advantage over other hiring managers who do not know they are ignoring important parts of the candidate market. Sometimes it's a simple failure of imagination (I have many such failures every day), and sometimes it's a bit deeper and more worrisome.

Geographic Bias

There are far more excellent engineers alive than those who live within commuting distance of your office, and whatever programmer paradise you find yourself recruiting in, there are dozens more great engineers to be found. To reach a truly wide array of highly capable engineers, you must reach out across a wide area.

It may seem like a hassle to attract and interview people who live at great distances, and your organization may not have a precedent for relocating candidates, but your hiring options are vastly improved when you do. All things considered, the total expense is usually fairly minimal, amounting to a fraction of an annual salary.

For better or worse, the world is separated by national boundaries, and there are unavoidable complications involved in hiring across many of them.

---

[4]For a disturbing example of how readily a person's judgment is influenced by apparently unrelated events two weeks prior, see J. Freedman and S. Fraser, Compliance without pressure: The foot-in-the-door technique. *Journal of Personality and Social Psychology*, 4 (1966), 195–202.

Acquiring a work visa can take substantial time and cost you substantial legal fees, so it should not be undertaken lightly.[5]

Eliminating Prejudice

You can actively loot parts of the candidate market that others do not or cannot access. Many people suffer from prejudices that inhibit fair judgment. You can take advantage of that fact and snag great candidates, if you can identify and work against your own prejudices.

Regardless of intentions, people carry prejudices that they are not even aware of.[6] They are not necessarily the result of any conscious decisions people have made, but can come from environment. When they do notice prejudice, people frequently make the assumption that because they *want* to act in an even, fair, and unbiased manner that they *actually will* be able to do so.

Discriminating between capable and incapable candidates is the hiring manager's duty; you must detect and act on differences between other people, anticipating their future activity. When it is legitimate, I refer to it as *differentiating*. Like most decision processes, much of it happens unconsciously,[7] and there's much more going on in your unconscious mind than you might imagine. Active, intentional elimination will help clear bias that does not aid your decisions, such as illegal or irrelevant discrimination. It will help you avoid using knowledge you have but should ignore, such as a candidate's gender. It's unlikely that you will completely succeed, being only human—but the better you eliminate inappropriate bias, the better you will hire.

Here are a few common prejudices people have. There are many more.

Ageism

In April 2011, Cisco announced that they were "incentivizing" employees to retire early as a cost-cutting measure.[8] The reasoning they employed was along the lines of "more experienced employees cost more." I didn't pay too much attention to their wordsmithing, because to me it seemed like a serious mistake, and I moved to take advantage of it right away.

---

[5]As a reminder, I am not a lawyer and proffer no legal advice in this area.
[6]Widely reported; see for example M. R. Banaji, Ordinary prejudice. *Psychological Science Agenda,* American Psychological Association, 14 (Jan–Feb 2001), 8-1.
[7]Chun Siong Soon, Marcel Brass, Hans-Jochen Heinze, and John-Dylan Haynes, Unconscious determinants of free decisions in the human brain. *Nature Neuroscience* (April 13, 2008).
[8]Network World, April 2011. www.networkworld.com/news/2011/042711-cisco-retirement.html.

More experienced employees do typically cost more, no arguing that. They are also typically the best deal. They can avoid mistakes because they have seen and made them already, and will act appropriately in circumstances you might never have even anticipated. Experienced engineers have moved through markets up and down and ridden gigantic technology and methodology shifts. They helped make these shifts happen.

An engineer with thirty years of experience frequently requires less than twice the salary of an engineer just out of school. When they keep your team from making the first million-dollar mistake, they've paid you for ten years of salary difference.

How can you detect ageism in practice? One clue is the comments that interviewers make when they evaluate candidates. For example (I have heard all of these several times):

"She should have gotten further in her career by now—a principal engineer, or a manager."

"His code will be spaghetti and unmaintainable."

"She's going to have a hard time learning new languages and techniques."

The idea that someone of any given age "should have" reached some career level, or switched careers or roles, is usually a manifestation of personal hopes. "*I* wouldn't respect myself if I wasn't a principal engineer by forty-five, so why should I respect this person?" It's pure projection and not a good basis for judging anyone.

When an interviewer makes a statement, ask yourself whether they could have real evidence that it's true. If you are in any doubt, ask for the root evidence behind the statement. If the interviewer can't produce evidence, it's often an assumption that has no basis in reality—and no place in your evaluation.

Sexism

Gender discrimination is sadly common. It continues to mystify me why this might be so, but if other hiring managers are reluctant to or ineffective in hiring female engineers, I am happy to take advantage of those managers' ignorance and hire great women engineers. In fact, I specifically tell sourcers to send me the résumés of recognizably female engineers (you can't always tell from letters on pages—a good thing) in the belief that if I can merely evaluate them more fairly than others, I have gained a hiring advantage.

You must detect it before you can correct it. The clues left by sex discrimination may be subtle, such as an interviewer interpreting the same technical answer less favorably from a woman candidate. As another example, I have observed interviewers label women "too shy" or "not assertive" for behavior that would be unremarkable in men.

As with ageism, discrimination against women has no place in any rational mind. Two of the ways I try to counteract sexism are including women interviewers and requiring all interviewers to make direct technical comparisons between candidate answers across interviews with different candidates.

Sexism extends to offers (for less pay),[9] reviews (fewer promotions),[10] and many other work life areas. Frankly, we shame ourselves.

Racism and Nationalism

Racism and nationalism discriminations are based on how candidates look and where they come from. Interviewers sometimes say that certain candidates have "communication difficulties" or strong accents, and they generally don't want to work with them.

This is deeply unfortunate, as my experience—and, I believe, broadly everyone's experience—is that talent and capability are universally distributed among all humans. Using generalizations instead of examinations is dangerous and wrong.

There are real cultural differences in different regions of the world, and these differences are reflected in education and business organization. But a cultural backdrop is not as relevant for an individual person, so you should consider the personality and performance you actually see in interviews. Look for the same capabilities and traits in all your candidates, regardless of their cultures or origins.

Something as seemingly harmless as a candidate's name has a measurable effect on how managers interpret résumés.[11] It may be a good idea to ask sourcers to strip out names before forwarding résumés for review.

I have observed nationalism in software companies, such as organizations that will avoid hiring immigrants or almost universally hire people from one particular country. It is a shortsighted and self-harming attitude, and this behavior is often illegal.[12]

---

[9]U.S. Department of Labor, Quick Stats on Women Workers, 2010. www.dol.gov/wb/factsheets/QS-womenwork2010.htm.
[10] M. Yap and A. M. Konrad, Gender and racial differentials in promotions: Is there a sticky floor, a mid-level bottleneck, or a glass ceiling? *Relations Industrielles/Industrial Relations* (RI-IR), 64 (fall 2009), 593–620. www.erudit.org/revue/ri/2009/v64/n4/038875ar.pdf.
[11]J. Cotton, B. O'Neill and A. Griffin, The "Name Game": Affective and Hiring Reactions to First Names, *Journal of Managerial Psychology,* 23, no. 1 (2008): 18-39
[12]Again, I am not a lawyer, and this does not constitute legal advice.

Educational Elitism

There are many fine academic courses of study in the world and many extraordinary institutions. There is no denying that Carnegie Mellon, Stanford University, and University of California at Berkley computer science graduates, among many others, are likely to know all they need to know and have useful skills to start their careers in software engineering. That statistical advantage carries forward throughout their careers, so even many years later it is worth noting that they graduated from a top school.

They are not the only institutions that produce great engineers. Great engineers don't always come out of computer science departments either. Software engineering is as much a practical art and craft as it is a science, composed of skills, techniques, and knowledge that it is possible to pick up on the job or incidentally during a technical course of study in math or science.

As a development manager, your chief concern is almost certainly creating wonderful products quickly. Your highly capable engineers are the key to making this happen, but the mix of inborn ability, skills, experiences, and opportunities that made your developers great are moot historical facts. You only need to examine and know these facts to the extent that they *signal* possible greatness for the purpose of sorting candidates. It should not be intrinsically important to you whether an engineer attended a top school or even any school at all.

The same reasoning applies to advanced degrees. Educational achievement is a useful signal, but only one among many. Overfocusing on it will eliminate many great candidates.

The Long-Term Plan

A great strategy guides you inexorably toward success, helping you identify what direction to move in under any foreseen or unforeseen circumstance. It keeps you on the move, advancing all the time, even when there's no emergency or urgent need. Building and acting on a long-term plan will benefit your recruiting substantially by providing great talent over time, continuously bringing in new talent, and increasing your recruiting capability.

Continuous Hiring

From a hiring manager's perspective, excellent engineers appear on the market at random times. As a result, the talent available during the time you are looking is random. Any person who is not available in the specific period you look will not be found.

You can give yourself access to every candidate by hiring continuously. That way, anyone who goes on the market at any time during your own employment becomes available to you.

It may not seem practical to hire continuously, because headcount is often allocated by project or fiscal year, and once you've hired a quota, you're done. If you are creative, you can work within or around this limitation. You might expand the team when you find great engineers, build new teams around great engineers, place great engineers on teams with open headcount, "horse-trade" open headcount, hire against a standard attrition rate (guessing that you will periodically lose even contented engineers), or leave headcount open. (Of course, the strategy of leaving headcount open strips you of the resources you've allocated for your projects and the problem simply returns immediately when you do make a hire.)

When you are looking less actively—because your headcount is effectively full—you have the opportunity to raise your hiring bar even further than usual. This reduces the interviewing load to a minimum but still exposes you to the best engineers in the market when they come up. You don't have to exhaust yourself and your team all the time to keep your hiring options open. Looking regularly and letting recruiters know you will always consider outstanding engineers may be enough.

Honeypot

There's a common saying: "if you build it, they will come"; as a general rule, it's entirely inaccurate. "They" will only come *if they know about it* and a lot of the work of the recruiting process is getting the right people to know that you're hiring and why they should be interested.

If you have a stream of highly qualified candidates coming to you with minimal effort, you can spend your energy on evaluating them and do a great job of it. But why would people just *know* about your team, your work, and your organization?

If you have a famously successful product, a lot of that work is already done. Potential candidates will check whether you're hiring without any prompting from you. Others will notice any messages you have sent, pay attention to them, and forward them. (It's my experience that forwarded job notices are much more likely to get a candidate interested than one that simply rolls by.)

As examples, many product groups at Apple have this advantage, as well as famous videogame companies such as Blizzard, and teams working on products of particular importance to many developers, such as Microsoft's C# group.

When your product or team is not already famous, you can evangelize. Showing off your product and technology whenever you have the opportunity will create positive impressions that pay off in the long run. Run a blog, present at conferences, attend and host local technology groups, write a book—even when you're not hiring. Yet.

Talent Attracts Talent

The better you hire, the better you will hire in the future. When a candidate interviews with your team, they also evaluate the team—a top candidate who walks away thinking "what a fascinating team, I want to learn from them!" is a lot more likely to accept an offer, should you extend one.

Set up this opportunity two ways. First, hire great engineers! Second, and this is critical, expose candidates to them. If you have a Fields medalist or Turing award winner on staff, flaunt it.

It's not exactly attraction, but hiring great engineers will naturally cause you to hire more engineers by raising the bar in your team. You don't want to lower the bar below the team's capability, ever, and neither will the team want to do so. That forces the minimum capability level you'll hire upward over time. If there are other teams around, they will notice. When you set and lift the standard, you may quietly lift the entire organization.

Incompetence Repels Talent

A corollary to talent attracting talent is that incompetence repels it. If you have underperforming engineers on staff, you always want to address that, but in the context of hiring it's especially dangerous. Capable engineers frequently sense the presence of incompetence (I'm sure you've seen this happen), and they will naturally and reasonably assume two things. First, they'll assume that the capability level of the team is low. Second, they assume they will learn nothing by working with the team, possibly leading to frustration and disappointment.

Candidates you hire might be disappointed if they join a team whose real capability is lower than it appeared during the interview process (or courtship, you might say). This leads to the conclusion that you should not hide the team's actual performance. Neither do you need to make an exception appear to be the rule by putting your one underperformer on an interview loop.

Do Something Interesting

Top engineers want top problems. They want to learn and create innovative technologies and get even better at what they do. To attract and keep these stars, you need to work on problems that require their skills. If you are building new products in new spaces, if you're at or building a startup, or if you're doing active research, you're already in that position.

If you are not working in an area that demands star performers, why not? What about your work and your problems is boring or behind the times? Can you reconceptualize and reengineer the work to make it attractive? Maybe you run a sustained engineering team that hunts down and fixes bugs in shipped products, sometimes relatively old products. Can you create a role tasked with *automating* bug fixes?

Maybe the technology required to automate or reengineer your problem set seems impossible. Star performers thrive on the impossible—or, at least, the seemingly impossible.

Résumés

Until we have something better, we are stuck with résumés as the fundamental unit of candidate information. This is a shame because they are not standardized in any meaningful way in either structure or contents. They are rarely designed to show you the information you want in the way you want it, so every résumé is unique. They remind me of the gunsmithing industry before Colt invented interchangeable parts: None of them are similar enough to allow processing at speed or useful automation.

Reading a Résumé

With no broadly standardized résumé formats, you're going to have to extract useful information yourself. Maybe you have an information extraction system or trained experts ahead of you in the résumé pipeline, which can pull out the relevant bits for you. If so, congrats! Perhaps that will become standard in the future, saving us all a lot of trouble.

Evaluating a Résumé

The only purpose of reading a résumé is to answer the question, "Can the candidate do the job?" There's not enough information in any résumé to tell you that, so you should expect to go through an interview to answer the question. Use a surrogate question you can answer: "Is there a 50 percent or better chance that this candidate will pass a phone screen?"

Using this question and this perspective can be justified by looking at the candidate pipeline as a whole. At any given step in the pipeline, only candidates who are likely to pass the next step move forward. The phone screen filters for interviews, and the résumé screen filters for the phone screen. You might be able to predict whether a candidate will be hired based on the résumé alone, but the margin of error on a prediction like that will be very large, even if you are highly practiced. Although you may set a different standard in terms of percentages, building a probability for just one step simplifies the evaluation process considerably.

A 50 percent chance of passing your phone screen may not sound like a high bar, but almost no one can pass your phone screen. If you're reading software developers' résumés, the odds go up, but even so, with a properly calibrated phone screen, only a small fraction of developers can pass. Better résumés lead to better pass rates, so finding high-quality potential candidates—in other words a source of good résumés—should be a top priority.

In my experience, about three in one hundred developer résumés qualify for a phone screen. When a sourcer finds and passes résumés on to me, I normally expect about one in four to pass. After working with expert sourcers for a while, I have noticed the pass rate for résumé screens approaching nine out of ten. That should emphasize the importance of providing great feedback, covered in detail in the "Feedback Loop" section of this chapter.

It's worth pointing out that the 50 percent chance of passing a phone screen goal is not a hard-and-fast rule. You can raise or lower it to suit your needs and use your pipeline's capacity; if you have a lot of phone screen time available, you can probably afford to be a little more generous with résumés, and similarly place limits when phone screen time is scarce.

Time Investment

It's said that recruiters and managers spend thirty seconds reading a résumé before making a decision.[1] I can't deny that under time pressure— and we are always under time pressure—it's tempting to scan through résumés with great speed, picking out a few key elements and moving on.

Spending a bit more time on each résumé allows you to reflect, study, cross-reference, and verify. It adds a deeper layer of analysis and allows you to avoid a common problem: overaccounting for the "prettiness" of a résumé.

I know that with a snap judgment, I am biased toward résumés that are crisp, well structured, and frankly look like my own résumé. But those elements are much less important than what I can learn by reading carefully, and that is particularly true because most engineers' résumés are poorly structured for my purposes. Crisp résumés stand out a bit too much.

---

[1]In fact, a recent eye-tracking showed that some recruiters spend 6 seconds on résumés. http://cdn.theladders.net/static/images/basicSite/pdfs/TheLadders-EyeTracking-StudyC2.pdf

Optionally, you can go another level and read articles, papers, dissertations, and books written by the applicant and listed on the résumé. I usually learn all I need to know from the title and existence of these documents, but I have never regretted spending the time to read further.

Developing Evaluation Skill

Quickly but effectively evaluating a résumé is a skill, and you should expect that it will take time to get proficient at it. Unlike the skill of standing on one leg, where you can tell immediately how you are doing by checking whether you're upright, résumé evaluation results have a long feedback loop. It takes a while to find out whether, metaphorically, raising your arms, leaning to one side, or holding your breath improves your results. It takes so long that you're likely to forget exactly what you tried, and you may try so many experiments and variations in the meantime that you can't tell which were useful, useless, or harmful.

Changing your evaluation technique may produce different results days or weeks in the future, so you need a skill-building strategy that anticipates the long feedback loop. For instance:

- Be analytical
- Be intentional
- Seek training
- Take notes
- Make and confirm predictions

You need to get it right quickly, with little trial-and-error iteration. There are complications: Making multiple changes at once means it is hard to determine what changes led to better or worse results, and making one change at a time means you have a very long feedback loop indeed.

If you haven't done this before, ask for help. Find someone with hiring experience, give him or her a handful of résumés, and ask them to explain how they evaluate them, their observations, and so on.

Red, Yellow, and Green Flags

A system of categorizing candidate information has helped me record, communicate, and quickly extract relevant information from résumés. A coworker introduced me to a flagging system: using red, yellow, and green flags on specific information.

- Red: bad signs
- Yellow: negative signs
- Green: good and positive signs

Tag information with these flags to improve your ability to find the information you need to make a decision. You can "add up" the flags to make a decision about the résumé using your own heuristics, such as two yellows make a red, there must be more green tags than red tags, and so on.

To hone this ability, read a few résumés and decide for each piece of information whether it is relevant, and if so, whether it is red, yellow, green, or simply neutral. It will train you to find this information quickly, and of course force you to consider what's specifically important to you. At the end of this chapter there are two résumés marked up with flags and notes as I make them.

After reading through a résumé, your flags (or whatever system you use) can form the basis of both constructive feedback, covered in the "Feedback Loop" section and a set of topics for a phone screen if you schedule one.

Look for Evidence

Delivered exceptional results through strategic thinking and innovative problem solving.

When a résumé makes a claim, look for evidence to back it up. When encountering the foregoing quote, look for specific examples of successful strategic thinking and innovation. If a programming languages section extols the extensive expertise the candidate has with C++, Ada, and Haskell, there ought to be specific jobs or projects called out in which the candidate applied this knowledge. If there's no evidence, the résumé is incomplete or the candidate is blustering. Unfortunately, the safe money is on blustering.

What I Look For

Résumé evaluation is your secret sauce. It's an important differentiating element from other hiring managers because it dictates how you spend most of your organization's hiring resources—on phone screens and interviews and debriefs and so on. It is the first gate and probably the most heavily trafficked, and your honed talents in screening make a tremendous difference. It may be the biggest lever you can pull to increase the quality of the developers you hire.

So you've got to make it your own, figure out for yourself what's important and not, what's a good sign and not. You won't just act differently from other hiring managers, you will act differently based on your company and team and the market itself. You'll move with the market, bending to circumstance, and set up your own rules.

What I present here are some of my methods—what works for me in some times and some places. I have felt free to adapt them, drop them, and add new ones as time goes on. I've reversed my position from time to time and may do so again.

Length of Experience

All things being equal, more is better. All things have never been equal.

To complicate matters, as a manager once told me, it's one thing to have ten years of experience, and another to have one year of experience ten times.

Relevant Experience

Perhaps it seems obvious, but I look for and count positively any domain knowledge a candidate has that will help with understanding and working with my team and our projects. By this I mean work experience in the same industry, with similar products, or with companies that operate in the same general marketplace, as well as the "sphere" of software, such as online transaction processing versus medical imaging. I don't value it extremely highly, and certainly not exclusively, but this kind of similarity is undeniably useful. Onboarding will be quicker.

In startup-like environments, I give less weight to candidates with large spans of experience at huge defense contractors and others that use regimented work environments I can't offer. Onboarding is slower and sometimes unsuccessful.

Education

Education isn't an absolute prerequisite for high-capability software developers, but it's an excellent sign. Doctorates and undergraduate degrees in computer science (or computer engineering or similar fields) are consistently good signs, followed closely by degrees in other highly technical fields such as physics and mathematics. Top-tier schools are found worldwide, and attending one does make a difference in early career development.

However, it's my experience that a master's degree in computer science has no effect on either passing interviews or on-the-job performance. Exactly why this is the case is not clear, but it's consistent. As a result, at this point I simply ignore the presence of a master's degree when evaluating résumés. Your mileage may vary.

Variety

Software developers with varied experience tend to learn faster and have more tools and resources to draw on to solve problems. I mean variation in careers, roles, and jobs, as well as working in different domains, such as embedded and financial, and with different technologies and languages. Deep specialization may work for some product teams, but mine are continuously faced with new challenges and need new and different ideas to succeed. Great developers synthesize knowledge from across their experiences, so having more than one or two work experiences helps them be resourceful and productive.

Fundamental CS Experience

A number of professionals and commentators have decried the evolution of "Java schools," by which they mean college curricula that emphasize high-level programming using APIs rather than deep programming in languages such as C and C++ where you have to "roll your own" tools and techniques from more granular components. The general argument is that it leaves students without an intuition for or cognitive tools to derive what's happening below the surface in APIs. To back that up, there are an abundance of stories and anecdotes about fresh computer science graduates who can't explain how binary searches work or reason about memory models.

They are entirely correct. Candidates whose résumés make no mention of Assembly, C, C++, Objective C, or something similar usually do not pass phone screens on my team. Some candidates just list these languages on their résumés without really understanding them, and of course they fail the interviews and waste time for both of us.

Patents and Publications

Software developers create valuable intellectual property as fast as any other professionals I know of. It's really the core of the job. That manifests as running software and also appears as patents and publications.

There is substantial and ongoing debate among software professionals on the value and ethics of software patents. Value and righteousness aside, these are an identifiable artifact of an engineer's effective intellectual engagement. Some companies and environments encourage creating these artifacts and make it relatively easy to file or publish them. The core of each idea comes from a developer's mental activity. You want that activity on your side, creating value for your business, whether you file patents or publish papers or neither.

Not all papers and patents are inherently valuable (if there is such a thing), but their presence is a useful sign of an active developer whom I may want on my team. In addition, when reading their publications, I sometimes come across information and ideas I find personally valuable. I skip investigating the patents for liability reasons.

Developers and others who build résumés tend to put patents and publications at the end of the document, as though they are the least important item on there. I find that aggravating, but at least it keeps me reading all the way through.

Responsibility

Great employees bring particular focus to achieving strategic goals and holding themselves and others accountable for it. It's all too easy to get lost in the details, miss the big picture, and forget that making the business thrive is the major part of your job. I look for clues that candidates have had experiences and responsibilities that may have provided them perspective or opportunities to develop a strong sense of personal responsibility.

Some indications are founding or owning a business and holding positions with profit and loss (P&L) responsibility or lead or management positions.

Build Your Own List

I urge you to develop your own set of criteria for evaluating résumés (or, frankly, we'll be fighting over the same people). You can do this by working backward from the résumés of current employees or recent hires. Fellow managers will have plenty of advice (much of which you'll have to politely ignore), as will the sourcers and recruiters you work with and even current team members. You might pick résumés virtually at random and interview those candidates to see what happens. Building an effective method for evaluating résumés is just that valuable.

As long as you keep harmful and illegal biases off your list, it doesn't matter what your criteria are if they work for you.

Bad Résumés

Some résumés are more difficult to read—they are apparently set up to be unreadable. In some cases it's clear that confusion was the intention! Some of the antipatterns these résumés use are simply bad signs. You might ignore these résumés, or send them back for reworking if there's something intriguing but you can't really use the résumé to make a decision. Here are some examples of unhelpful patterns I've found in resumes.

Wall of Words

Résumés may be stuffed with words that don't say or mean very much or are simple definitions of technologies and techniques the candidate may have used at some point. There's little indication of why the terms are important, and often they are not.

Book Length

I automatically discard any résumé with more pages than the candidate has years of experience. They are inevitably project-by-project listings of company names, acronyms, and technologies. They are "full of sound and fury, signifying nothing." No such candidate has passed a technical phone screen for my teams.

Final Decision

Ultimately you weigh up the positives and negatives and see if there's a net positive strong enough to justify moving forward with a resource-consuming phone screen. Call out risks, highlight especially good signs, and decide whether to move forward.

You will make many mistakes; most people you move past the résumé review stage will not wind up working on your team. That's perfectly all right. A strong recruiting system expects to make many attempts before getting it right, and in the meantime you get to hone your selection skill.

As in every other evaluation stage, there will be decisions you feel are easy and obvious, and others where you are ambivalent or undecided. You can err on the side of safety, if you have a solid source of strong résumés, or lean more toward taking a bit of risk when you have have a weaker resume source source, limited market, or lots of hiring bandwidth.

Regardless, in any situation except the most hard-pressed, I take a few long shots. I sometimes screen engineers whose résumés fail to meet apparently basic criteria, but who stand out in some special way. Enough long shots and you may make a very valuable hire, particularly if you go after the sort of person who may have trouble passing *any* résumé screen in the industry: basket-weaving majors and the like.

Résumé Reading Pitfalls

As if decoding résumés isn't difficult enough, a number of subtle problems commonly appear when reading résumés. They are full of information you don't want to know, and some common practices, such as asking about gaps in employment, are more harmful than helpful.

Confirmation Bias

We frequently make a decision and then find supporting evidence to back it up. For instance, the first thing we notice about a résumé—say, a good school or a failed company—may set an initial impression in our minds. We look for supporting evidence, and the impression becomes a decision. Because you have found reasons, a snap judgment looks like sound reasoning, but it's not.

The obvious problem is that you'll miss great candidates due to chance—you happened to look first at one thing and not another. To gain an advantage over those who fall victim to this problem, keep a clear head and suspend judgment as long as you can. Gather evidence impartially, and then look at the whole. The problem is not gone, but it is better managed.

Irrelevant Information

Much of every résumé has to be simply ignored. There will be a lot of irrelevant data: definitions, locations of former employers, unrelated volunteer work, unnamed awards, and the like.

Some personal information may be useful within the bounds of your company policy. A black belt in a martial art may indicate perseverance, for example, or community dispute-resolution service may indicate communication skills. I only count this sort of thing in a candidate's favor, or not at all, but never against them.

Troublesome Information

If there is information that you must specifically ignore because you can't use it to discriminate between candidates—such as, in my jurisdiction, marital status—check with your human resources team. In the absence of a company policy, I send it back to the source and ask for such information to be removed. If I have doubt as to whether I can make an impartial decision at that point, I am upfront about this and pass on the (cleaned) résumé to someone else for judgment.

I most frequently find this sort of information—spouse, kids, and so on—on résumés made outside of the United States, where laws and practices presumably differ.

Errors and Confusion

Résumés frequently have nonsalient problems like spelling errors. Native and non-native speakers of your language may make grammatical errors and use unfamiliar colloquialisms, use style and words inconsistently, and so on. The errors may be the result of honest original mistakes or were introduced through editing, translation software, or by editing or reformatting done by a third party, such as a recruiter. It's better to ignore this sort of thing than consider it an indicator of a candidate's capability; even for a position where language fluency and written communication are critical parts of the job, there are too many sources of error in the résumé you get to adequately judge the candidate based on small problems. There are exceptions; if a résumé is illegible or unclear on important points, definitely ask for clarification.

Horns and Halos

Many great engineers have worked on terrific products and for famous and successful companies, but not everyone involved was necessarily high-caliber. Such experience is not direct evidence for a candidate's capabilities, outside their actual contribution and expertise, so it's necessary to evaluate them as if the illustrious names did not appear on their résumés.

There have also been many famous flops and failures, which can in some cases be directly attributed to individuals, but many great minds have worked on them as well. Apollo Computer is long defunct, but if the designers of its AEGIS operating system's amazing distributed file system show up at your door, give them an interview. I can attest from direct personal experience that excellent technical design does not always result in a product that's successful in the marketplace.

Personally, I count it as a point in someone's favor if they have recently worked at a company or in a team that I know has a very high standard for hiring. They passed a high bar not long ago, so there's a decent chance that they will pass my high bar, too. Companies make hiring mistakes and everyone changes for better or worse over time, of course, so I use the same thorough interview process as always.

References

Though commonly requested of candidates in the software industry, candidate-supplied references are essentially worthless. Only your colleagues and friends have real incentive to be honest with you. References are selected by candidates for their bias already, and those references have an incentive to speak well of the candidate, as they can expect reciprocation in the future.

A professional network, aided by social and professional online networking tools such as LinkedIn can help provide the information you want. Reach out to your network to find out about a candidate, speaking directly with people you know. Use caution and judgment when using these probably more reliable references, and take care to not ask about irrelevant information. Confirm by interview, whenever possible, any positive or negative evidence you gather about the candidate.

Remember that people change. You are not the person you were five years ago, and hopefully you are better and more effective in every dimension. Candidates have the same opportunity to improve. Out-of-date information should be ignored.

Searching the Internet

Managers commonly conduct an Internet search on a given candidate to see what they find. That could reveal useful information, but it's quite likely to reveal irrelevant personal information or things you must not consider in the hiring process. Among other things, you may find slander, mistakes, obsolete content, political or religious activity, information about a different person with a similar name, or the (irrelevant) activity of friends and family members.

For instance, no engineer should be the target of a slander campaign or attack against them in a job interview. There's no reason to punish an innocent applicant by refusing to hire them based on a relative's criminal activities!

Poking around the Internet for information about a candidate is likely to misinform or poison your opinion with biases, so I recommend avoiding a general Internet search or you will miss out on great hires.

Verification

Candidates may and probably should reveal on their résumés any relevant papers they have authored, articles, dissertations, website portfolios, patents, and so on. Find and read the ones they list: you may learn something useful in general, as well as getting a feel for the candidate's general contribution.

Use caution when researching patents. Your company may have an intellectual property search policy that forbids or discourages patent searches, as this can lead to legal complications. Consult your HR or legal department; better yet, simply avoid it.

Most major software products are the result of many people working in concert, so evaluating the quality or success of an engineer by the quality or success of the product they worked on is likely to be misleading. Still, small, specialized applications can be the product of one person, and sometimes these entrepreneurs look for a job. In this case it may be valuable to find and study their software product.

You should expect an SDET's application to have few bugs and meet customer expectations, a UI specialist's app should be clean and neat, and so on. Areas outside their specialty may be of less interest to you and to the candidate. Many people simply don't care to put the time into building a pretty UI for their personal work and are happy with an ugly one. If it's not a UI specialist you're looking for, it doesn't indicate that the work they do for you will be ugly as well.

Evaluation Horror Story

Verification is a tricky business, and doing it poorly may be much worse than not doing it at all. Even more perniciously, we automatically and unconsciously analyze candidate information if we happen to have related knowledge.

A few years ago, I asked friends and colleagues for leads and referrals to find a new job for myself. One peer asked to send my résumé with a strong recommendation to a former employer. After looking at a job description, I altered my résumé to make sure the relevant information was prominent and obvious, and then sent it off. Normally I hear back within a few days, but after about ten days I pinged my friend to ask if he had heard anything. In response, he received and forwarded to me a message from his contact.

The note revealed that the hiring manager had attempted some verification, which is a responsible activity, but made important mistakes that destroyed its validity as well as my interest in working with him. He made poor assumptions, checked the wrong sources, and didn't ask me for clarification. I'm happy to report that I hire engineers from the same market as the company that employs this manager.

Don't Mind the Gap

Natural curiosity leads us to wonder and speculate about missing data. If there is a multimonth or multiyear gap in recorded experience on a résumé, or several gaps, it is tempting to consider this a warning factor while evaluating. For example, this record may provoke questions:

- 5/2007–[Six months ago]: Research Scientist, Analog Analogics Inc.

- 5/2001–7/2006: Associate Research Scientist, Digital Digitalics, Inc.

- 9/1995–5/1999: Associate Eng. Scientist, Quantum Quantics Corp.

Your attention may be naturally drawn to a ten-month gap and a two-year gap—particularly if those gaps lead up to the present day. Pure curiosity may drive you to ask for an explanation, or perhaps you're worried that the candidate tends to remain unemployed for long periods due to being unable to find a job because of poor skill or some other potentially important reason.

If you were to ask, you might get back any sort of answer, including for example:

- I took family leave.

- I spent time raising my special-needs kids.

- I spent two years writing a novel.
- I was recovering from a major illness.
- I took a job in another field.
- I spent time building wells in the third world.

Each of these answers may satisfy your curiosity, but you won't learn anything you can use to evaluate the candidate. In fact, you may have provoked the disclosure of information you must not use for evaluation, which you were better off not knowing.

If there *was* relevant information to be found in those gaps, the candidate would have volunteered it—and if they did not, digging for that information yourself is pointless and dangerous. The gaps were included on purpose.

You care about the candidate's capability, and the presence of gaps tells you little, so the best course of action is to simply ignore them.

Minimize Bias

We all have biases and make inappropriate generalizations, often hidden from our awareness. Actively combating these biases will aid you in effective evaluation. Some biases are unfortunately quite common, and others will be specific to you, your organization, or your industry.

Some common biases include sex, race, nationality, and age. You should work actively against these biases at the sourcing stage (discussed in Chapter 4) as well as during all stages of evaluation. It doesn't do much good to find candidates you're not willing to hire. Depending on where you are, these biases might be illegal discrimination. Consult HR.

Individuals have their own biases. In addition to all the foregoing ones, I have encountered bias against PhDs, against master's degrees, against second-tier universities, against multiple-career workers, against people out of work more than two months, against people currently working, and against people working at large corporations.

Bias can be useful in the general sense that you weigh some facts as more important than other facts, but it is harmful in any situation in which it does not meaningfully and effectively help differentiate capability in engineers.

To manage harmful biases, make a list of what concerns you when you look at a résumé. Talk with your colleagues and ask them what worries them about candidates and what sort of résumés they discard. Maybe you share concerns. Make your own list and update it periodically and whenever you notice a bias.

Analyze the list. What's actually, definitely helpful, and what's hearsay, or based on a few selective samples? If you've heard that people with PhDs "can't really work, they just theorize"—is that actually true? Alternatively, are you just going with what you've heard, or someone you've worked with, and making an inappropriate generalization?

Feedback Loop

Whenever you receive a résumé, identify and list a set of specific reasons the résumé is good or bad, or a list of pros and cons. Send this list to the sourcer or recruiter you work with (or write it down, anyway), whether you continue to a phone screen or not. Be honest and direct and include the most salient differentiating factors—all the elements of the résumé that lead you to believe that the candidate is more or less likely to pass a phone screen and ultimately receive an offer from your team.

When a given candidate passes the phone screen, and again when she passes an on-site interview, revisit the résumé. Look for bits of evidence that you were counting as inconclusive or bad signs and for clues to good signs you should start looking for. I don't suggest you revise your whole approach based on one candidate, but with some diligence you can revise and improve your résumé evaluation criteria over time.

Sample Feedback for a Rejected Résumé

Pros:

- germane experience
- computer science degree
- continuing development of education

Cons:

- no languages used other than Java and Visual Basic
- wall of words; little apparent substance

Sample Feedback for an Accepted Résumé

Pros:

- germane experience
- varied experience
- length of experience
- substantial C, C++, Java experience
- technical degree

Cons:

- not a CS degree

- extensive experience at culturally different company

As candidates pass and fail, look to their sources. Some sources and sourcers will produce better candidates for you, and it's a good idea to find out why. For sources, what sort of engineer winds up in that channel, such as sets of keyword search results or a particular career board? Can you expand your attention in that channel? For performing sourcers, why do they find more appropriate candidates? Are they better trained, receiving better feedback, tap superior contacts—or do they just have a different approach and disposition? Is there anything you can apply to other sourcers, or can you expand your relationship and get more of what you're getting?

When sources are underperforming, perhaps you can turn them around, or you can simply drop them and find better ways to focus your energy and spend precious time.

Sample Résumé Evaluations

This is a sort of guided tour through two résumés: the first one accepted and the other rejected. As I read through them, I put in annotations to note what stood out and what I was learning. The annotated parts are not the only ones I read—I read over all of it, of course—but they're the ones I felt I learned something from. The rest was mostly noise.

When I analyze candidate résumés, I don't mark them up at this level. I annotated these in extra detail to show what parts drew my attention and how I interpret what I find, as well as where I put red, yellow, and green flags.

Résumé 1: Accepted

BORIS GOODENOUGH

PROFESSIONAL EXPERTISE HIGHLIGHTS

Broadly experienced software engineer.[2] Thriving in constantly changing, dynamic environments. Strong team player. Enjoys self-development and learning new things. Areas of achievements include:

Test Automation[3]: backend and frontend; cross-platform; building frameworks; model-based tests.

Performance testing and capacity planning in high-load low-latency distributed[4] environment.

---

[2]Relevant title.
[3]Relevant expertise.
[4]Relevant expertise.

Testing: white-box to black-box; planning and design.

Software Development: wide variety of languages and methodologies.

TECHNICAL SKILLS

Development Processes: Agile[5] (based on SCRUM, MSF, XP), ISO 9001.

Platforms: Win32, Mac OS X, Web, Multi-tier, High-load/low-latency.

Data: MS SQL Server, map-reduce6.

Testing: Performance and memory profilers, code coverage[7], bug trackers, network/protocol analyzers, Selenium, xUnit, Rational Robot, Redstone Eggplant, Mercury QuickTest Pro, Hammer IT.

Programming: C#, C++[8], SCOPE, Python, JavaScript, T-SQL, AppleScript.

Other: Perforce/SourceDepot, ClearCase, Crystal Reports, Networking (Cisco 2611, Cisco IOS 12.xx).

WORK HISTORY

February 2008–Present[9]

[Huge Software Company, USA][10]

Project description: Web Search,[11] ads, data quality, ranking, related searches, speller. C#, C++,[12] Python, map-reduce.

April 2011–Present, Software Design Engineer II[13]

- Improved performance and stability of speller. Reduced 99 percentile latency by 21%,[14] debugged and fixed crashes found in production, tracked down and fixed memory leaks.

---

[5]Cultural similarity (green flag).
[6]Relevant expertise.
[7]Commitment to quality (green flag).
[8]High- and low-level language experience, including C++. Note: look for evidence in the résumé body.
[9]Four years.
[10]This company frequently hires strong engineers (green flag).
[11]Establishes context.
[12]Evidence of C++ language expertise (green flag).
[13]Relevant title.
[14]Concrete evidence of delivering value. Relevant experience, commitment to quality.

- Improved speller's experimentation by adding support for codeless, precalculated machine-learned features. Integrated speller with a key-value data store.

- Team's expert in topics[15] related to infrastructure, integration with other services, testing, performance, and troubleshooting.

February 2008–April 2011, Software Design Engineer in Test II[16]

- Defined approach for defects detection[17] and measurement in the data sets. Developed framework and reusable heuristics. Integrated with data generation pipeline for related searches. Reduced defects in related searches data by 23%.[18]

- Developed framework for analysis of changes in answers ranking. Improved experimentation agility by enabling 90% of experiments to run without online A|B testing.

Owned all aspects of testing[19] of v.1 online ads system (patent pending). Contributed to architecture and algo,[20] developed tests, planned capacity and tested performance.

April 2000–January 2008[21]

[Small Software Company, USA]

Project description: Software package allowing design studios, prepress and printing companies to automate their business processes. Selenium, Python, JavaScript, T-SQL, Crystal Reports, AppleScript.

January 2005–January 2008, Lead Test Engineer[22]

- Led teams of three to five engineers[23] in an agile cross-functional environment. Allocated resources, defined tasks and techniques necessary to finish iterations

---

[15]Shares expertise, developing others.
[16]Relevant expertise. Change in job title; has held multiple technical roles. Potentially valuable perspective.
[17]Responsibility, commitment to quality.
[18]Concrete evidence of delivering value.
[19]Ownership.
[20]Contributing outside of scope of role (green flag).
[21]Eight years. Running total of twelve.
[22]Job title explained. Relevant title. Lead may indicate greater responsibility.
[23]Team leadership, mentoring.

on time. Provided hands-on leadership and technical expertise.[24] Interviewed, hired, and mentored new team members.[25] Automated collection of project metrics to improve tracking of project progress.

- Designed and implemented framework for automation[26] of functional testing of [Product 1]. Implemented 45+ test suites/500+ test cases covering crucial business cases and 80% of the regression tests. Fixed and extended Selenium, contributed to Selenium community.

January 2004–December 2004, Professional Services, Senior Software Engineer[27]

- Led a team of three engineers[28] during the largest (1 year, $2M+) and most complex (400 concurrent users on 30 plants across the US) implementation of the [Product 2]. Developed product-specific UI framework that minimized time to market and was reused for other professional services projects. Trained customer's team to[29] maintain and extend the system.

April 2000–January 2004, Test Engineer[30]

- Introduced and implemented changes in the software development process[31] that reduced number of support incidents by 50%[32] in the one-year period.

- Automated testing of combinatorial-heavy subsystems. Used model-based approach and combinatorial techniques. Found root causes for numerous problems reported as random issues[33] by beta users.

---

[24]Responsibility. Mentoring.

[25]Managerial responsibility. Another job role. Potentially valuable perspective.

[26]Design experience, architectural responsibility.

[27]Another role change. Relevant title, but why the changes? (yellow flag)

[28]Team leadership.

[29]Direct interaction with customers. Good experience.

[30]Role change.

[31]I didn't consider this important until I read the next bullet item.

[32]Concrete evidence of delivering value. Particularly interesting due to the method used (in the above item). Indicates high-level problem-solving approach.

[33]Somewhat concrete evidence of delivery. Also, this task is difficult for most engineers.

July 1999–March 2000,[34] **Senior QA Engineer**

[Small Financial Company, Russia]

- Tested [Product 3], functionality, internationalization, Y2K compatibility, and integration with other company products. Used Perl, Rational Purify. [Product 3] automates deployment of security applications and policies.[35]

March 1997–June 1999,[36] **Test Automation Engineer**

[Small Security Company, Russia]

Project description: Debit calling card system with wide integration capabilities.

- Led a team of three engineers.[37] Developed test scripts and created documentation for the project. Covered 95% of the automatable regression tests for client-side applications, reduced time-to-market for maintenance releases.[38] Used Rational Robot and T-SQL.

- Automated regression testing of voice responses of [Product 4].

February 1998–August 1998, Software Developer

- Implemented UI[39] for remote configuration of HIL-to-TAPI service provider. Used Java, JavaScript, HTML.

October 1996–March 1997, Software Developer

[Tiny Software Company, Russia]

- Automated business processes for customs legislation consulting company.

- Ported [Product 5] database applications from Clipper for DOS to Visual Basic for Windows.

---

[34]Part of a year.
[35]Security products are complex and difficult to test.
[36]Total years of experience up to about sixteen.
[37]Glancing ahead to total experience, this looks very early for leading a team.
[38]Somewhat concrete evidence for delivery. Repeating this motif throughout the résumé indicates that the engineer understands the point of software development—delivering value—and cares about producing useful results.
[39]UI development is a different software skill set from others present, indicating a variety of experiences.

ADDITIONAL INFO

B.Sc., M.Sc. in computer science;[40] Saint Petersburg State Polytechnical University, Russia[41]

[Invention] John Doe, et al. Patent pending.[42]

[Web link for other details on applicant's outside work][43]

I am a permanent resident of the United States and authorized to work for any employer in the U.S.[44]

Commentary on Résumé 1

This résumé passed my screen. The most important positive notes are:

- Strong CS education
- Varied experience in different roles
- Low-level and high-level programming experience
- Experience relevant to the job
- Numerous leadership experiences, ownership, responsibility
- Goal-oriented problem-solving approach

Negative notes:

- Numerous role changes may indicate instability
- Extensive test experience, but the team needs a dedicated SDE
- Does not have experience with the language we are using now

---

[40]Computer science degrees.
[41]I don't recognize the school. A search indicates it is known as "the Russian MIT." Good sign, noted for future use (green flag).
[42]Creates intellectual property. I am not going to look up the patent (green flag).
[43]Following the link, I find that the developer assists others using Selenium on a public website.
[44]Work status is good to know.

Sample Résumé 2: Rejected

JOHN BADENOV

SUMMARY

Applications architect,[45] team lead, and database administrator with over 15 years'[46] experience.

Extensive multi-platform[47] technical background and experience working with large global companies.[48]

EXPERIENCE SUMMARY

Expertise in design, development, and management of J2EE applications[49] using SDLC[50] involving tasks like Requirement Analysis, Application Architecture, Design, Database Design, Web Development, and Quality Assurance.

Rational Unified Process/RUP and SEI-CMM Level-5[51] software development experience for building complex software applications with strong hands-on knowledge of the J2EE stack in large and scaled implementations.

J2EE server side java architecting[52] (design), programming (code), deploying, and testing distributed applications[53] using Java, J2EE, XML APIs and frameworks with myriad application servers and databases.

Demonstrated expertise with SOA, Web Services, MQSI, XML-based implementations.

Domain expertise in the insurance industry and CRM.

Led and mentored development teams[54] in enterprise-level projects. Great team player with refined communication skills, experience presenting to upper management, and attention to detail. Strong desire to learn new technologies and concepts.

Designed solutions for (Master Data Management) MDM/CDI and coordinated with vendors.

---

[45]Relevant-sounding title but vague.
[46]Extensive experience. Confirm in résumé body.
[47]Multi-platform experience (green flag).
[48]Possible cultural mismatch (red flag).
[49]Relevant experience. We are currently using Java.
[50]This buzzword is present for keyword searches and otherwise says nothing.
[51]Possible cultural mismatch.
[52]Relevant experience.
[53]Relevant experience.
[54]Unable to find evidence in résumé body.

Subject Matter Expert (SME) to reconcile and supervise vendor implementations with client's vision.

Skills[55]

Job Roles	Team Lead, Architect, DBA, Designer, Onsite Coordinator, Developer, 24x7 support lead
Java & J2EE Tech.	Java,[56] J2EE, EJB 2.0, JDBC, JNI, JSP, Java Mail, JAXP, Servlets, JMS, JNDI, JAAS, MDB, JUnit, Hibernate, AJAX
Microsoft Tech.	IIS, ASP
Application Servers	Tomcat, WebSphere 7, Weblogic 10, Oracle 9iAS
Languages/Utilities	Java, XML+XSL, DTD, HTML4/5, CSS, Ajax, Javascript, PL/SQL, Windows Powershell, Jacl, Perl, J2EE
Design Patterns	Front Controller, Business Delegate, Session Façade, Service locator, DAO, etc.
Databases	DB2 UDB , Oracle 10 + 11, SQL Server 5+, IDMS II, MySQL[57]
Web Protocols	SOAP/WSDL, UDDI, JAXP, AXIS, SCA
UML Artifact Diagrams	Activity, Use Case, Class, Package, Timing, Sequencing, Interaction Overview
Frameworks Used	MVC, Struts, Log4J, ANT, Grail, Maven
Case Tools	Rational Rose, Requisite Pro, Enterprise Architect
Messaging Systems	Weblogic and WebSphere JMS, Tibco EMS 4.3, MQSeries 5
Version Control	CVS, VSS, SVN, ChangeMan
Operating Systems	Solaris, HP-UX , Windows NT/2000+, AIX, Red Hat Enterprise

---

[55]The more they show, the less they know. This is nearly useless alphabet soup full of specific technologies. The point of résumé review is to understand general engineering capability, and this shows none. If the author has deep expertise with so many technologies, that would be something, but there's no indication (yellow flag).

[56]Heavy experience with Java throughout the résumé, limited exposure to other compiled languages (red flag).

[57]Relevant experience. We're using MySQL now. But it's listed last of five databases.

Degrees

University of Bengal, India   Master of Computer Applications,[58] 1994

University of Calcutta, India   Bachelor of Science: Physics,[59] 1991

WORKSHOPS[60]

Six Sigma; IBM MQSeries; CMM; Techniques to Technical Proposals; WCC 7.0 from IBM.

EMPLOYMENT HISTORY, EXPERIENCE/PROJECT SUMMARY

Large Consultancy Company, USA   Jan 2007[61]–present

Lead Developer Consultant[62]

Assignment: Software development lead[63] at Sunny Days Corporation

Wrote functional and technical design documents.[64]

Developed Java services using IBM WAS feature pack for SCA using spring injection to decouple services.

Developed shared libraries and APIs for in-house services.

Assignment: SDE at Shady Nights Inc.

Created detailed design documents from high-level design.

Wrote a Quality Stage adapter/converter customization[65] in MDM to include critical data elements.

Worked with developers to integrate MDM with the website.

Developed code using existing frameworks, maintained a Grail build system.

Developed several composite transactions and associated test cases.

Worked on externalized rules for search, collapse, survive, update.

Developed primary schema and physical data plan.

Assignment: SDE and Sys Admin at Bendy Rivers

---

[58]Didn't recognize the degree. Search reveals it is similar to a CS degree.
[59]Technical degree.
[60]Continuing education (green flag).
[61]Five years of experience.
[62]Technical consulting. Valuable experience, but possible cultural mismatch (green flag).
[63]Responsibility.
[64]Technical writing capability.
[65]This is unfortunately meaningless to me. Is it something the author did? How?

Installed Weblogic 8.1, Tibco Runtime Agent 5.4 (Hawk), Tibco PortalBuilder 5.2, custom authentication, and portal authentication in clustered Windows.

Reviewed a composite transactions specification. Worked on representing contracts in WCC.

Worked on fixing a bug in redirection that caused a session drop.[66]

Installed WCC 7.0.1 with Rational Application Developer/RAD 6 & 7.

Design unit test cases.[67]

Environment[68]: Java, JSP, Hibernate, Apache Axis, JSON, Struts, HTML, WML, EJB, WSDL, Oracle 10g, DB2, SQL Server, MySQL, Ant, Grail, Perl, Linux, EA Weblogic 8.1, Tomcat , MVC, Struts, Log4J, Tibco EMS 4.3, MQSeries 5.

Medium Software Company, USA   Sep 2000[69]–Dec 2006

Software Engineer[70]

Worked with offshore team[71] to divide projects and offload deployments.

Wrote specifications for existing and new data interchange systems.

Scoped and estimated projects with stakeholders and developers.

Built reports and data exporters for multiple databases.

Installed and configured cryptography services for authenticating services and authorizing access.

Environment: Java, JSP, Struts, HTML, WML, EJB, WSDL, Oracle , DB2, MySQL, Ant, Perl, Linux, EA Weblogic, Tomcat.

Medium Insurance Company, USA   Apr 1999[72]–Sep 2000

Environment support (24x7) lead[73]

Installed a development debugging environment.[74]

---

[66]Would be concrete evidence if the author mentioned the result.
[67]Not a meaningful accomplishment.
[68]Alphabet soup. (red flag)
[69]Running total of twelve years.
[70]Relevant title.
[71]Valuable, relevant experience. We have some remote team members (green flag).
[72]Running total of thirteen years.
[73]Not a strongly relevant title, but operations experience is valuable. Role change.
[74]Not important. What did the author accomplish in seventeen months? (yellow flag)

Create integration component using XML over HTTP[75] for a legacy system on Windows.

Environment: Java, JSP, Corba, JacORB, C++,[76] IDL, Oracle, Perl.

Large Entertainment Company, USA Nov 1997[77]–Apr 1998

Programmer[78]

The project requirement was to capture[79] title, product, and SKUs into a database and manage user, territory, and license data for home office, domestic, and 90+ countries and territories.

3-Tier MVC solution[80] with servlets upfront, business layer, authentication through X.500 and LDAP, and data stored in DB2.

Requirements gathering, meta-study of analysis and design documents, and project estimation.

Praised for improving key algorithm performance.[81]

UI and vertical development with Java Servlets.

Developed integration components for using XML and software services.

Delivered a SQL script to reconcile desynchronized database tables.[82]

Trained the operations team and wrote a runbook.[83]

Environment: Java, Servlets, LDAP, X.500, DB2 (materialized views), JNDI.

Commentary on Sample Résumé 2

This résumé did not pass my screen. The most important positive notes:

- Strong CS education
- Varied experience in different roles

---

[75]Somewhat concrete evidence.
[76]There's no concrete evidence for this claim. Discounting it.
[77]Running total of sixteen years—there is a gap.
[78]No leadership evidence in this job. Discounting it.
[79]Establishes context.
[80]None of this tells me what the author accomplished.
[81]Somewhat concrete evidence. Noting praise indicates pride in work.
[82]Concrete evidence of experience with SQL.
[83]Valuable experience. Operations perspective. Contribution outside scope of role? (green flag)

- Experience relevant to the job
- More than 10 years of experience
- Has experience with the language we are using now

Negative notes:

- Likely cultural mismatch with the team
- Few notable accomplishments
- Mostly Java experience, no low-level programming
- Extensive test experience, but the team needs a dedicated SDE

Interviews

Honing your interviewing process will allow you to build a competitive advantage. When you can differentiate well, you will identify strong, highly capable candidates whom your competitors will overlook or mismeasure.

Once you enter the interview stage, the total cost of evaluating a candidate increases substantially, so it's critical to do it once per candidate and get it right. This chapter addresses measurement, building and running interview teams, scheduling and running interviews, phone screens, and on-site interviews.

Measuring People

All measurements from instruments in the real world have a margin of error, whether the instrument is figuring the distance between galaxies or the rate of nuclear decay in atoms. The measured system's complexity and the desired accuracy drive the cost of producing a measurement.

For example, if you want to know the width of a table to within one centimeter, you can cheaply use a tape measure. If you want to know the width to within one micron, you need sensitive calipers and a temperature- and pressure-controlled environment. If you want to measure it within one nanometer, you're going to need an electron microscope as well. Cost mounts rapidly.

People are a lot more complex than tables and have many more dimensions for potential measurement. Each dimension you want to measure adds cost, and each increase in accuracy adds cost. Without a bottomless checkbook, you must choose the dimensions and levels of accuracy you need and learn to work within a certain amount of fuzzy knowledge and some doubt.

You will not learn everything you want to know about candidates, but you can expect to learn what you need to know to make a sound hiring decision. It is important to be informed about the accuracy of your knowledge, and you should establish confidence by using the best instruments you can, which at this point are interview questions. You will still be in the dark about many aspects of each candidate, and worse, you cannot be totally certain what you don't know about, as interview measurements will be inaccurate in unknown directions and to unknown degrees.

The simplest way to work with unknowns about candidates is to assume the worst and err on the side of hiring safety: When you don't know, assume a candidate has weak skills, low capability, little knowledge, and a flaky personality. You will miss some good hires, but you will frequently avoid bad hires. The wider your margin of error and safety, the more candidates you will miss, particularly candidates with capabilities that are not obvious under examination.

Revisiting Candidate as Customer

When candidates are customers, the main feature of your service is the interview. That's where you and they have the most interaction in the process, and it's where the candidates' participation counts most. The interview is not just an evaluation technique, it's your best opportunity to establish your organization's competence with candidates, build a reputation for a great experience, and lay the groundwork for candidates to view any offer you might present in the most favorable light.

Interviews are a focal point of your reputation because candidates tend to report about them to others. You must nail it, so put great attention on the candidate experience: Make the process as transparent as you can and as comfortable as possible considering the candidate is subjected to many difficult tests in succession.

Transparency with Candidate Guides

Customers want to know what to expect when they interact with your process. One way to set these expectations is to create and distribute a comprehensive guide to your interviewing process—a guide that reduces confusion and preempts questions that otherwise consume your time. Your guide may also address or counter stories and legends about your interviews in circulation. Such stories—the meat of your reputation—are usually reported by rejected candidates. They are often biased and negative, sometimes simply false, and likely out of date, so countering them with an inside perspective and facts gives you another means of building a good reputation as an employer that won't frustrate and humiliate candidates.

I recommend you include any service level agreements you have committed to, such as how much time may lapse between an interview and a hiring decision. It further sets expectations and helps you stick to the commitment (just as when you've set expectations with a customer).

A recruiter once asked me for help preparing candidates. When I sent a comprehensive, multipage guide, she said, "This is the most complete answer I've ever gotten to any question!" That's exactly the sort of relationship you want with recruiting allies: They know you're totally and uncommonly committed to success.

There is an example of a candidate guide in the appendix. It details a specific process I've used and is meant to be a useful starting point. Write your own to reflect your experience and procedures. I send mine by email to candidates early in the process.

Candidate Experience Horror Story

This is a personal story of a poor experience, which shaped my attitude about customer experiences. You should be concerned if you recognize something of your own process in this.

In 2005 I had a series of phone screens with a large online retailer for a software development engineer position. They arranged three screens, one at a time, over a period of two weeks, and each had significant problems.

The first interviewer did not call. A few days later, it was rescheduled, and a rather haughty interviewer gave me an otherwise decent interview ending with a difficult brainteaser. This was deeply frustrating because the job is not about solving brainteasers quickly, and it's easy to stop making progress on such a puzzle until you have a sudden breakthrough. If you don't get it in the time allotted, you feel like an idiot.

The second interviewer called twenty minutes late and asked me some tricky technical questions that I definitely nailed, and then gave me a series of brainteasers of increasing difficulty. Overall, this was as frustrating as the first caller.

The third interviewer examined me for a system administration job, which is not my profession, asking a series of questions that I could answer only vaguely and refusing to respond to my concern that he was not talking to the right person.

All of this was followed by a no-thank-you call from a different impolite recruiter. The total experience was excruciating, so for the next three years I advised everyone I worked with or met who mentioned this particular company that those folks were a bunch of clowns who didn't know what they were doing and not to bother with them. I don't know how much damage this did to their recruiting pipeline (probably not very much). However, it's often appropriate to assume your experience is typical, and this is borne out by many anecdotes about this company from that period, so they likely typically irritated candidates. That fact most certainly damaged their recruiting efforts for a long time.

Interview Teams

Unless you're going it alone—and you shouldn't be—interviewing is a team effort that requires coordination. An effective team has multiple distinct roles, though as usual some may be filled by the same person wearing several hats.

Hiring managers should construct interview teams from trained and qualified interviewers. This section provides a description of the roles in an interview team, how to qualify and disqualify interviewers, training, and organizing interview teams in pools and for particular interviews.

Roles

Just as there are separate roles in the overall hiring process, there are definite roles in the interview. If you are explicit about who owns a role, you know who's responsible for doing it well and you can reassign or delegate it all at once.

Coordinator

The coordinator makes sure all the other roles are in place, orders food and drink if necessary, and monitors the interview to verify that it is running smoothly. This person usually does simple setup, such as stocking a whiteboard with markers and an eraser. The role is sometimes filled by the recruiting process scheduler.

Greeter

This person greets the candidate and starts the interview process for the day, either proceeding to an interview themselves, or escorting the candidate to an interviewer. If you need a nondisclosure (NDA) or other confidentiality agreement signed, this is the person to present and collect it.

Hiring Manager

This person is as vital to the interview as the candidate, of course, and is usually also an interviewer. (Please interview candidates yourself before hiring them!) Of course, the hiring manager fills in the other roles as needed.

Interviewer

These are the stalwart folks who question and evaluate candidates. They may develop software on the side.

Qualifying Interviewers

Always choose interviewers who are roughly qualified in relation to each candidate. For interviewing software developers, this is almost always another software developer, so interview teams should be heavily stocked with working software developers and not overloaded with human resources or development managers.

You can help candidates find a comfort zone during interviews by using interviewers who are in some sense like the candidate. That may also make it easier for candidates to fairly evaluate offers, if they can see that the new environment won't be composed of entirely alien people. Unfortunately, the effect works in reverse as well—interviewers may develop an unjustifiable positive bias toward the candidate.

The Dunning-Kruger Effect

In their 1999 paper "Unskilled and Unaware of It: How Difficulties in Recognizing One's Own Incompetence Leads to Inflated Self-Assessments,"[1] David Dunning and Justin Kruger described how people who have little competence in a given field frequently cannot recognize substantial competence.

A straightforward extension of this phenomenon (which I have witnessed many times) is that even otherwise competent people may not recognize superior competence. A junior engineer may not be able to tell the difference between a senior and a principal engineer and may even make the mistake of not recognizing competence at all. The approach and solutions created by a greatly superior engineer may have unrecognizable nuance and subtlety, anticipating problems the more junior interviewer hasn't seen and couldn't foresee without guidance.

My interpretation of the Dunning-Kruger effect and my experience are that with a little training, most people can fairly evaluate candidates who are a little bit more or a little bit less skilled and experienced than they are. Evaluating engineers outside this natural range takes practice, and not everyone seems to develop a knack for it.

Some interviewers will be particularly good at interviewing certain kinds of candidates and not others. For example, I know a principal engineer who excels at evaluating college candidates but consistently gives overly critical evaluations of industry veterans.

---

[1]David Dunning and Justin Kruger, "Unskilled and Unaware of It: How Difficulties in Recognizing One's Own Incompetence Leads to Inflated Self-Assessments," *Journal of Personality and Social Psychology* 77(6) (1999): 1121–34.

Language

The language of the interview is also an important consideration. The mental gymnastics of an interview are complex enough without forcing candidates to speak in languages they cannot use fluently, so use interviewers who are fluent with the language the candidate is expected to use in the ordinary course of work (such as English).

Field of Expertise

Often overlooked, there is a special challenge to hiring for new roles and specialist roles—the sort that you don't have on your team already. That might be someone like a molecular biologist to design computational models for a new gene network analysis tool or just your first software developer. For candidates with fields of expertise you have difficulty evaluating, you may be able to find and ask questions that match the skills you need for the role, but interpreting the answers is another issue. Careful interpretation generally requires another specialist.

You can make do with what you have if the new field of expertise is relatively close to ones you already have. It may be more effective if you can provide some training, such as teaching software engineers to evaluate software test engineers.

If you still have no qualified interviewers, find someone you trust who is qualified to evaluate the candidate in the area of specialization required. It could be someone from another department, a consultant, or someone you know personally. If none of these are available, you might substitute qualification signals, such as peer-reviewed publications, followed by candidate references. Finally, you may have to do your best to determine whether candidates are at least comfortable and articulate when discussing their specialty and make a hire on faith, then evaluate the success of the hire by his or her performance.

Another option is to take on a specialist as a contractor, if the person is willing. You are stuck with the same evaluation problem, but it may be cheaper to conduct trial-and-error searches.

Disqualifying Interviewers

Some people should not be allowed to interview candidates. You've met them: the disgruntled, the underperforming, and employees on their way out, as well as anyone who feels threatened by bringing on new employees. Highly introverted engineers and the chronically surly tend to be poor interviewers and make negative impressions on candidates.

There's a pernicious type of employee who uses interviews as opportunities to show how much smarter they are than candidates. These egotists will ask questions that rely on obscure knowledge or that are inappropriately complex, or will hold answers to an impossibly high standard. They have no interest in actually evaluating candidates. They can be overbearing or intimidating. These interviewers are dangerous to your hiring process, so root them out and cut them out of the process as soon as you can.

Don't be afraid to take troublesome people off interview loops and out of your interview team. If an interviewer has an irreconcilable difference of opinion with you over basic procedure or evaluation philosophy, you should certainly hear them out, but don't let it become a source of continuous frustration. Make the cut and move on.

Training Interviewers

Some people become excellent at interviewing, developing superb intuition and critical insight into candidates with little training. Others have already received training before you met them and gained experience that honed their interviewing skills to a fine degree, so they will need little or no help from you. In either case, such people are rare, so it's likely you will have to build this capability in interviewers.

All interviewers must understand the interviewing and hiring policies of the company and applicable laws, including the types of questions they must not ask, questions they should not answer, and unacceptable interviewing behaviors. They should know the essentials of the recruiting process and know to treat candidates as customers. Additionally, your team's interviewers should share an understanding of the local process and the team's standards. The more they know beyond that and the more skills they accumulate, the better they will differentiate between candidates. Various methods are available for making great interviewers.

Shadowing

In my experience, having new interviewers shadow interviews is the most effective way to build competence and confidence in their ability to effectively interview and evaluate candidates. It exposes them to the real deal in a relatively safe manner and gives them examples to draw from, and access to experienced interviewers to confer with and ask specific questions.

Shadowing a phone screen is simple. Put another person in the room with the interviewer and conduct the interview via speakerphone, with the shadow remaining quiet. It isn't necessary to introduce the shadow. Both the interviewer and shadower have the opportunity to press the mute button for short periods to comment on or discuss the interview as it progresses, and the candidate will not need to be concerned about having a third party listen to the conversation.

The presence of a third person during an on-site interview can make candidates uneasy, but they usually relax if they understand the purpose. Introduce the shadow at the beginning of the interview; the shadow should greet the candidate and say something to the effect of "I'm here to sit quietly in the back and learn about interviewing. Please pay me no attention." Then the shadow should do just that and take notes. You might also consider asking candidates before they arrive whether they would mind having shadow interviewers.

In either circumstance, the shadow and interviewer should discuss the interview immediately after, talk about the techniques and questions used in the interview, and share their evaluation of the candidate. When I am the primary interviewer, I try to ask the shadow for feedback on my performance. Feedback from fresh perspectives has helped me improve my interviewing in many ways, such as pronouncing words more clearly, speaking at a steadier pace, and patiently drawing more detailed answers from candidates.

Sending a new or experienced interviewer to shadow interviews conducted by another team may also be enlightening, showing new techniques and ideas. Your interviewer may be able to provide useful feedback in return.

Classes and Workshops

How much you can teach via distributed documents, lectures, and hands-on workshops will depend on your organization's culture and your team's learning styles. My experience is that hands-on workshops are an effective way to distribute important structured information and build skills at the same time.

It's almost certainly a worthwhile investment to conduct a small workshop for your team: reviewing the fundamental theory of hiring and highlights of how to hire, modeling questions and evaluations, practicing interviewing each other, and giving an opportunity to ask questions in context.

Documents and Guides

In some organizations, nothing is real until it's written down. Whether or not that is your situation, it is true that documents are longer-lived than oral instruction, workshops, examples, and word of mouth. Writing down the essentials of your process in a friendly, easy-to-follow guide will help create a consistent system of concepts that will cause effective hiring, allow people to teach and refresh each other, and create a wake behind you.

I suggest you document, distribute, and archive only what you think people on your team will actually read, which in most circumstances is not very much. Consider writing or gathering a summary of the interviewing process from first candidate contact to offer, a summary of the organization's basic hiring philosophy and standards, a list of examples of good questions, a phone screen guide or sample transcript, and a set of advice on evaluating candidates. Make these things succinct to increase the likelihood that someone will use them.

Coaching

I have also asked interviewers to shadow in reverse, sending a great interviewer to observe a less experienced interviewer. Then they discuss the interview. This coaching provides an avenue for constructive feedback and leads to rapid improvement, as long as the two interviewers have a strong relationship and both see the process as collaboration.

Practice Interviews

I have found that shadowing and coaching gives my team strong interviewing skills quickly, and practice interviews reinforce these skills. These are simply role-playing sessions in which one person takes the role of an interviewer and the other the role of a candidate. Most people have fun with this kind of practice.

The technique appears to be particularly useful when you limit the mock interview to asking and answering a single technical question. It helps the interviewer gain practice at asking a particular question before asking a candidate, and it helps calibrate the question to the team's needs. (Chapter 7 has more information on question calibration.)

Tracking and Profiling Interviewers

On an interview team there will be interviewers with various different personalities, strengths, and weaknesses. Taking full advantage of all the interviewers will require understanding and tracking their differences—such as who usually gives overly negative feedback, who can interview SDETs, and so on. A spreadsheet may help you organize this information as well help you select and organize an interview team for any particular interview.

Standing and Dynamic Interview Teams

An interview team can be composed of the same people for interview after interview—a standing team—or it can be a temporary team, drawn together for one interview from a pool of interviewers. Both approaches have advantages: a standing team establishes a rhythm and may develop a more consistent evaluation style (not necessarily a better one); a dynamically composed team may spread the interview load more widely and in my observation develops a more creative approach to evaluation due to differing styles that are not yet comfortably meshed.

Scheduling a standing team is straightforward because you know who needs to attend. Putting together dynamic teams from a large pool of interviewers requires careful consideration for each interview. A meta-schedule can help guide building each individual interview from an interviewer pool.

A meta-schedule is a set of instructions for creating and scheduling a team out of many possible team members. It should be comprehensive enough that anyone with access to the team members' calendars can set up the interview meetings. The instructions can have several line items, each of which says "draw x from y" where x is a person and y is the interviewer pool. The following example should make this clear.

A-Team Interview Schedule

For each interview, schedule four contiguous interview sessions at fifty minutes each. The order is not important, except that where it is convenient we would prefer to have the hiring manager interviewing first or last. Schedule all of them either before or after lunch, but if scheduling over lunchtime is necessary, schedule the hiring manager for the lunch session.

Sessions:

- Hiring manager (required) and one from Pool A
- Two from Pool B
- Two (others) from Pool B
- Two from Pool C and one shadow from Pool D

Interviewer pools:

- A: (technical program managers): Bujor, Christi, Devon (in order of preference)
- B: (SDEs): Eliza, Franklin, Genna, Hiram, Ilsa, Johann, Katrina (pick randomly)
- C: (Senior SDEs): Bujor, Ilsa, Larry, Melissandra (pick randomly)
- D: Namit, Ophelia, Patri (shadowers)

Interview Structure

Chapter 3 explores the overall structure of the recruiting process and how you can create, adapt, and tweak it. This section discusses the internal structure of interview elements of the process: prequalifying, phone screens, and on-site interviews.

Prequalifiers: Barriers to Entry

To focus their time on candidates more likely to pass interviews, some hiring managers place proof-of-competency tests at the head of the candidate pipeline. The approach is most appropriate when you receive a big ratio of unqualified to qualified solicited applicants. If the ratio is not huge, but you feel pressed for time, this might work for you.

Prequalifiers are usually assignments: tests that candidates take and submit along with their application before it is considered, or as a preliminary step before interviews. They can be questionnaires, multiple-choice tests, coding assignments, design exercises, and so on. These barriers reduce the number of applicants, possibly quite dramatically. The bigger and more complex the assignment, the higher the barrier, so fewer engineers will apply.

In this sense the theory is sound: Engineers who cannot complete the assignment will not become candidates. It may also keep out engineers who are qualified but are simply too busy to take the assignment.

From the candidate's perspective, she has many jobs she can apply for. A barrier that requires substantial effort to cross may keep out the engineers with the most choices; these are often the best engineers.

The developers who get through the prequalifying barriers are the ones who have an overwhelming interest in your particular job, as well as those with enough time on their hands. Having a lot of time on one's hands isn't always a good sign in a candidate.

Phone Screens

The purpose of a technical phone screen is to admit candidates who have a certain chance of passing an on-site interview. You should set a target ratio and publish it to the team, such as one in four: one hire per four in-house interviews.

The ratio you aim for is your balance point for interviewing efficiency, determining how much time, on average, you spend evaluating each candidate. More on-site interviews per candidate costs you more interviewer time, so that's the trade-off between avoiding interviewing people who are unlikely to pass your interviews and accidentally failing to continue interviewing great engineers.

Calling the candidate is easy, but conducting a useful phone screen takes planning and practice. Each role you interview for has idiosyncratic requirements, but in general for software engineers you should plan to learn:

- Whether the candidate can communicate clearly,

- Whether the candidate can code, and

- Whether the candidate can create and think about algorithms.

These capabilities are broadly—perhaps universally—useful, and understanding a candidate's ability will let you roughly estimate the odds that he or she will pass an on-site interview. To learn about these capabilities, develop and include questions that you find over time will differentiate between candidates who pass on-site interviews and those that do not.

To keep the admittance to on-site ratio at your target, use feedback from further along in the interview process. Do you typically end up rejecting engineers after the on-site interview because they cannot code well? Step up the difficulty of coding questions on your phone screens—or at least reevaluate the ones you use. In the other direction, to increase the number of candidates who get to on-site interviews, you can relax difficulty in areas that are not common failure modes for candidates you interview.

Phone Screen Structure

Using a consistent structure for phone screens will make it easy on you and the candidate, covering all the important points and leaving your attention on the important part: learning what's different about this person. There's a full sample phone screen transcript included in the appendix. Here is a highly compressed abstract.

1. Greeting

   - "Hi, this is Patrick calling from ExampleCompany. May I speak with Chaz Fernandez? . . . Is this still a good time to talk?"

2. Introduction and Verification

   - "I'm a software development manager and I'm calling to do a phone screen for a software development engineer position. Is that what you expected?"

   - "Do you have something to write with or an Internet-connected computer?"

3. Set Expectations

- "I'm going to introduce our company and team, ask you some technical and nontechnical questions, then let you ask me whatever you like."

4. Brief Overview

- "ExampleCompany is in the software as a service industry, and our team is responsible for developing and maintaining a public distributed computation and caching service."

5. Interview Questions

- "Please write me some code that . . ."

6. Candidate Questions

- "What would you like to know about us?"

7. Next Steps

- "I'm going to review my notes carefully, and we'll get back to you shortly."

8. Wrap-Up

- "Thanks for your time today. Have a great evening."

9. Prepare Feedback or Record Notes

I recommend keeping notes as you conduct a phone screen, which you can refer to later when you prepare specific feedback, update a candidate book, or prepare for a hiring decision. Typing them directly into a computer saves some transcription time, and I use a template to do so. My template is an otherwise empty document with a list of the questions I intend to ask. Notes go in between; I save the document, and I have everything I need to create feedback and pass the notes on to future interviewers.

I have also found myself wondering after an on-site interview, "Why did I decide to bring this person in?" Thorough interview notes provide a clear (if not always flattering) answer.

Missing Context

Phone screens can be strange and scary even to experienced interviewers, and it seems that both sides of the conversation are at a disadvantage. First, you talk with a stranger. Second, there's a substantial power imbalance between the participants. Third, the participants have differing motives. Fourth, the communication channel is unnaturally narrow.

Normal human interaction is substantially nonverbal. Stance or posture, direction of attention, placement and movement of hands, eye contact, facial expressions, micro expressions, and much more set the context of communication and reframe it as the conversation goes on. All of that information is stripped away when we talk on the phone, and we are left with only auditory communication cues such as inflection, timing, volume, and words.

Because nonverbal signals guide others to interpreting our words as we mean them, miscommunication is much more likely over the phone. You may have noticed this. Be careful to speak clearly and listen generously.

Problem Complexity

Solving problems over the phone seems to be universally more difficult than solving them in person, so an otherwise simple question can become difficult, and a tricky question can become virtually unsolvable. Some classes of question are nearly useless in a phone screen; coding problems in particular require special care.

Problematic Questions

In person, a candidate can closely monitor the interviewer for clues and feedback as they start to respond, asking clarifying questions or producing an answer. Over the phone, uncertainty does not resolve easily, so candidates frequently go off track when presented with slightly vague or ambiguous questions. When they are on track, they will often wonder how they are doing.

I find that the interview becomes a lot more difficult when asking questions that involve large design spaces, ask the candidate to work in an unfamiliar domain, or can only be answered well after several rounds of back-and-forth discussion or extensive requirement gathering by the candidate.

Great phone screen questions are briefly posed and briefly solved, easily stated, and have an answer form that's either highly verbal or expressed in short pieces of code.

Knowing what not to ask about will save time and keep unimportant information out of your head. I don't ask:

- All about their most recent project.
- A litany of skills and buzzwords.
- What they did on their summer vacation.
- Their childhood pet's middle name.

The answers to these kind of questions are distracting, take valuable screening time, and are usually not relevant. If you really need to know any of that stuff, you can cover it on-site.

A major class of questions to avoid asking in phone screens is any open-ended inquiry about the candidate's experience. Such questions pass control of the conversation to the interviewee, and you really shouldn't let that happen. You are in charge, and the candidate should spend their time answering your questions or asking their own at your invitation, not retelling stories. When the candidate controls the interview, the time will be spent on their interests, so you won't learn what you need to know.

Coding Questions

On the phone it's critical to ask coding problems that can be easily and readily explained, coded quickly, and evaluated quickly. I only ask coding questions that can be posed in less than one minute (usually less than thirty seconds), which good candidates can understand rapidly with no confusion. These questions have elegant solutions that are no more than a handful of lines of code, giving the candidate a fair chance to design and code a solution. Wide varieties of coding problems meet these conditions and differentiate among candidates, highlighting those most likely to succeed.

Chapter 7 has more discussion of designing, choosing, and evaluating interview questions.

Paper and Pencil

My personal practice is to keep coding questions short and straightforward, such that most solutions can be written with a few lines of code. These can be worked out easily with pencil and paper.

Candidates can acquire and use simple writing tools wherever they are. They are also kept off computers; where there may be a temptation (or even an involuntary reflex) to look up answers and other information they may use to perform better on the question than a candidate without these resources.

The disadvantage is unfamiliarity; it is uncommon for software developers to work out code solutions in anything other than an IDE or at least a text editor. It may feel a bit unnatural for them. Acknowledging up front that it's going to feel unnatural relaxes most candidates.

Online/Shared Screens

Screen-sharing lets you share screens or live online documents with a candidate. This gives you the opportunity to see her work progress as well as the end product immediately, with much less chance for miscommunication. No one has to read code out loud over the phone. It is especially useful for code that is verbose or complex, such as regular expressions or HTML.

However, a downside is that shared screens require the candidate to have an Internet-connected computer with them, sometimes particular software installed, and a hands-free phone or headset. That limits the circumstances under which they can screen. The computer in front of the candidate also gives her an excellent opportunity to quickly look up information to respond to questions you otherwise expected them to answer without aid and tempts many to cheat by searching for source code.

Personally, I've never been sure of what I have learned by watching candidates type. Everyone seems to think a slightly different way, often nonlinearly, and this makes them jump back and forth, refactor, rename, and so on. All I can learn is that they seem to be actually working on it, and I see little else of use about their process and results that can't be learned in other ways.

There are many ways to accomplish screen sharing using tools such as Google Docs (http://docs.google.com), See[Mike]Code (http://i.seemikecode.com/), and general desktop sharing applications such as Fog Creek Copilot (www.copilot.com).

Antipatterns and Pitfalls

Some difficulties come up repeatedly with phone screens. These are problems I have coached people through many times: staying on too long, working with senior candidates, handling candidate expectations, and candidates who talk too much.

Staying on Too Long

You wisely arrange your phone screens to cover the truly important and most differentiating aspects of the interview first, so you may have the opportunity to detect early that a candidate simply will not pass the rest of the phone screen. You need to get off the phone because you have other things to do— like find more candidates.

Cutting a phone screen short can feel quite rude, and if you do it abruptly and with no compassion it will be a poor experience for the candidate. Candidates seem to universally appreciate honesty, and their time is valuable as well. When you are certain there's no hope, go ahead and let the candidate know. Avoid platitudes or false flattery. For example, here is how I halted a recent phone screen:

"Based on how the interview is going so far, I think it's pretty clear that this position requires substantially more fluency with algorithm design. So there's not really a match possible here. I know your time is valuable, so what I'm going to do is end the interview now. Thank you for talking with us."

Senior Candidates and Complex Questions

Experienced engineers accumulate lots of information and many skills, which is why you want to hire them, and they often expect to have these skills put to test in interviews. Phone interviews, however, are not a very good place to ask the complex and nuanced questions that will engage a candidate's deeper knowledge and hard-earned skills, so they may feel underchallenged. It is not rare to hear a senior candidate report that they felt they were interviewed for a junior position rather than one that would challenge them and demand their skills.

I simply advise them that the purpose of the phone interview is to screen out candidates who are unlikely to pass an on-site interview, and it's the basics that commonly drive on-site interview failures. At the on-site, we ask the sort of questions that will demand and exercise their well-developed skills.

Candidate Expectations

Candidates may have preset notions about how interviews should function and what their role is. For example, they may expect to be asked detailed questions about past projects, and if your interview does not meet those expectations, they may come away disappointed or frustrated.

You can only spend so much time setting expectations, so you will inevitably disappoint some people. A candidate guide, as described earlier, can help inform people about your intentions, though this won't stop them from disagreeing with your methods if they choose to do so.

Candidates Who Have Something to Tell You

I don't ask for it, but if they volunteer, I let candidates spend a few moments telling me why they are a great fit for the job. However, I politely stop them before they get very far. It's not a question I asked, and the answer is usually not enlightening. I know from their résumé what they have worked on recently, and they demonstrate the skills and capabilities that are the most important for the role by performing during the interview.

On-Site Interviews

Once you decide to bring someone in for an on-site interview, costs mount quickly. Your organization invests the time of all interviewers for the interviews, their feedback preparation, and recap meetings, as well as whatever capital it takes to bring candidates to your location. With this much at stake, you want to get it right and do it the minimum number of times per hire.

Location

Organizations have various approaches to locating interviews at their sites—from individual offices to cafeterias to conference rooms.

Individual offices have the merit of being easily booked, because they are usually plentiful and interviewers often have their own. In their own offices, however, interviewers may be "too comfortable" and too easily distracted. Email and visitors are constant distractors, and it is very natural to have the candidate sit across the desk from the interviewer. Desks create a psychological barrier that may hinder effective communication,[2] so when I must have a desk or small table in a room I try not to sit across from the candidate, but side by side or at a corner.

Cafeterias are common settings for interviews, particularly during lunch. But cafeterias are designed for getting a large number of people fed quickly, not for privacy or quiet. In a crowd, people tend to raise their voices to be heard, and raised voices can easily lead to raised emotions. I recommend you bring lunch to a candidate in a more intimate setting, such as a conference room or office, or at a quiet restaurant where you can talk naturally and the chairs are not designed to make people uncomfortable after twenty-five minutes.

All in all, I strongly recommend using conference rooms.

Schedule a conference room or spacious office for the duration of the interview, with lots of natural light and comfortable furniture. Using one room for the entire interview day is efficient and reduces the chance of scheduling errors, getting lost, or spending valuable time navigating between rooms. The candidate will appreciate not being yanked from room to room and will have the opportunity to get more comfortable as the day proceeds.

Ensure that you have lots of whiteboard space—whole walls of whiteboard, if possible. If you find yourself with a tiny whiteboard, you can make do, but you're better off bringing in a large portable board from somewhere else or, if you have time, nailing a bigger board to the wall.

Accessibility

Evaluate your interviewing facilities for general accessibility and in particular for any candidate you know has a specific disability. Not everyone can stand

---

[2]Eric Sundstrom and Mary Graehl Sundstrom, *Work Places: The Psychology of the Physical Environment in Offices and Factories* (New York: Cambridge University Press, 1986).

at a whiteboard for long periods of time, or indeed stand at all. Not everyone can hold a marker steady, or hear you clearly, or hear you at all. And so on with any number of disabilities you may have to accommodate.

I was recently embarrassed to realize that a whiteboard I found uncomfortably high was impossibly high for one candidate, who could barely reach it, and yet it was a whiteboard-intensive engineering interview. Afterward, the facilities team brought in a portable whiteboard that went to the floor, but it was too late to avoid making a poor impression on the candidate as well as complicating our evaluation.

Disabilities are not always obvious or volunteered. On one occasion I had a team full of people who disliked a candidate because he spoke very loudly during interviews; interviewers felt that he was trying to be intimidating or had underdeveloped interpersonal skills. Someone realized that he was probably losing his hearing. He had asked all of us to speak up at one point or another—so we were looking at a disability, not a distasteful personality trait.

Length of Interview Day

Human endurance is alarmingly finite, so you should organize the interview to get the most information you reasonably can about the candidate without spoiling the data with overexhaustion. Four to six hours with several breaks seems to be the most you can expect. Even so, you may find the candidate flagging near the end of the interviews.

Candidates who have to travel far to the interview site may start with fatigue or jet lag, so factor this into the length of the day and your start time. If you have to fly candidates quite far, it's a good idea to book an overnight stay and an interview the following morning.

Number and Length of Interview Sessions

Introductions, establishing a rapport, and creating interview rhythm takes several minutes of each session. Set aside a few minutes for candidates to ask questions in each session, and expect to spend some time each hour on breaks and fetching beverages. If the interview sessions are not all in one location, travel also consumes time.

Answering technical questions requires substantial concentration, so it is difficult to get a technical read on a candidate with a session length of less than forty-five minutes. More than sixty minutes seems to fatigue candidates and interviewers, so a session length of forty-five to sixty minutes works well most of the time.

You may be able to use shorter spans for interviews focused on nontechnical matters that don't require intense or uninterrupted thinking time. This might include interviews that focus on collaboration or for sessions with HR or managers who look for background information, ask about compensation expectations, or intend to answer general questions. Generally, it seems that thirty minutes works well for nontechnical sessions.

Hand-off Models

How you transition from one interview session to the next seems to have a surprisingly large effect on the process of evaluation. When an interview session is finished and the candidate is ready for another round, interviewers have several options for passing on what they have learned to the next interviewer. They can go without comment, provide preliminary feedback to the next interviewers or the hiring manager, or broadcast their feedback to all remaining interviewers.

Each approach has merit, and what you do may come down to a matter of organizational style and history.

The silent hand-off lets each interviewer form an unbiased opinion (at least unbiased by feedback from other interviewers).

Hand-off with comments gives interviewers an opportunity to pass on suggestions as to what topics they may want to explore, perhaps because their interview did not cover them well, or to look for even more depth in an area of strength. It has the drawback of being preliminary. Passing comments along can also cause a bias cascade, in which one interviewer causes the next to start the interview with a bias. That prior bias affects the interview, which affects what the interviewer tells the next one, and so on. The first interviewer of the day can have enormous, nearly invisible influence with this effect.

Broadcasting comments can give all future interviewers for the day the same information. It may not reach them all before the interviews, but it is particularly effective at spreading bias.

The silent hand-off model is currently prevalent for hiring at Amazon.com, and both the comments and broadcast models are commonly used at Microsoft.

Choose a method or hybridize to suit your purpose. On my interview loops, I ask the interviewers to contact me if they strongly believe that a candidate will not succeed, so we have the opportunity to halt early if appropriate, but otherwise not to pass on comments throughout the day, or to discuss their opinion with other interviewers before they have settled on their own decisions and written feedback.

Interviewers that hear about candidates before their own interviews are automatically and unavoidably biased by the people they talk with. Silent hand-offs are an excellent way to eliminate this bias.

Lunch Interviews

It's easy to interview candidates and have lunch at the same time, but it's also easy to misuse the time. The candidate and interviewer are distracted by their meals, so it shouldn't be used as a regular interview session. Don't ask critical technical questions at lunch. Don't ask coding questions. Let the candidate eat; take turns asking nontechnical questions so you can both eat. Use it as a selling time.

Feed the candidate. Don't make the candidate pay for lunch or anything else during the evaluation process. Making the candidate pay will make you look cheap, thoughtless, broke, or all of the above.

Briefing Interviewers

Every interviewer in the loop should know what role you are trying to fill on your team and your hiring bar. They should have a copy of the job description (or whatever variant of that concept you are using), the candidate's résumé, notes or transcripts from phone screens or previous on-site interviews, and the entire interview schedule.

You should also brief team members on your hiring philosophy as well as lay ground rules and expectations. For instance, you might remind the interviewers that you are not hiring for skill in a *particular* language but facility with any of several languages. You might tell them when you expect to receive written feedback following the interview.

This is a good time to make sure you've disqualified all the interviewers who will not perform the way you need, as described in the section "Disqualifying Interviewers."

I've seen effective reinforcement of this approach when hiring managers send a morning-of-briefing email with the documentation and a reminder of who is responsible for what aspects of the interviews.

Dividing Responsibility

Maximize the use of interviewer time by avoiding unnecessary repetition. Repetition that leads to stronger analysis is fine, but repeatedly asking the same question or close variants of it can waste valuable interview time.

Set expectations explicitly by briefing each interviewer, letting them know what information you expect them to have when they leave the interview. A question plan, described in Chapter 7, will help prevent duplication and encourage covering all important candidate capabilities.

How Many Interviewers?

You need enough interviewers to evaluate every aspect of the candidate's performance that you care about. In my experience, this is five to six people, including a development manager. Interviewers who have conducted more than fifty interviews can pull a lot of information from candidates, so it's safe to use four to five experienced interviewers.

Interviewers per Session

Fit the number of interviewers to the job requirements. If the role involves working with groups, such as an architect who must present designs and defend decisions to executive teams, use at least one committee interview with three or more interviewers. This forces the candidate to perform as they would on the job.

In general, committee interviews can create a layer of difficulty that may obscure the candidate's capability. The candidate must not only consider and answer questions but also efficiently switch attention among a group of people. Without context about the interviewers' social structure and the varying communication patterns and cues they use, this might result in hurt feelings ("He ignored me!") or "social overload" for the candidate. There's also the potential for a group/outsider effect occurring, in which the team unconsciously bands against the "interloping" candidate.

If you have inexperienced interviewers, or if you need to gather many different opinions but have limited time, use pair interviews. Two interviewers (not just one shadowing the other) at a time can be quite effective when they know each other, work together, and ideally have done pair interviews together before.

Most of the time I use single interviewers in each session, sometimes with a shadow interviewer attending.

Running the Interview

Great customer service is driven by attention to detail and empathizing with the candidate/customer.

Preparation

- Have an NDA prepared and ready, in case of incidental discussion and observations, contents of whiteboards, and any comments about the future or anticipated directions, technologies, or products.
- Send a copy of the NDA to the candidate ahead of time so they have a chance to review it.

- Stock whiteboards with markers and erasers, and stock any other consumable or portable resources you'll need.

- The coordinator arranges for a greeter to meet the candidate in the reception area, the lobby, parking garage, lounge, arrival gate, taxi stand, sidewalk, and so on.

- The coordinator arranges for a single interview room or, if necessary, two rooms, before and after lunch.

Arrival

- Greet the candidate warmly.

- Confirm that it's still a good day for the interview (no pressing concerns).

- Ask when they have to leave.

- Offer the candidate water, coffee, and whatever else you have available.

- Offer a trip to the restroom.

- Present and ask the candidate to sign the NDA.

- If appropriate, present a lunch menu or restaurant options. This will let the candidate take dietary restrictions into account without requiring them to volunteer that information, which you don't otherwise need.

- Validate parking, and take care of other such logistical issues.

- Set the candidate's expectations by saying how many interviews they will have (if there is a fixed number) and how long each interview will last if they are fixed in length.

Sessions

Each interviewer should prepare a list of questions that would normally greatly exceed the length of the interview. That keeps them from running out, which can occur for any of a number of reasons, such as the candidate admitting to having prepared for a particular question, discovering that another interviewer has already asked a similar question, or that one or more prepared questions turn out to be inappropriate for the candidate or circumstances.

Just as candidates are well advised to prepare for common or expected interview questions, interviewers are well advised to consider and prepare responses for common candidate questions. Interviewers should speak from the heart and be honest, but organizing thoughts ahead of time will make responses succinct and internally consistent.

Candidates frequently ask:

- Why do you enjoy working here?
- What is the work/life balance?
- What is a typical day like?
- What are the opportunities for advancement?
- What is your group working on? What's next?

The last question deserves particular thought because interviewers should not divulge business plans to candidates no matter what confidentiality agreement they have signed. In my opinion, NDAs are really a formality, because once a secret is out, it's out. Interviewers should give direct and honest answers that reveal nothing confidential.

During Session

The basic process is to make the candidate comfortable, ask challenging questions, and give them the opportunity to conclude that you are awesome. Here's the basic structure of a typical interview session.

Session Stages

Greet: Give your name, describe your role and team.

1. Offer break and beverage.
   a. "Can we get you some water or coffee or similar? Or a trip to the restroom?"
2. Ask questions.
   b. "Create an algorithm for connecting DNA segments found via shotgun sequencing."
3. Answer candidate questions.
   c. "What would you like to know?"
4. Sell the organization and job.
   d. "Let me tell you more about why you should work here ..."

Hand off to next interviewer or escort candidate out.

Time Management

Interviewers should keep a clock in view or, if no clock is available, check the time on a watch or phone. Don't be discreet about it—announce it. In some cultures, discreetly checking the time is a social signal that you're bored or have something else to do. Saying, "Excuse me, I have to check our schedule" preempts that signal.

Between Interviews

Offer a restroom break and a beverage. Interviews involve a lot of talking, and talking is thirsty work! That drives trips to the restroom later, too. Be sure to escort the candidate to and from the restroom area, for reasons explained next.

Leaving the Candidate Alone

Do not leave the candidate alone for more than a few moments, unless they are in a one-exit conference room and you're on the other side of the door or you're waiting for them outside the restroom. This accomplishes two important goals: to make the candidate feel welcome and cared for, and to minimize security risk. Candidates left alone can readily walk away with secrets or other valuables, whether or not they signed an NDA. Each interviewer has the responsibility for a live, in-person hand-off of the candidate to the next interviewer or to escort the candidate out.

Calling a Halt

A major purpose of intentionally designing and managing the interview process is to respect and optimize your team's time spent on interviews. The amount of engineer-hours invested in an interview increases throughout the day, so it's worthwhile to check whether you can save time and frustration for all parties (interviewers and candidate) by halting the interview day early.

- Have a manager interview before calling a halt.

- Protect against flukes by having more than one interviewer interview the candidate before making this call.

- Let only hiring managers and experienced interviewers decide whether to stop.

Troubleshooting

With enough interviews, you can safely assume that anything could happen: Candidates will be injured, the building will catch on fire, and so on. Be your normal, well-prepared, level-headed self and everything will be fine. When dealing with an unusual circumstance, keep in mind that the candidate is a customer and deserves deference, all else being equal.

Certain situations seem to consistently trouble or confound new interviewers. Here's how I interpret and deal with some of the ones I encounter from time to time.

Candidate Acts Inappropriately

Check with HR on this point. In my jurisdiction, it is the employer's responsibility to take reasonable action to stop workplace harassment,[3] including when it's caused by an outsider, such as a vendor or a candidate. Interviewers should feel free to cut their interview short if they are offended by candidate behavior.

Candidates that make off-color or otherwise inappropriate jokes in interviews will likely be even more informal after hiring. I never take a risk of that happening. Rude language, on the other hand, is frequently an automatic habit that seems to be easily retrained.

Candidate Acts Threateningly

Your safety and your team's safety are more important than any candidate or interview. If you or any interviewer feels threatened, halt the interview immediately. Call security (or police) and notify HR so they can record the incident and proceed with any necessary next steps.

Candidate Attempts to Take Over

Act and speak with confidence and you are likely to retain control of the interview. But sometimes candidates don't understand, expect, or respond to the structure you try to create for the interview session. On a few occasions I've had to reestablish control explicitly by telling the candidate, "That's fascinating and I wouldn't normally interrupt you, but I do need to ask a few more specific questions due to limited time."

Assertive personalities are fine and valuable, but there is a social context and business purpose for interviews that candidates must respect. When they don't respect your guidance of the interview and work in the context you provide, they can interfere with your ability to evaluate them. More worryingly, it signals a personality that may not collaborate effectively.

---

[3]Again, I'm not a lawyer. Review your company's policies and relevant laws with HR if you need clarification and guidance.

Candidate Is Caught in a Lie

Depending on how you define lying, 28 percent to 90 percent of undergraduate job candidates lie during interviews,[4] and it seems a safe assumption that veterans might lie at a similar rate. When you discover a lie, the interview could go off the rails immediately and never get back on track.

I have encountered different philosophies for dealing with lying, from being blasé about it to being extremely critical. Most of the time I aim for more of a middle ground. (Some of this may be due to a direct personal experience I described in Chapter 5.)

When I spot an apparent lie, I take a moment to verify the facts and suss out assumptions. I ask a clarifying question to find the root, and then ask the candidate directly to reconcile the contradictory evidence. Most candidates make some sort of admission at that point, ascribing it to a misunderstanding, misstatement, or unintentional exaggeration. Whether this is really the source of the problem is a judgment call, but it gives candidates a fair opportunity to address the contradiction, and sometimes they clearly resolve the issue right away.

If the discrepancy is major and unresolved, I politely point out that the contradiction is worrisome and has raised serious doubts about the candidate's trustworthiness. I end the interview and escort the candidate out. Remember, it's not personal—there is a lot at stake for many people when it comes to getting jobs, and pressure makes people do strange and unethical things. You probably don't want people who crack like this on your team, but neither are they necessarily inherently evil or trying to harm you.

Candidate Completely Off Track or Answers the Wrong Question

Sometimes a candidate will give you an answer to a question that is only similar to what you asked, not the question you asked. This can be unconscious; they may hope or expect you to ask a different question, or they are unknowingly using the availability heuristic.[5] They essentially hear you ask an easier or different question. In my experience, all of these are more likely to happen when asking subtle variants on common questions, so patiently explaining that the question is different and repeating or rephrasing it usually brings the candidate back on track.

---

[4]Julia Levashina and Michael Campion, "Measuring Faking in the Employment Interview: Development and Validation of an Interview Faking Behavior Scale," *Journal of Applied Psychology* 92(6) (2007)

[5]Daniel Kahneman, "Maps of Bounded Rationality: A Perspective on Intuitive Judgment and Choice," Nobel Prize Lecture, 2002, www.nobelprize.org/nobel_prizes/economics/laureates/2002/kahnemann-lecture.pdf.

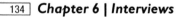
Still, sometimes multiple repeats and rephrasings are not enough. If the question is not critical, and you can replace it with another that informs you just as much, it may be worthwhile to move on rather than stalling on one question.

Candidate Gets Distracted

Candidates show up to an interview with their whole world going on around them, which could be in any shape and state. Your own life is no less complicated.

I've interviewed candidates distracted by family problems, ongoing emergencies, illness, and more. If a candidate's life is saturated with distraction and disaster, it will certainly affect their performance, but how can you know that from one incident around the time of interviews?

When candidates indicate that they are acting under outside stress, I suggest offering to reschedule the interview to when they can give it full attention. Be sincere and understanding and the candidate will appreciate it, whether or not they accept the offer to reschedule. It lifts the customer experience and gives you a chance to fairly evaluate the candidate later.

Candidate Is Inarticulate

Brilliant engineers can consistently discuss complex topics. Candidates who cannot do so indicate a disorganized mind or dramatically underdeveloped communication skills. I do not know of any way to work effectively with a cognitively disorganized engineer.

Verbal disorganization might be caused by interview jitters or hasty, excited speech; so take some to calm the candidate and guide him or her to speak slowly and precisely.

Candidate Is Incomprehensible

Very rarely, you may come across a candidate you cannot understand or who does not seem to understand apparently straightforward questions and discussion. In my experience this has been caused by low capability in the interview language. Consider treating the problem in the manner described in the "Thick Accent" section. If it does not improve, consider halting the interview. You're not learning anything.

Always interview candidates in the language you expect them to use in the ordinary course of the job.

Candidate Needs Mulligans

Even an exceptionally qualified candidate may make an obvious or ridiculous mistake during an interview. Be prepared to forgive one of these; the interview situation is artificial and stressful. You make errors from time to time, too, and not always under so much pressure. Besides, errors are opportunities to learn and grow (unless they are catastrophic).

Candidate Is Nervous

Consider the interview from the candidate's point of view. It's stressful and they may have a lot on the line—mortgage and tuition payments overdue, or an intense and long-standing frustration they're trying to leave behind. Their incentive for landing a job may extend far beyond looking for more interesting or comfortable work. Nerves are quite understandable.

In addition, an interview is highly artificial situation, far removed from what you expect from developers on a daily basis. They do need to complete the interviews, of course, and you can make it easier for them. Through basic empathy, people take anxiety signals from those around them, so stay relaxed as much as you can. Be friendly and understanding, but don't draw too much attention to the candidate's nervousness—that can amplify the problem. Mention or address the nervous behavior and then don't mention it again, so the candidate has a chance to calm down.

In this kind of situation, I give the candidate a win by pointing out that they are being successful, for example, in providing a key insight or solving a problem. Success seems to foster relaxation. There is an art to putting people at ease, so if this is a recurring problem in your interviews, do some research and practice.

Finally, not everyone is as nervous as they look. I've interviewed brilliant engineers who couldn't stop moving and fidgeting but solved complex, nuanced problems without difficulty.

Candidate Has Strange Mannerisms

Interviews bring out twitchiness and nervous tics in candidates. It's best to simply ignore these little quirks; interviews can be intensely stressful to some people, eliciting rare behavior. More important, some mannerisms can be caused by medical conditions (e.g., restless legs syndrome) that should not factor into your decision-making process anyway.

Candidate Has Thick Accent

Candidates typically need to speak some language or another in common with your team—maybe more than one—so there's a baseline speaking capability required. Accents are a fact of life and everybody has one, but some are more difficult for a typical listener to puzzle out.

The key to communicating with someone with a thick accent is patience. Listen intently, repeat what you have heard, and ask the speaker to restate what they've said. Stow any frustration; treat the communication as if it were a puzzle and you will establish a communication path.

Even an accent quite difficult to follow when you first hear it will become easy after days and weeks of exposure. Because it's just a temporary adjustment for team members, I have yet to disqualify a candidate for having a difficult accent.

Uncomfortable Silence

In Western cultures, silence during conversation can cause discomfort.[6] A conundrum of technical interviews is that they are both conversations and tests, and the test parts demand some concentration. Not everyone can talk and concentrate at the same time—some candidates are comfortable narrating their internal problem-solving process, and some are not. A narrative gives you access to their mental states; you can see they are making progress, and you have an opportunity to provide meaningful hints and steer candidates away from unimportant tangents. Helpfully, some people even talk aloud as part of their thinking strategy.

Candidates can't always produce a narrative, perhaps because it interferes with their thought processes or their problem-solving process is difficult to verbalize. They will quietly look at a whiteboard or stare into the distance, and time passes in silence. Just wait. If they are able to make progress, so be it. Wait a while to let them concentrate, and then you can ask what they are thinking about, whether there are potential solutions they are exploring or have discarded, or if they want a hint.

Embracing a little silence won't hurt anyone.

Remote Interviews

After a candidate passes your initial screen, you would normally conduct an on-site interview, but sometimes you can't. Conducting a remote interview is an option when a candidate is particularly distant or unable to travel, or you just don't have the budget to transport the candidate to your office.

---

[6]"Brief Silence in Conversation Evokes Negative Emotions," University of Groningen, January 20, 2011

If you get to the offer stage but are reluctant to make an offer because you didn't have a "normal" interview, then you may have wasted considerable time and energy. Before starting down that path, you must establish a bar for the candidate to meet and commit yourself to making the hire if the candidate meets that bar. If you need buy-in from your management or HR, get it first.

With a commitment in hand, use all available technology to make the remote interview as much like your on-site interview as possible. That makes it easier to evaluate the candidate in the same context as all other candidates, or as similar as it can be. Keep the process similar, too; for instance, schedule it in a contiguous block with short breaks.

If remote interviews are the exception for your interviewing team, their unfamiliarity makes it an intrinsically higher risk to hire based on remote interviews. You can offset this effect by insisting on holding to a very high standard. That will reduce the odds of a bad hire, though it does also increase the odds of missing a good hire. Such is life.

Before considering a remote interview, I look for at least two positive phones screens measured against a high bar.

Record Keeping

Your HR department might have specific policies regarding what you may record about interviews, what you may not, and when you must destroy the records. Even restrictive policies should allow you to keep anonymized notes, in which you have stripped out the candidate's name and other identifying information.

Use records to reflect on and discuss the candidate's interviews, and later as an information source you can mine. In the absence of specific policy, I recommend that you write and keep for each candidate the following key memoranda: what you asked, the essence of the response, and your interpretation.

To allow you to share the exact answers with others (rather than interpretation or vague recollection), transcribe or take pictures of source code and pertinent diagrams or charts the candidate creates as part of their answers. With an exact record, you can get fresh opinions and comments from others at any time.

If your interviews are generally getting off track—if you are rejecting many otherwise apparently qualified candidates, or accepting those who aren't—you can use records to help you find out what's going on. For example, reading individual feedback lets you understand the consistent patterns each interviewer has established and how recap meetings affect their decisions.

By using strong statistical techniques to protect yourself from outliers and unjusti-fied conclusions, you might discover other interesting and useful phenomena—for instance, that early morning interviews are more likely to result in a positive hiring decision.[7]

---

[7]Shai Danziger, Jonathan Levav, and Liora Avnaim-Pesso,"Extraneous Factors in Judicial Decisions, *Proceedings of the National Academy of Sciences USA* 108(17) (2011): 6889–92, doi:10.1073/pnas.1018033108.

Interview Questions

Interview questions are the most discussed and least understood part of the hiring process everywhere I have worked. Despite their importance as the heart of an interview, few people can succinctly describe why we ask particular questions, how to create them, and how to interpret responses. This chapter describes a method for choosing, building, and asking questions and for evaluating candidate responses. It also shows you how to avoid several pitfalls in question design and answer evaluation.

Probing a Black Box

It is notoriously difficult to evaluate a knowledge worker's on-the-job performance.[1] It is even more difficult to predict a candidate's *future* performance in a new job. This is complicated further by the likelihood that the nature of the work will evolve as your product and its technology change.

If we could look directly inside a candidate's mind, we would look for traits and capabilities that we believe will drive success or failure in our organizations. Because we can't do this, we probe their minds by sending in signals and watching what comes out. In the ideal situation, we would send in signals exactly like those we expect on the job: problems and tasks the candidates will need to resolve. Unfortunately, those problems are usually complex and situation-dependent, requiring lots of context to understand and solve.

---

[1]Robert D. Austin, *Measuring and Managing Performance in Organizations* (New York: Dorset House, 1996).

Instead, we select and send in simplified but representative signals and examine the responses for clues about the behaviors and capabilities in those candidates' minds. Candidates' responses form the basis for guessing how they will act on the job.

Since we are making inferences from simplified signals, the process is noisy, and the results are often indistinct and difficult to interpret. It is somewhat surprising that interviews work at all; certainly in many instances, they do not provide accurate results. Even so, a careful approach to building probing signals (questions) and interpreting results (answers) will minimize errors and give you sufficiently reliable information to make sound hiring decisions.

Crafting or Choosing Questions

The purpose of an interview question is to measure a candidate's ability in an area you care about. With such an area in mind, you find or create questions that force the candidate to demonstrate his or her ability with a specific response. The response is the evidence you use to estimate underlying capability.

Use this sequence for all interview questions, and each question you ask will be specifically chosen to provide evidence you can use in your evaluation. You will extract the maximum amount of relevant information in the time available and avoid asking questions that won't help you.

There is much lore regarding interview questions, and an Internet search will reveal thousands of questions. Some of them are good, some are useless, and some are awful—inappropriate, muddled, and likely to produce unreliable evidence. If you choose to adopt an existing question, take care to analyze it to make sure it probes an ability you care about and test it just as you would if you crafted it yourself.

If you have time, create your own questions either from scratch or by making variations of preexisting ones. Creating your own question gives you full control and substantial insight into the question itself and how it can be solved. More specific tips on creating interview questions are found later in this chapter.

Whether you select a preexisting question or make a new one, asking a new-to-you question introduces the problem of calibration: Answers should be evaluated in comparison to other answers you have encountered. Calibration is also covered in some detail further in this chapter.

Candidates may have encountered any given question, and even new questions you create will eventually "leak." Because there's no meaningful way to compare the quality of answers produced by candidates who have already encountered a question with those seeing it the first time, you will need to distinguish between them when you can. Not everyone realizes they should volunteer this information! The best way I know of to handle this is to instruct candidates to tell you when a question is familiar. Then you can skip the question.

Candidates may lie about their familiarity with a question. Direct lie detection is usually unreliable, so the best defense is to create your own questions that candidates could not reasonably be familiar with. When using off-the-shelf questions, you can use more than one technical question to measure each area you care about and compare the performances between them. Substantial differences on related questions could reveal deceit.

Question Plans

To be successful, consider using a question plan: a document that collects the questions that interviewers intend to ask during a particular interview day or across interviews for a certain job. A question plan will help you avoid unnecessary duplication across interview sessions. You don't want your team to ask the same question twice, or very similar questions, or ask so many questions in a particular ability area that you stop learning something new each time. As an example of overdoing it, many companies present a candidate with several interviews in which they only ask coding questions. Each interviewer should prepare a set of questions that does not overlap with any other interviewer's. Sharing the questions with each other will help prevent overlap, and it has the added benefit of allowing a bit of peer review.

The sum of all prepared questions should cover every trait and skill your hire must have, and probe for negative attributes as well. Be sure to leave time in any interview to ask at least one new question so you can alter and improve your effective repertoire all the time.

An example of a question plan is included in the appendix.

Ask Lists and No-Ask Lists

A list of questions the team has had success with and experience in evaluating will come in handy for onboarding new interview team members. Similarly, keeping a list of no-ask list of questions will help your team accumulate knowledge and avoid repeating mistakes.

Good Questions

Good questions

- measure a specific capability.
- are quick and easy to ask.

- clearly specify the expected form of the answer.

- do not contain tricks.

- do not require specialized knowledge (unless you are specifically testing for that particular knowledge as a critical element of the interview).

- do not require sudden leaps of intuition (a ha! or satori moments) to solve.

- have answers that can be readily recorded, evaluated, and compared.

- are neither trivial nor incredibly difficult.

- provide differentiation in useful dimensions between candidates.

You usually can't tell at a glance how a question measures up to all these criteria. You need to calibrate most questions before you know whether you've got a good one.

Calibration

A question is properly calibrated when you know what it reveals about candidates, how well the question differentiates between candidates, and the correlations of different solutions to real capability. Calibration also reveals whether a question is too simple, too complex, too vague, irrelevant, or in other ways not the best sort of question you can ask.

Calibrations don't last forever, so questions should be recalibrated over time. Your organization and team's standards change, and a question's effectiveness at differentiation may fall due to widespread adoption of a similar question, by full expositions appearing in interviewing books and popular websites, or by question leakage from candidates or recruiters.

Calibrating Questions

There is no absolute and universal "challenge level" we can assign to a question in the absence of testing it out on candidates. Some online research may tell you about a given question's familiarity and, if applicable, how difficult candidates typically find it. But you are better off testing the question with yourself and your team members.

Questions that you (or at least your competent engineers) cannot solve in a reasonable, interview-length period are probably not within the calibration range of your group. Questions that difficult may work for another team or organization, but such a hard question compromises your ability to empathize with candidates' problem-solving processes and accurately evaluate their performance. Candidates who do solve questions more difficult than your team can solve are operating at a different, higher level; as discussed in Chapter 6, large capability differences make evaluation less reliable.

Asking questions of your team is important but not sufficient. There are too many possible biases and sources of error. For example, the interview pressure is vastly diminished when you tackle a problem in front of or for team members who work with you all the time. You must also calibrate with real candidates.

To calibrate against candidates, you can ask the question and record the answers carefully, but—and this is where some serious discipline comes in—you must ignore the answers. Do not consider the question to be part of each interview, because you don't yet know whether it is a good, useful question. Apparently stellar answers may turn out to be common, or, inversely, the question may be too hard or too far out of left field for just about everyone, including the candidates you want to hire.

Calibration is not just about finding the difficulty of a problem. For any given question, measuring any given capability, you also need to know whether it meaningfully differentiates between developers. For example, juggling ability (in the literal rather than metaphorical sense) varies widely among developers, but whether a candidate can juggle three balls is probably not a signal of job performance.[2] To understand a question's differentiating utility, you must correlate the answers you get with on-the-job performance over long periods of time.

Target Complexity

Interviews are tests, and all tests have a minimum and maximum level of capability they can reliably measure, also known as floors and ceilings.

When you need to identify capability at relatively low levels, use a test with a low floor. For example, a series of questions ranging from the incredibly trivial upward may have a very low floor. If you need to identify capability at relatively high levels, use a test with a high ceiling. Long strings of questions of complexity and subtlety that require careful consideration and nuance will get this information.

Few tests have both a low floor and a high ceiling, because they tend to frustrate everyone: high scorers get bored with the easy questions and low scorers

---

[2] I do know a former circus clown who juggles quite well *and* is great engineer, but that's only one data point.

can't tackle the difficult ones. Tests that cover a wide range of ability are usually adaptive, including, for instance, triggers to halt the test after a certain number of wrong answers.

Interviewing great candidates lets you eliminate the need to maintain a low floor: You can skip trivial questions and halt the interview if the candidate isn't faring relatively well. Still, you do have a floor, and it must not be set above the level you need to find a minimally capable ("least great") candidate for the given position.

Interview questions also have a ceiling. Perhaps unexpectedly, this is where I frequently see interview teams run into problems. When a candidate passes an interview without stumbling on some questions, you can't know their limits. For instance, a candidate that passes a set of interviews geared for entry-level engineers may not respond well to an offer for (or thrive after taking) a position with entry-level expectations. That candidate might also have passed a much more challenging interview with questions designed to measure engineers up to principal level.

The lesson from test floors and ceilings is to prepare and ask questions with difficulty varying from challenging to extremely challenging, but not expect all candidates to solve all questions. If you set up an interview to measure a broad spectrum of capability, you will not underestimate fantastic engineers. A consequence of that approach is that many great engineers may have unsatisfactory performance on your most challenging questions yet still be worthy hires.

Question Types

Most questions fall into a few broad types: direct performance, behavioral, negative attribute probes, chains, and open-ended questions.

Direct Performance Questions

You hire employees so they will do the job, so you must know that they *can* do the job. The easiest way to tell whether they can is to observe them performing.

On a day-to-day basis, you need your developers to estimate, evaluate, design, create, follow through, and coordinate, so that's what you should measure. You can ask a candidate to do one or more of these things. Where that's not feasible, you can ask them to describe specific, actual, and concrete past instances where they demonstrated their abilities—in enough detail that it establishes beyond a shadow of a doubt that they not only applied a particular skill before but can do it again on demand.

Hiring managers commonly ask candidates to describe past projects and the companies they worked for. However, while working, developers do not normally need to relate these experiences verbally—they incorporate them into their ordinary work. When the candidates show you how they work, all that experience is incorporated and instantiated, so you do not need to ask about it. Most of the questions you ask should model direct performance. Ask questions about experience when you specifically want to learn something about behaviors that are difficult to elicit.

Behavioral Questions

Not every capability can be readily observed by simulated performance, such as resolving conflict or lobbying on behalf of customers. To gather evidence of how candidates will behave on the job, probe their past behaviors with questions about how they acted in certain situations. Within reasonable limits, and not accounting for personal growth, a candidate's past behavior is a fair indicator of how they will behave in similar situations in the future.[3]

Discovering the details of a candidate's past is tricky because you usually only have their word. In my experience, however, most people will tell mostly the truth when you ask about specific past situations. The result is not entirely reliable and is probably a bit rosy-colored. Candidates will also sometimes describe incidents that paint them in a surprisingly negative light, and those seem easier to believe.

Get specific details about past performances. For instance, instead of saying "Tell me how you got along with coworkers," you could say, "Describe the last time you had a major dispute with a colleague. Where and when did it happen, and what were your roles? Tell me about a particular dispute with a specific real person."

Negative Attribute Questions

Your organization has a set of core ideas, principles, and behaviors guiding short-term and long-term decisions that make it different. These are the building blocks of your culture, and new hires are indoctrinated during the

---

[3]Henk Aarts, Bas Verplanken, and Ad van Knippenberg, "Predicting Future Behavior From Actions in the Past: Repeated Decision Making or a Matter of Habit?" *Journal of Applied Social Psychology*, 28, (15) (1998):1355–74.

onboarding process. Still, you can inculcate only so much; isolated behaviors can change, but personality usually does not.[4]

Most people do not have the attitudes and skills you need for your teams. Of the ones who do, some have other attitudes and skills you do not want. Such undesirable attributes would entrain destructive and passively or actively harmful effects on your teams. The sad reality is that a single bad individual can quickly demoralize and destabilize a whole team,[5] setting you back months or even causing a permanent rift. Candidates who are just untalented and unskilled have a much more manageable impact on the team than those who can poison it with these negative attributes. As a result, even a candidate with phenomenal capability in many competencies is still not a good hire if he is bitter, cruel, and quick to anger.

Look for patterns of destructive behavior that you have observed throughout your career and, most important, such patterns you've seen on and around your team. You have direct evidence they don't work here and now. Negative attributes can be subtle, such as an unwillingness to resolve conflict, indolence, or manipulative behavior; they can be more obvious, such as irascibility or a combative attitude.

People are generally good at keeping a game face for a few hours, but asking direct behavioral questions seems to reveal incidental attitudes about coworkers, such as disdain and anger. The safe assumption is that palpable signals in these areas—anything you can corroborate with a second observation or through references—are real and substantial. You might end up reacting to some misleading signals and turn down a candidate who is not in fact a toxic liability, but this is an unavoidable loss.

Chained Questions

Chains are sets of questions where one question leads naturally to another, the next one often being a deeper or continued exploration of the same theme. Questions like these have great appeal. The transition from one to the next is smooth; the candidate has the problem frame in mind already, so she can potentially solve more complex problems; and it lays a clear path to walk

---

[4] J. J. Conley, "Longitudinal Stability of Personality Traits: A Multitrait-Multimethod-Multioccasion Analysis," *Journal of Personality and Social Psychology*, 49 (1985):1266–82. Some people change more than others; see Spiro Mroczek III, "Modeling Intraindividual Change in Personality Traits: Findings from the Normative Aging Study," *Journal of Gerontology: Psychological Sciences,* 58B (2003):P153–56.
[5] Will Felps, Terence R. Mitchell, and Eliza Byington, "How, When, and Why Bad Apples Spoil the Barrell: Negative Group Members and Dysfunctional Groups," *Research in Organizational Behavior*, 27 (2006):175–222.

so you can find where the candidate's capability ends. A drawback is that if a candidate takes the answer in a direction you didn't anticipate, you have to bring them back onto the chain so you can compare their set of responses with those of others.

As an example, a game chain might look like this. First, describe a simple game, and then ask the candidate to:

1. Model the game's data structure.

2. Score a finished game, or determine a winner.

3. Write a game player or solver.

As another example, you may ask the candidate to use and manipulate a data structure in increasingly complex ways, as in asking the candidate to:

1. Model a binary tree.

2. Traverse the tree to find a value.

3. Save and restore the tree.

4. Rebalance the tree.

Open-Ended Questions

Open-ended questions test a candidate's ability to respond to and deal with ambiguity, and they work in a situation in which there's no clearly defined goal. These questions are usually "what if?" or scenario questions—such as "Suppose that we are three-quarters of the way through a large project when we discover that we absolutely cannot use Java. It's all Java so far. What do we need to do?"

Sorting out how to behave in a novel situation with no book answer is an important capability because it happens frequently at work. Great employees can sort out what needs to be done and create their own sensible and strategically consistent goals, negotiate and explain them, and strive to achieve them.

Candidates usually expect closed questions for which there are known good, better, and best answers. Present candidates with a question that has no obvious "right answer" and many will search for *your* right answer instead of exploring the solution space freely. You may have to state explicitly that you expect *their* answer.

It is difficult to evaluate the strength of answers to open-ended questions. Because the solution space is all but unlimited, calibrating against others' answers may be misleading. Expect the sort of answer that developers on your team give, and you may be accidentally testing for a lack of originality!

Here's how I evaluate these questions. I use them to test whether candidates can think comfortably about vague problems, and I ignore the particulars of their answer. I examine their comfort level with resolving ambiguity and their technique: whether they look for constraints, compare the situation to ones they have encountered before, draw on abstract principles, and explore different possible answers. Less capable candidates may immediately narrow focus to a specific minor problem and its solution or might fail to make any conceptual progress, such as characterizing the problem in a manner that could be solved.

Capabilities

Developers must start out in your organization with a minimum core set of capabilities. Your list of must-have capabilities may vary greatly with time, organization, and circumstance. The stable set of capabilities I make certain to test for in developers includes coding, collaborating, designing, estimating, gathering requirements, learning, and selecting tasks. Let's look at the value of and techniques for measuring some instructive capabilities: knowing, learning, collaborating, fitting in, designing, estimating, and coding.

Knowing

Knowing is just having some facts in your head, and a knowledge question tries to detect them. In general, it is not incredibly important because technical facts are easy to find. We're drowning in facts. What's important is that candidates can apply the facts to their work with clarity and judgment. The best way I have found to determine whether someone can judiciously apply existing knowledge is to ask them to perform in response to, for example, coding or design questions.

There are circumstances in which particular knowledge reveals a depth of experience or a pattern of engagement with technologies and techniques. Examples of such "deep knowledge" are details of design and implementation choices in various programming languages or a particularly extensive repertoire of data structures and algorithms at immediate command. Candidates with this level of knowledge seem to enjoy getting into the details as well as understanding the larger picture of software design problems, and they may make valuable employees.

An important and common use of knowledge questions is to verify statements made on a résumé or during an interview. With time at a premium, I keep these to a minimum, but I do take easy opportunities for them.

Knowing (Academic)

At this point in history, day-to-day programming in most jobs consists largely of gluing other software components together and manipulating data with simple, preexisting libraries. Even the challenging and cutting-edge work your team hopefully engages in is probably mostly configuring and tying other software bits together, with interesting parts between them.

Because that is the standard performance you probably need, it makes sense to ask candidates to do just that in interviews: glue software together. Instead, we much more frequently ask coding questions more "academic" in nature. Typically these questions require candidates to directly manipulate data structures in ways they have rarely needed to and may not need to do again. Why this discrepancy? Does simulating problems the candidate won't normally be expected to solve tell us anything useful about the candidate's real-life capabilities, or does it distract us from what we need to know and cause us to pass over perfectly qualified candidates?

In my experience, academic questions do reveal fundamental software development capabilities. The most common explanation I have seen is that candidates who are able to work with difficult, unusual academic problems can also likely work with everything a standard team might do day to day. It's like asking a professional weightlifter to lift 500 kilos overhead when you expect to have only 200-kilo objects most of the time; the weightlifter who struggles at 200 kilos may not be a consistent performer, but the one who can lift 500 kilos will have no difficulty with 200 kilos most of the time.

On the other hand, you may feel like you're wasting the capabilities of engineers who can (metaphorically) lift 500 kilos if you ask much less from them. When you test candidates with difficult academic questions, any developers you hire will probably have more capacity than you needed. That is more of an opportunity than a problem.

Learning

Software developers have to learn mountains of information and hone many skills just to get started in their careers. To become truly proficient, and develop high general engineering capability, developers must have quick ways to pick up even more information and skills whenever they needed, on demand. To become and stay productive, a developer must learn and build better tools and methods all the time. As a sort of meta-skill that takes time to exercise, the ability to learn is trickier to measure directly than coding or designing, but you can look to a candidate's past behavior and current attitudes for evidence.

Developers who work across domains, use different languages for different jobs (or for different tasks and goals within the same job), or have developed or contributed to new tools and techniques probably have the right attitude about learning and trying new things. The same may be true of candidates who apply and interview for roles that clearly involve the use of new languages and computing platforms, showing they can leave their comfort zone when they want or need to do so.

Collaborating

Collaborating is a universally valuable skill, so it is useful to test for it in interviews, but it is challenging to provoke performance with this skill. After all, we interview candidates one at a time, so how can they collaborate in front of us?

An interviewer who poses a problem cannot genuinely collaborate with a candidate to solve it, but he or she can participate in a collaborative manner. She can stand at the whiteboard, follow along with the candidate, ask for explanations, make suggestions, and point out errors in a nonconfrontational manner. Candidates who respond well to feedback, explain their work, and pick up suggestions may be able to cooperate with peers. Whether candidates respond to hints and ask for feedback has been a strong indicator of collaboration skill in my interviews.

Still, it's not a great method, and it prompts an important point: Sometimes we should stop and rethink our assumptions. Maybe it's possible to observe real collaboration in interviews. Could we have an uninformed employee genuinely collaborate with the candidate to solve an interview question? Is it strictly necessary to interview only one candidate at a time, or could we bring in two or more and give them a problem to collaborate on so we can observe them working together or trying to work together?

Fitting In

Attitudes and behaviors can be probed, but it seems there's an indefinable feeling people who like to work together get when they meet—an intuition built from hundreds of essentially imperceptible signals. With the same mechanism, sometimes people get a "bad vibe," which is hard to justify or defend but is also hard to let go.

Unfortunately, letting vibes influence hiring decisions is seriously problematic, because vibes are a major conduit for biases that harm thinking and encourage bad decisions. Biases cause unease, "the creeps," distaste, and a general sense of "otherness" that can discount or ruin all the hard work put into gathering real and valuable evidence about candidates.

Effective, capable people typically enjoy working together. They challenge each other to do better and be better every day, learn from each other, and develop ever-growing respect. Proximity alone does wonders in allowing people to adapt to each others' quirks and vibes.[6] I have never regretted ignoring a negative vibe.

Designing

Because designing is a major part of a developer's job—and possibly the most important and most difficult task a developer will undertake—it is critical to evaluate design skill.

I recommend asking design questions in the domains you care about and your team creates or frequently works with, such as APIs, web services, user interfaces, federated identity, embedded operating systems, and so on. It is easier to evaluate design work in domains you're familiar with or within the sort of problems your team deals with regularly. An opposite but common tactic is to ask questions about parking garages, elevators, and traffic lights, but when the topic lies outside the domain of both the interviewer and candidate, it is harder to reliably evaluate success.

Estimating

"How many squirrels live within six kilometers of Seattle's Space Needle?"

Estimation of effort is a core skill for engineers, because it's one of the major inputs of the project planning process. In the case of the sample question above, variations of which are quite famous and common, the question domain isn't within the problem space in which an engineer is likely to work. Engineers are more commonly called on to estimate the effort required to build software or operational resource requirements, so it may be useful to ask for estimations in these immediately relevant domains.

Developers are frequently called on to estimate *difficulty* and *time to completion*. To measure those, you might ask directly how long it would take to write a complex feature, but all you would learn is the basic method the candidate uses to create estimates. You won't learn how accurate the estimate is because you can't observe the candidate writing a complex feature. It is possible to learn whether he can estimate *anything at all* by asking for something verifiable. For instance, you can present a coding problem and ask the candidate to estimate how long it will take to solve *before* she solves it.

---

[6]Leon Festinger, Stanley Schachter, and Kurt Back, *Social Pressures in Informal Groups: A Study of Human Factors in Housing* (London: Tavistock, 1963).

Coding

Because coding is a critical part of most software developers' work, and it is a rare and difficult skill, you'll definitely want to evaluate each candidate's ability. Aside from being a job task, coding is composed of a number of subskills that are useful in a variety of knowledge-worker situations. Good coders have a tendency to be good engineers all around (but not inevitably; there are great coders you don't want to hire).

Valuable coding subskills include tracking multiple variables simultaneously, evaluating and altering an automated process, reading others' code, debugging, thinking at multiple levels almost simultaneously, and more.

Great engineers select, learn, and use programming languages that let them express and solve particular problems in elegant and effective ways. Whether or not your team is completely flexible with languages, you must pose questions and expect solutions in some particular language that both you and the candidate understand well. Some sort of common ground is necessary for this communication, even if it's in a language you don't use or intend to use for your products. All else being equal, I have found success favoring the language the candidate knows best. The comfort of working in a familiar syntax will aid the problem-solving process.

One caveat on letting the candidate choose a language (provided the interviewer is sufficiently proficient) is that some languages support solving certain classes of problem so well that there's almost no point asking for a solution. As an example, basic text file manipulation is no challenge in Perl, but is a lot more interesting and error-prone in C. Your question plan will have to take that into account.

Question Elements

A question is targeted at measuring a certain capability. It has a source and context, an intended presentation, and expected answer form, solutions, and evaluation criteria. Explicitly documenting these aspects of the questions you ask will give you and your team an opportunity to review the questions for correctness, clarity, and subject coverage. The very act of writing them down will force interviewers to analyze each question. The resulting documentation allows the question to become widely reused throughout your organization.

These are the five essential elements of an interview question.

Capability

Capabilities are broad skill sets and the ability to acquire and use skills. Often they are roughly equivalent to "competencies" as defined in some organizations. Some examples are coding, clarifying requirements, building test plans, estimating design time, and creating travel itineraries. What counts as an important capability for any given role can be determined by company policy, the criteria used in annual reviews, or your best judgment. Deconstructing capabilities as actions gives you a path toward testability, because you can elicit and observe an action; having an action to provoke gives you a way to build questions.

Background

An interview question's background comprehends the source of the question, calibration notes, and (if it's not obvious) why the question reveals the candidate's capability in this area.

Presentation and Expected Form

The verbal and visual presentation of an interview question needs to be fixed in however many parts are necessary to elicit a suitable answer.

Specify the sort of answer you expect to receive and record. For example: verbal, written, coded, pseudo-coded, or diagrammed.

Solutions

The known or expected solutions of an interview question should be annotated with comments on how you would evaluate each answer. Evaluations are set by question calibration.

Evaluation Criteria

Comments on evaluating answers to an interview question may go beyond analysis of the specific solutions. For example, note any behavioral traits you consider important or instrumental in solving the problem that you expect or hope to see and rate how they should affect overall evaluation.

How to Design a Question

Designing a question has only a few steps.

- Select an important capability to test.
- Identify a task or performance that uses the capability.
- Create a way to elicit the performance.
- Calibrate it to establish usefulness and accurate evaluation criteria.

To identify a task and create a way to provoke it, you can plumb your own experience. Take an inventory of the times you have exercised the capability. For each incident, consider whether you can isolate and simplify it, so you can describe the problem you solved succinctly and without much context. If your own history doesn't have enough examples to draw on, ask your peers and software developers for examples.

Examples of question constructions follow for assessing the capabilities of selecting tasks and proceeding under uncertainty.

Capability: Selecting Tasks

Background: Engineers have a bewildering array of possible things to do at in any given project and at any moment. They can code, write documentation, consult with colleagues, consult with customers, learn about a technology or tool, improve their process, and so on without end. Even the most meticulously planned development team's developers each have hundreds of opportunities a day to decide what to do next to further the business. Capable developers will choose wisely among their options with the aid of guiding principles such as customer focus, increasing capability, and avoiding technical debt.

Performance: The candidate decides what to do in a presented scenario, then explains and defends the choice.

Question: Your team is working on an enterprise disk backup system, but you have a few days of unstructured time. Recently, the team has been struggling with builds breaking and integration test failures. Some of the product's code was inherited from another team with no unit tests. After someone was hired recently, you found that it takes days to set up a development environment. What do you spend your time on?

Evaluation: Look for capability to establish the context, use fundamental principles and structure around the decision, and defend the decision. Capable candidates should present excellent reasons for their choices. Less capable developers may rely on habit and strict direction, limiting innovation and requiring management overhead.

Capability: Proceeding under Uncertainty

Background: There are always many unknowns in life and work. Even a project that's simply rebuilding the same software a second time has unknowns, introduced by changes in the environment and personnel. Every project has risks and uncertainties from not knowing product requirements well (maybe nobody does) to being unsure of software design and technical direction.

The importance and necessary willingness to proceed under uncertainty will vary with your software domain and organization's attitudes, of course. This question is designed to measure the candidate's attitude and current proclivities.

Performance: The candidate decides whether and how to reduce uncertainty through direct action.

Question: Think about the last time you were expected to create software despite not having enough information to do so effectively. Tell me about the exact situation, what you did, and the result.

Evaluation: Great developers want their work to be important and meaningful, so they care that the software they create is useful. Typically, these capable developers learn at least enough to make sure they are not wasting their time and then begin to build. They adjust and adapt to changes in understanding rather than trying to anticipate every last detail up front.

Excellent answers describe the situation's context without including irrelevant details. They tell you what sort of information was missing, how they usually expected to get it, and why it was not automatically available. Then they show how the developer acted, such as building prototypes, constructing tests first, writing a strawman specification, tracking down stakeholders, and so on. Last, they include a verification step: how they quickly discovered whether their work was proceeding in the right direction and, if necessary, made corrections.

Sample Questions

Nota bene: All the examples in this book are in C# because I like C#.

A good coding problem is:

- Usually posed in one minute or less.

- Usually takes more than five minutes to solve.

- Solvable by competent developers in ten minutes or less.

A good coding problem does *not*:

- Suggest a similar but different problem.

- Require specialized or arcane knowledge to solve.[7]

- Require a long series of clarifications.

---

[7]What counts as specialized varies, but calculus, geometry more complex than slopes and area, astrophysics, and the board game Monopoly were all too arcane to produce consistent results for me.

Work performance for some skills is relatively easy to evaluate; if you sharpen pencils all day, I can measure how sharp the pencils are, how many you sharpen, how many are ruined in the process, and so on. In all likelihood there's a sufficiently excellent way to sharpen pencils that I can determine whether you will be successful by carefully watching you follow a particular process with well-defined steps. Unfortunately, programming is such a creative endeavor that there's no way to watch a candidate follow any particular process and know whether they will create great code day after day by following that process. We are left with examining the end product.

We can be reasonably certain that in any successful coding exercise, capable developers will:

- Meticulously define the intent and purpose of the code.
- Pay careful attention to detail such as fenceposts.
- Test against well-defined and known good inputs and outputs.
- Anticipate and handle failures and misuse.
- Use appropriate and restrictive data types.
- Efficiently use (or not waste) computational resources.
- Produce readable code.[8]

These are general principles that can be applied to evaluating any code independent of the specific solution for any particular question.

---

[8]As in using descriptive names and concise, straightforward syntax—not in as in good penmanship.

"Code a Fibonacci Sequencer" Question

Difficulty

Easy

Competency

Coding (algorithms)

Background

This tests the candidate's ability to build a simple, easily understood method. It is easy to state and understand, and the code can be quickly written and evaluated. There are multiple different answers.

This question is so well known that many candidates can be expected to remember a whole answer rather than build one from scratch.

Presentation

Name and describe the Fibonacci sequence with examples and list the first seven members (0, 1, 1, 2, 3, 5, 8). Ask the candidate to write production-level code in a C-derived language such as C++, Java, or C#, which determines the value of the nth member of the Fibonacci sequence.

The sequence is defined as:

$$f_n = f_{n-1} + f_{n-2} \text{ with } f_0 = 0, f_1 = 1, f_2 = 1$$

The method signature is int Fibonacci(int n);

Solutions

A: Iterative

```
static int FibonacciIterate(int n)
{
    if (n < 2)
        return n;
    int x = 1, y = 0, z = 0;
    for (int i = 1; i < n; i++)
    {
        z = x + y;
        y = x;
        x = z;
    }
    return z;
}
```

Or, better:

```
static uint FibonacciIterateBetter(uint n)
{
    if (n < 2)
        return n;
    uint less1 = 1, less2 = 0, current = 0;
    for (int i = 1; i < n; i++)
    {
        if (uint.MaxValue - less1 < less2)
            throw new ArgumentOutOfRangeException(
                "n", "" + n +
                "th Fibonacci number is larger " +
                "than a maximum unsigned integer value.");
        current = less1 + less2;
        less2 = less1;
        less1 = current;
    }
    return current;
}
```

Evaluation: This code is straightforward and succinct. It is an O(n) algorithm, which is reasonable when n can't be very large, but it could have been further optimized. The second version is closer to production code, as it has reasonable variable names, uses more appropriate data types, and checks for error conditions. Although the second version changes the requested method signature, it does so in a helpful and clarifying way. Overall, the second shows a level of attention to detail that you would expect in great engineers.

B: Recursive

```
static int FibonacciRecurse(int n)
{
    if (n == 0)
        return 0;
    if (n == 1)
        return 1;
    return (FibonacciRecurse(n - 1)
        + FibonacciRecurse(n - 2));
}
```

Evaluation: A well-prepared candidate may know this solution. It is a fine example of recursive programming, although—since there are other elegant and less resource intensive solutions available—it is not appropriate for production systems. It is also an O(2^n) exponential time complexity algorithm, the sort of time complexity that would be horrifying under most circumstances.

This code can be improved to O(*n*) runtime by memoizing the results into a lookup table. That's quite an improvement, but a full lookup table is just as feasible, as in solution D.

C: Closed Form

```
static double Phi = (0.5 * (1+Math.Sqrt(5)));
static int FibonacciClosedForm(int n)
{
    return
        (int)(Math.Round(
            Math.Pow(Phi, n) / Math.Sqrt(5)));
}
```

Evaluation: This closed-form solution is based on Binet's formula, and it's the sort of answer you would expect from a mathematician. The code could be improved with error checking and unsigned data types. It is effectively an O(1) algorithm.

D: Lookup

```
static int FibonacciLookup(int n)
{
    int[] sequence = new int[] { 0, 1, 1, 2, 3,
        5, 8, 13, 21, 34, 55, 89, 144, 233, 377,
        610, 987, 1597, 2584, 4181, 6765, 10946,
        17711, 28657, 46368, 75025, 121393, 196418,
        317811, 514229, 832040, 1346269, 2178309,
        3524578, 5702887, 9227465, 14930352,
        24157817, 39088169, 63245986, 102334155,
        165580141, 267914296, 433494437, 701408733,
        1134903170, 1836311903};
    return sequence[n];
}
```

Evaluation: Because the sequence[9] does not vary and only the first forty-seven numbers in the Fibonacci sequence are less than the largest number that can be represented by a thirty-two-bit integer, it's sensible to simply store the answers and look them up. The same approach is feasible for sixty-four-bit integers, as only ninety-three Fibonacci numbers are less than that maximum value. This implementation could be improved with an unsigned data type but

---

[9]This sequence was queried from Wolfram Alpha. http://www.wolframalpha.com/.

is the fastest possible solution, in O(1) with the only calculation being to find an index in the answer array.

Evaluation Criteria

This is not a difficult problem to solve, so the evaluation focus is on the fundamental style of code planning and implementation, and all general considerations for questions and coding questions apply.

"Code a Binary Tree Depth Finder" Question

Difficulty

Moderate

Competency

Coding (algorithms)

Background

Tests the candidate's ability to write code using a standard, predefined data structure (binary trees). It is relatively easy to state and understand, and the code can be written fairly quickly and evaluated quickly. There are multiple correct answers.

This question is well known enough that some candidates will be prepared and "solve" it quickly. Should they solve it in less than a few minutes, switch to a less common variation.

Presentation

Verify that the candidate understands binary trees. Ask them to write production-level code that finds the maximum depth of a binary tree, given a root node. (Some candidates will think of this as the maximum height of the tree.)

The method signature is int getDepth(Node node);

Definition of Node:

```java
public class Node
{
    public Node left;
    public Node right;
    public Node() { }
    public Node(Node left, Node right)
    {
        this.left = left;
        this.right = right;
    }
}
```

Solutions

A: Concise Recursive

```
public static int getDepth(Node node)
{
    return node == null ? 0 :
        Math.Max(
                getDepth(node.left),
                getDepth(node.right)
                ) + 1;
}
```

Evaluation: This method uses a simple depth-first traversal, pushing information back up the stack. It is concise and clean—the closest thing to a "book solution"—and very strong coders will often come up with this solution. It is also the answer that a well-prepared candidate who knows the problem will provide, so it is not necessarily a clear signal of developer strength.

B: Verbose Recursive

```
public static int getDepth(Node node)
{
    if (node == null)
        return 0;

    int leftDepth = 0;
    int rightDepth = 0;

    if (node.left != null)
        leftDepth = getDepth(node.left) + 1;

    if (node.right != null)
        rightDepth = getDepth(node.right) + 1;

    if (leftDepth > rightDepth)
        return leftDepth;
    else
        return rightDepth;
}
```

Evaluation: Structurally the same as answer A, it's more verbose and more natural to write before optimizing for visual clarity. Candidates who are not well prepared for the question frequently work through the problem and arrive at this solution. It is thus a better signal of developer strength than solution A.

C: Stack-Based Iterative

```
public static int getDepth(Node root)
{
    if (root == null)
        return 0;
    Stack<Node>nextLevel = new Stack<Node>();
    Stack<Node>currentLevel = new Stack<Node>();
    currentLevel.Push(root);

    int levels = 0;
    while (currentLevel.Count>0)
    {
        Node node = currentLevel.Pop();
        if (node.left != null )
            nextLevel.Push(node.left);
        if (node.right != null)
            nextLevel.Push(node.right);
        if (currentLevel.Count == 0)
        {
            currentLevel=nextLevel;
            nextLevel=new Stack<Node>();
            levels++;
        }
    }
    return levels;
}
```

Evaluation: This method traverses the binary tree with a breadth-first sweep, keeping its own stack. The approach avoids direct recursion, and has a memory use profile different from the recursive solution, tracking the tree level by level instead of path by path. Based on interview experience, candidates who create this solution have almost certainly *not* prepared for this question. This is a creative approach: The candidate understood the principles of tree traversal and selected an efficient algorithm. It is the rarest solution and the best signal of developer strength.

D: Top-Down Recursive

```
public static int getDepth(Node node)
{
    if (node == null)
        return 0;

    int maxDepth = 1;
    getDepthHelper(node, 1, ref maxDepth);
    return maxDepth;
}
```

```
public static void getDepthHelper(Node node,
                          int myDepth, ref int maxDepth)
{
    if (node == null)
        return;

    if (myDepth > maxDepth)
        maxDepth = myDepth;

    getDepthHelper(node.left, myDepth+1, ref maxDepth);
    getDepthHelper(node.right, myDepth+1, ref maxDepth);
}
```

Evaluation: This method recurses into the tree, passing the current height of the tree and the maximum height yet found forward. At each node, the method may set its current node depth as the deepest found.

Recursion can often be programmed as either top-down or bottom-up, depending on which way the information flows most naturally. Developers whose intuition is to push data down the tree code this solution. However, to meet the question's method signature, a helper method must do most of the work. It's a pattern familiar to most developers.

Choosing the right approach is an important part of solving any problem. Because pushing the data in the other direction is simpler and requires less information juggling, that method is preferred over this one. Once the candidate selects this approach, its complexity makes it more difficult to implement, and fewer developers will create working code.

Candidates who create this solution have almost certainly *not* prepared for this question. That makes this answer a more reliable signal of developer coding strength than solutions A and B.

E: Top-Down Recursive with Static Variable

```
static int depth = 0;
public static int getDepth(Node node)
{
    depth = 0;
    if (node == null)
        return 0;

    getDepthHelper(node, 1);
    return depth;
}
public static void getDepthHelper(Node node, int myDepth)
{
    if (node == null)
        return;
```

```
        if (myDepth > depth)
            depth = myDepth;

        getDepthHelper(node.left, myDepth + 1);
        getDepthHelper(node.right, myDepth + 1);
    }
```

Evaluation: Similar in concept to solution D, this method solves the need to push information down the recursion stack by taking it outside the recursion method. It lets methods communicate the "best-known answer" no matter where they are in the tree, but it also introduces a substantial drawback: The method is no longer threadsafe.

Candidates who create this solution have almost certainly *not* prepared for this question. However, this is the poorest correct solution I have encountered.

Evaluation Criteria

The time goal for this coding problem is ten minutes.

Candidates should be familiar with tree data structures and options for traversing them. Candidates typically fall into three categories with this question: easy, struggling, or reinvention. Candidates for whom this question is easy are well prepared, either for this specific question or due to experience with coding to binary trees (which is relatively unusual when you're not studying them for school, but it does happen.) To gauge whether a performance was likely to be from specific preparation, move on to a more difficult coding question. If the candidate struggles with a close variant of the problem, they were specifically prepared and their answer should be discarded. You may want to set expectations with these candidates about telling you how they solve the problem—on demand or through memory.

Other candidates struggle with the question. They haven't written code to work with binary trees in a while, and their grasp of solution patterns like recursion or breadth-first search is weak. They will take some time to work through the problem, perhaps taking multiple fresh starts; almost certainly they will draw and use example trees to ground their understanding and test their code. If they move through the problem with some confidence and produce a correct solution without many false starts, they are probably strong coders. If it takes more than fifteen minutes or no solution appears, they are probably weak coders.

A few candidates seem to find binary trees novel but work their way through the problem and find a solution anyway. These people are both fascinating and concerning. To be successful in software engineering usually requires a foundation of general knowledge that includes binary trees, so that lack is a signal of low capability, but solving a problem like this from "first principles" is a tremendous feat, indicating a powerful intellect. I call it a wash at that point.

"Find the Bad Code" Question

Difficulty

Moderate

Competency

Debugging systems

Background

Tests the candidate's ability to debug systems, solve technical problems at multiple levels, and work with postcompilation software products. This scenario-based question is somewhat tricky to state and understand, and the candidate will need lots of direct feedback and collaborative participation. There are multiple different answers.

This question is virtually unknown, so candidates are unlikely to be prepared.

Presentation

Imagine this situation: We have 50,000 Java executables whose source code is lost. A developer discovers that we have been using a weak random number generator (RNG) to build security artifacts in an unknown number of places. Worse, the pattern from the code we do have is clear: It was not abstracted into libraries, just source-pasted in place from elsewhere. The RNG is quite bad and produces predictable output. Do you think this is a problem? How can you determine what executables are affected? Tell me your answer in terms of the principles and process you will use, but do not write source code.

Note: This question can be asked for native code, .NET, and other platforms, but should specify which up front.

Solutions

Weak RNGs are a problem in this context because security artifacts such as encryption keys depend on randomness or near-randomness to create secrets. The Java compiler produces an intermediate executable form called bytecode, which are the actual instructions the Java runtime is expected to follow. All active source code is represented as bytecode, which is highly structured, so any compiled RNG can be found in a Java executable in a relatively predictable form. A known example of the source code can be compiled so the bytecode form is identified, then a custom program reads in the 50,000 Java executables and finds candidate RNG sections. An engineer confirms them by eye.

Evaluation Criteria

The time goal for this problem is ten to fifteen minutes.

This question gives the candidate the opportunity to show a number of positive signals. The more signals, the better he or she did.

- Agrees that there is a problem because security depends on secrets created with strongly random data.

- Knowing or realizing that compilers for all languages in which you can throw away the source code create an artifact you can analyze.

- Automates the solution as much as possible so that having 50,000 executables is not impossible to deal with.

- Does not settle on a solution that involves observing the output of each executable to see if it produces a predictable pattern; it is unreliable and can't be automated.

- Considers the possibility of different compiler versions and settings producing different bytecode patterns, and the possibility that the RNG source was altered from to time. This may lead to caveats or an altered approach that uses statistical comparisons.

- Bonus: expresses dismay at the copy/paste pattern and loss of source code.

"Design an API" Question

Difficulty

Moderate

Competency

Designing system components

Background

This question is designed to measure how a candidate approaches and executes on a common and important development task: designing an API.

Presentation

Ask: "I'd like you to design the API for a spellchecker for me. The spellchecker will be a library shared by two products: a spreadsheet program and a word processor. The products are developed by two teams that you work with. I'd like you to tell me what sort of API you would present for their use, in terms of the classes and methods a developer would use. They will expect an object-oriented interface. I don't need you to describe or build a specific implementation. In other words, don't write a spellchecker for me, just the API for a spellchecker."

What makes this question difficult and effective is that it does not provide every piece of information the candidate needs up front, though it does provide all the pointers and problems. Great engineers will notice the holes and look for necessary information.

Candidates may ask whether the two customers have different usage patterns. Reply: "The spreadsheet team expects to have lots of small pieces of text and many nonwords. The word processor team expects to have large bodies of text, mostly real words, and they want to check entire documents at once, or at least very quickly. Assume 50,000 words at a time."

If candidates ask about grammar checking and spelling correction, reply that they are out of scope.

Solutions

A common solution pattern is to jump to defining a simple method that meets a simple assumed use. This frequently looks like:

```
bool checkspelling(string word);
```

or:

```
int check(char* word);
```

Unfortunately, this is jumping the gun by several minutes. It assumes one particular usage pattern and data exchange. Highly capable developers should pick up on some important clues in the presentation to guide them into requirements-gathering mode. One critical element is that there are two different customers who may have different needs, so a developer should consider what those needs are and how they can be satisfied at once—or, if necessary, satisfied separately. In this case, the API should be able to handle bulk requests as the word processor team wants to check up to 50,000 words at a time.

Another possible misstep has to do with separating responsibilities between client and service. The API has limited information about the clients' information structures, so it must ask for sharply defined input data. It cannot determine what portions of a string are intended to be words, for example. This means that the client must provide an iterator or split the words itself. An example of an API method that makes the wrong assumption—that the client and service have exactly the same ideas about what constitutes a word—is:

```
bool[] checkWords(Document document);
```

This method is meant to examine an incoming document, parse out the words, and return a yes/no spelling check for each word. A variation of this attempt in which the developer returns only an array (or alternately, a list) of strings that are bad:

```
string[] checkWords(Document document);
```

Another frequent assumption is that the spellchecker must return a set of suggested corrections for each word it detects as misspelled, which leads to contraptions that return sets of corrections of words, that is:

```
string[][] checkWords(Document document);
```

In each of these cases, the candidate is focusing on one core use case, but there are more considerations. API clients may wish to specify a reference language, custom dictionaries, and so on. Some level of configuration setting and management is necessary, as in:

```
public class SpellChecker
{
    public SpellChecker(Language targetLanguage,
                    Dictionary customDictionary) { }
}
```

This brings up other important points. How expensive is it to instantiate a spellchecker? Is it meant to be mutable, so clients can set and reset target languages for multilanguage documents?

Good solutions vary substantially. This question provokes the act of designing, not producing a specific pattern of code. However, good solutions typically share these characteristics:

- Object-oriented.

- Allow clients to specify languages.

- Have a clear and justified data exchange.

- Resolve the "what is a word?" question.

- Support both individual word checks and bulk checks.

Evaluation Criteria

Solutions hinge on defining the problem by understanding usage patterns. The neatest approaches start with the customer's expectations and then design an API to meet them. Because implementation is left out, it's not necessary for a developer to go into any detail in terms of how that might be accomplished, but it's reasonable to expect that they consider whether the API they have designed can be implemented at all.

Expect candidates to refer to and use general principles of design and coding while they work on this problem. Specific experience defining public-facing APIs will aid candidates in solving this problem.

Candidates with experience designing high-profile APIs or spellcheckers should perform exceptionally well.

Positive signals:

- Considers customer usage patterns and expectations.

- Considers concurrency requirements.

- Considers service level agreements, such as latency, transactions per second.

- Considers the requirements imposed by various human languages and character encodings.

- Uses idioms and patterns such as immutability, factories, division of responsibility, iteration, visitation.

Negative signals:

- Fails to account for differing customer requirements.

- Fails to use a fundamentally object-oriented approach (as requested).

"Test a System Design" Question

Difficulty

Moderate

Competency

Designing for testability

Background

This question provokes the performance of examining a system design and suggesting alterations to achieve engineering goals.

Presentation

Ask: "We have designed a small subsystem that I'd like you to look at. Please recommend ways we can make this system more testable, or what design features you would expect or request to make it a very testable system?

"We need to summarize a software server's activity by looking at its logs. However, the system it runs on in production is expected to always be very busy, so we will do the analysis elsewhere. Our subsystem moves log files to a different server using the 'rsync' network file synchronization program. The log files are many nearly identical lines with several delimited fields. Once they are on a different machine, our analyzer program reads the logs and produces an average value for two different fields for each day of logs. It writes those into a database table, with the database residing on the same machine."

As described in more detail in the Evaluation Criteria section, candidates are likely to ask a large number of clarifying questions. It's not necessary to answer all of them, only to acknowledge the question and prompt them for more—why do you want to know that? What else did you need to know?

Solutions

Testable systems share several characteristics. They can be decomposed into components, those individual components can be tested in isolation, and they can be replaced with mocks. Each component will have configurable logging modes, can be run in debuggers, and actively reports failures. Expect developers to suggest most or all of these things.

Taking a closer look at the system, highly capable developers will typically focus on actions that can go wrong, such as network connections, writing to and reading from disk, concurrent access or request attempts, input/output (I/O) and computation bottlenecks, and so on. These should be safeguarded with good coding practices, monitored, and tested thoroughly.

The engineer who tests the system will want the ability to alter permissions on the file system and database and to alter the file system and database schemas to add, remove, and lock elements, or "hooks" and mocks they can use to simulate these and other failures. They will ask for the ability to redirect I/O, so they can for instance configure the initial logging service to write to different areas.

Evaluation Criteria

Before people can test something, they need to understand what it's supposed to do. That's the conundrum that professional test engineers deal with every day, and they typically spend a lot of time trying to figure out and document "correct" behavior. Obviously incorrect behavior they can account for, but whether it's meeting customer expectations is a matter of requirements and specification. Because of this fundamental aspect of testing, expect candidates to ask what the system is for. What happens to the values after they are put in a database? Who uses it? How often does the system run, or does it run continuously? What are the consequences of the values being late or wrong? If it can't operate correctly due to persistent failure, what should it do?

What's most important to observe is that candidates spend time trying to understand the system and looking for its weak points. They will apply universal principles of engineering over those and more thinly across the whole system.

Poor Questions

Some types of questions simply fail calibration over and over again, whereas others may have some value but actively irritate candidates. Here are a few examples.

Too Simple

"What is four plus four?"

Because: The answer will not differentiate between candidates because it is too easy. Everyone will solve it. Better: "Write a method that sums two integers."

Too Complex

"Resolve the Riemann hypothesis."

Because: The answer will not differentiate because it is too hard. No one will solve it. Better: "Write a method that alphabetizes the letters in the string 'Resolve the Riemann hypothesis.'"

Too Vague

"Write a function that sorts strings."

Because: There's not nearly enough information in the question to get started, and two correct answers could be incomparable. Where do the strings come from and go? How many are there? Are there performance constraints? Are the strings book or movie titles or names? Better: "Write a function that sorts a long, singly linked list of short strings alphabetically."

Questions should generally be specific enough that you can directly compare candidates' answers. If one writes a modern cache-aware burst sort algorithm that's neutral on content but amazingly fast, and another calls quick sort with a sophisticated library-style comparator (e.g., "McCuller" and "MacCuller" are sorted as if identical), the results are nearly incomparable.

Ask specific or open-ended questions instead of vague questions.

Too General

"How would you resolve a technical dispute with another engineer?"

Because: The question doesn't provoke performance or find evidence of past performance. The answer given may bear no resemblance to reality. Better: "Tell me the last technical dispute you had with a developer colleague and exactly how you resolved it."

Kobayashi Maru

Named after a test given to Star Fleet students in the *Star Trek* universe, the Kobayashi Maru is a test purposefully designed to be unpassable.[10] There's no winning solution. An example of this class of question would be to ask for a sublinear integer sorting algorithm, although provably there are none available.

These can be extremely stressful for candidates. Do not ask such a question without knowing exactly what you hope to learn, such as whether the

---

[10]*Star Trek.* Various movies, episodes, and books, starting with *Star Trek II: The Wrath of Khan.*

candidate recognizes classically unsolvable or undecidable problems, whether they know to push back on a tough problem or situation, whether they can think about creative alternatives, or how far they will explore a situation and how many avenues they will try before giving up.

In a more abusive form I recommend you avoid, I have seen interviewers ask strings of confrontational questions designed to continually stymie the candidate. It seems pointless and mean, reveals little useful, forces a poor customer experience, and damages the organization's reputation for fair interviewing.

Test of Backbone

You may want to find out whether candidates will stand behind their ideas or fold under external pressure. For instance, you could ask a candidate to "find the error" in a section of code they wrote that you know is perfectly fine. The candidate may study it and calmly assure you that they see no error, and ask you to point out what you see. Or she may study it, doubt herself, and panic. Either way, you will learn something about her fortitude.

The reason I don't use these kinds of questions is that interviews can already provoke uncertainty and doubt, so compounding the candidate's doubt on purpose may elicit a false signal. A candidate that would stay assured under any regular circumstance may buckle under the added pressure of being in an interview. Because I don't know exactly how much pressure the interview places on each person, I can't determine the candidate's real fortitude. Also, it strikes me as inhumane to deliberately overstress a candidate unless it is unequivocally necessary to establish that the person stays cool under *very* stressful conditions.

The ability to collaborate is indispensable, and an important aspect of it is responding to feedback and guidance. It must be safe and effective to point out errors and question assumptions with colleagues. You will have the chance to see how the candidate responds to feedback and stress in the normal course of the interview with no special effort.

Too Theoretical

The theory behind asking behavioral questions is sound. A decent prediction heuristic is that the near future will be similar to the near past, including predicting how individuals behave. If you find out how a candidate has behaved in certain situations in the past, you can make a reasonable extrapolation to the future.

Virtually everyone has a lot more theoretical knowledge about how their jobs are performed and work gets done than they actually practice. If you ask a candidate how to deal with personality clashes, many will give you perfectly fine advice that they never have and might never personally follow. To find out how they actually behave, you should ask for a particular, specific situation. Most people will report the truth of what happened, if in perhaps a bit of a positive light, when they describe a specific circumstance.

Literally asking for a particular, specific circumstance is almost always necessary, as is listening for clues that a candidate is speaking in the theoretical mode. I frequently must restate that I want to know what actually happened somewhere at some time.

Requires Implicit Knowledge

If you take my advice and do not heavily evaluate candidates against specific, tool-focused knowledge, then your questions need to probe more general classes of capability. Many questions require knowing intimate details of specific tools, such as asking how the Java garbage collector works and how you can use various memory models to guide its action. Better questions might ask how garbage collection works in general, or how the candidate would design a garbage collector for a theoretical language.

Asking

Trial lawyers are advised to never ask a witness a question they don't already know the answer to. This greatly lowers the chance that they'll be surprised and lose control of the examination. Interviewers are well advised to do the same thing: They should not only know the answer, they should know several answers they derived themselves.

In other words, solve every problem yourself before you ask a candidate.

Practice presenting the problem clearly. You can do this by yourself by speaking the question aloud or with help from team members. Have someone ask you the question in a mock interview so you can see how the question comes across, and you may see opportunities for improving your succinctness and clarity.

Inexperienced interviewers learn the most about candidates when they ask straightforward, highly structured questions from a preset list. After a few dozen interviews, they should be comfortable with going off-list, asking broad and open-ended questions, while essentially keeping the interview on track and continuing to gather useful evidence.

Evaluating Answers

In general you should not look for the *best answers* to questions; you should look for the *best signals*—those answers (and their means of production) that tell you the most about a candidate's capabilities.

When you ask a candidate to write code that, for instance, calculates the three-dimensional area of a hypersphere of specified hyper-volume, your goal isn't to fill a whiteboard with correct code. You want to see how the candidate develops and implements an algorithm to solve the problem. You should observe multiple phases of problem solving in action, such as recognition, characterization, deconstruction, and application of knowledge, experimentation, verification, decision, construction, and final verification of the solution.

Great engineers efficiently and confidently break problems into pieces they can solve, build those pieces into a working solution, and then verify the solution. Sometimes this happens faster than you can notice, as if by magic. That's a good sign if they produce a strong answer, but you may have to prompt some candidates to explain how they arrived at a conclusion, particularly if they got it wrong.

You'll recognize bad signs immediately. Software developers and their managers are usually so good at recognizing errors and mistakes that if you're not careful and looking for ways to credit the candidate for progress, it may be all you see. Stumbling, blocking, stubbornly solving the wrong problem, refusing to cooperate with interviewers, hoping for or expecting a sudden realization of a correct answer instead of applying method, using inappropriate tools and concepts, and failing to recognize or check for errors are all common mistakes and problems that point away from high capability, indicating developers who may be ineffective or are still developing their ability to take an engineering approach to solve problems.

I have observed—and sometimes fallen prey to—several general pitfalls in evaluating answers: not taking into account question familiarity, not recognizing correct solutions, discounting nonoptimal solutions, posing the wrong question, focusing on pet answers, and missing creative answers.

Question Familiarity

If you ask a candidate a problem and she casually writes out the answer, you have learned that she has a ready store of mathematical and algorithmic information, and perhaps the exact code of the answer, but the only phases of problem solving you have seen are recognition and application of knowledge. That's useful information, but you need to see the whole package. Continue to pose problems until the candidate must actually consider and solve one.

Not Recognizing Correct Answers

When interviewers haven't studied and personally solved the questions they ask, they may not recognize correct answers (or nearly correct answers) that take a different approach from what they expect. They are also stuck reasoning about potential answers entirely on the fly during the interview, which can leave the poor (and accurate) impression that the interviewer was unprepared and maybe not all that competent.

Discounting Nonoptimal Solutions

If the problem at hand is to calculate the Huffman code of the inaugural address of each U.S. president and print them out in order of the first sixteen bits in the code, then sorting the codes is not the interesting part of the problem. Software developers have a responsibility to know the performance characteristics of algorithms used to solve everyday problems such as sorting lists and to select algorithms that meet their performance requirements. In this case you can safely represent the bits as integers, and it doesn't really matter whether you sort them by $O(n \log n)$ with merge sort or by $O(n)$ with radix sort. It would be a shame to toss out a candidate who focuses on solving the heart of the problem but misses some optimizations.

Brilliant engineers won't always discover deep optimization opportunities in the time frame of an interview session. Even if you specifically ask for optimizations on some unique problem, I suggest keeping in perspective that optimal answers look a lot more obvious from the other side of certain knowledge.

Posing the Wrong Question

The brightest and best-prepared student can fail a test if the answer key doesn't match the questions. An ill-prepared interviewer can ask the wrong question, and the interviewee has no way to know whether what they were asked is what the interviewer *meant* to ask. Candidates will sometimes restate and rephrase a question before answering it, which can help catch these problems. Otherwise, it's just wasted time at best because you talked but learned nothing.

Focusing on Pet Answers

My own solution to a problem usually seems to me to be the best one, whether it's the first correct answer I came up with or one I arrived at after much thought. Sometimes it's a book answer, an especially space- or time-efficient solution, or one expressed in succinct and pretty syntax.

Favorite answers are not always the best answers. Take care not to undervalue simple, direct, or naive approaches, if they work. Ask for the reasoning behind apparently overly complex answers, as they may be the result of candidates thinking through implications and corner cases you missed or discounted. Last, a totally original or odd answer may be a sign of a valuable divergent intellect.

Missing Creativity

Sometimes we get so used to seeing a problem solved one way that other ways look strange and wrong. For example, in solving the binary node question earlier in this chapter, candidates can choose from two styles of recursive implementation: pushing information either down the stack or back up the stack. If you are used to thinking of the problem in terms of pushing data up the stack, and candidates have always taken this approach, you may be quite surprised to see a candidate start with a push-down approach. It will look wrong. That possibility makes it important to stay on your toes even when you ask a question for the fiftieth time, because you may get a successful approach you never expected, and it would be a shame to miss out on that creativity.

Even an attempt to solve a problem from an angle that doesn't pan out may be an important sign of a playfully creative mind that will tackle tough problems with an endless string of new approaches until they find one that works.

Hiring Decisions

After gathering extensive information about a candidate, it's time to make a hiring decision. This chapter reviews the goal of hiring and then advises when to hire and when specifically not to hire, gives examples of some difficult decisions and their outcomes, and describes a number of common problems and pitfalls.

Try to get to this phase without a strong inclination for either option (hiring or not hiring). All around you throughout the hiring process, people are forming and sharing their opinions, sometimes quite vociferously. You will need a clear head to make the best decision.

The Goal

Most of the people in the world are not great engineers, and in all likelihood most of the people you interview are not great engineers *and* not great for your team. The default stance is usually "do not hire."

There are some circumstances in which you *can't* hire, but in every case you must decide clearly whether you *want* to hire. Evaluate each candidate until you have a *definite hire* or a *definite no hire* result. To be definite, you must have clearly articulated reasons, and producing those reasons forces you to be thorough and to learn from each interviewing experience.

Decision Time

You know how to make decisions. You do it many times a day, and the fundamental process is straightforward: collect evidence, weigh it against a preset measure, and see how the balance tips. The candidate meets your needs? Hire. Doesn't meet your needs? No hire. Compared to many decisions in life, such as whether and whom to marry, this one is relatively simple.

To be more analytical about it, you might choose from any sort of analytic decision method, such as multidecision criteria analysis and an analytic hierarchy process.

Even the best decision-making system and the best personal judgment are crippled when your data are bad or you carry biases. To make the *best* call, you need to keep your goal in mind, be rational, evaluate the evidence fairly, and avoid a host of potential errors and pitfalls. It's not necessary to avoid every potential problem, but every one you dodge improves your decision.

There will be times when the best decision you can make with the information available does not turn out to be the *right* decision. The candidate would have benefited your team and you didn't hire them, or they did not thrive after you did hire. It's all right to make hiring mistakes when you can correct them—particularly when you can learn from them.

Accounting for Margin of Error

Your data are only accurate within some margin. Unfortunately, you don't usually know the size of the margin, but you can account for its presence by biasing your judgment toward a safe decision. All things being equal, I urge you not to hire a candidate who appears to precisely meet your needs. The evidence is unreliable, so the candidate might in reality somewhat exceed your needs or might fail to meet your needs.

Taking the safe side of hiring decisions will stretch the total time it takes to staff a team, but the resulting team will be stronger. Hiring a poor performer is quickly correctable, but when you hire an average performer, you may be stuck with that person for a while. It is psychologically difficult to fire someone for doing just an all-right job, and your organization's policies may make it impossible.

Rationality

We like to think of ourselves as rational beings, or at least rational when we really need to be. But we are not, and there are strong indications that humans have evolved neural architectures that create apparently irrational behavior.[1] This gives you an opportunity for an advantage over other hiring managers by being just a bit more rational.

---

[1]Based on evidence from studies of human and primate behavior. See Venkat Lakshminarayanan and Laurie R. Santos, "Evolved Irrationality? Equity and the Origins of Human Economic Behavior," in *Mind the Gap: Tracing the Origins of Human Universals*, ed. Peter M. Kappeler and Joan Silk (Berlin: Springer, 2010).

What I mean by "rational" is decision making based on facts, free of biases and hidden motivations. We suffer from a wide variety of cognitive biases that can drive us away from optimal decisions. On top of that, we all carry personal biases that influence us above and below the surface of conscious thought.

You can combat these troublemaking biases with careful vigilance and self-awareness. When you are aware of a bias, you can eliminate or at least adjust for it.

Others in the hiring process will not stay rational, and you probably can't teach them to be. It seems that people need to come to rationality in their own time, but you have the opportunity to set your interviewers on the right path. Be up front about the reality of biases and be subtle as you point them out. The middle of a hiring discussion is poor timing for this conversation; it is tough to accept that any particular opinion is based on bias, not facts.

Take special care to understand that the information and opinions the interview team provide you are not completely rational. You will get bad data and must strip away bias to reveal the important truths. This book addresses some biases, several of which are described in Chapter 4, but there are many others.

When to Hire

Hire the candidates who appear to be almost all the things you want and almost none of the things you don't want.

When you have some doubt, you have the opportunity to apply the benefit of the doubt in the candidate's favor. I apply benefit of the doubt in small increments on individual pieces of evidence, which gives me the ability to verify and corroborate my assumptions. Applying benefit of the doubt at the end of the hiring process, while making a final decision, means that the verification comes after the hire. The cost of a mistake peaks at that moment, so if in doubt over some evidence or even across the board at decision time, do not hire.

If a candidate is right for the job, the job is also right for them. Explain to yourself—and you can use this as a selling point later—how the job and environment will help the person be productive and happy. Why will they enjoy it? How does it fit their needs, their vision of their future?

If it's not easy to describe why a candidate will benefit from taking the job, it is possible that you need more information about the candidate or more time to reflect on what you know, or it may be that the candidate is not a good fit after all.

Deal Breakers: People Not to Hire

In my experience, hiring people with the following behaviors has led to disastrous performance and early termination. Think carefully before making offers to such people and, of course, add your own types and observations to this list.

Slams Former Employer

Candidates may express distaste or disappointment with current or recent employers. This is natural and expected, because it's rare to interview people who are totally satisfied with their current employment. You do want honest and direct people.

Sometimes candidates are *quite* bitter and express that wholeheartedly. That puts you in an awkward position, and it's natural to think a candidate may malign you and your company some day when they eventually seek other employment. That's concerning; in addition, it's an indication that the candidate may not be *ready* for another job.

Readiness means taking purposeful action to fulfill goals, and a candidate in uncontrollable distress will make poor decisions. They will take jobs they should not take, and when they do, they will start badly. First impressions will be sour, and negative precedents will haunt them.

Candidates in such a state rarely understand what they really want. They want "Not that!"—but without a clear and thoughtful consideration of their needs and desires, they will repeat their errors in employer selection and performance.

Severely Irritates Anyone

Sometimes even otherwise well-qualified and capable candidates have a distinctly bad interaction with an interviewer. The interviewer walks away with a bitter taste, which shapes their evaluations of the candidate.

Bitterness will also shape their future interactions with the candidate if he or she becomes an employee. In addition, most candidates feel obligated to be "on good behavior" during an interview—and if that good behavior leads to a strongly negative reaction, it's a fair bet that day-to-day interactions will go badly without a strong "best behavior" influence.

It can be frustrating to pass on a candidate with exquisite technical skills, deep knowledge, and a lightning-quick brain, but the alternative is working with a jerk.

Lies or Deceives

Miscommunication is unfortunately very common. Many apparently irreconcilable statements and intimations are the result of us naturally trying to interpret and reconcile what we experience. We should exercise caution before *assuming* that someone is trying to deceive us.

The average person's accuracy in detecting a direct lie in conversation is only 54 percent, just slightly better than flipping a coin.[2] As a result, I don't trust intuition or analysis for lie detection, so I verify any statement that I genuinely care about and assume the rest are only somewhat likely to be true.

Some lies are immaterial exaggerations. It is unimportant whether someone has five or six years of Java development experience and the discrepancy can be attributed to generous rounding in any case (such as $5.001 \approx 6$). There is no point worrying about things like that because you can focus on testing *performance*, and it's a lot more difficult to lie about programming skill while building a program.

Deeply incongruous statements are much more troubling, such as rounding 2.001 up to 6, or claiming to have graduated from a fictitious university. Material deception during an interview process is a strong indicator of a personality that will continue to trouble you and your team over time. I do not hesitate to pass on such candidates, let my recruiters know, and put them on a five-year blacklist.

Ignores Goals

At some point in your life, you probably reached out to a napkin dispenser to find that it was overstuffed to the point that getting a napkin out at all was very difficult. If you managed to dig in and yank one out, you got five to thirty at once. You may have also found that the napkins were inserted backward so their flap was facing inward, giving you no straightforward way to pull one out. In that moment you encountered the handiwork and hallmark of a sort of people you do not want to hire.

Employees were once instructed to fill the napkin dispensers. They did so, and not so cleverly minimized their future efforts by overstuffing them so they didn't have to refill them as often. They may also have inserted the napkins backward, which fulfills the instruction "fill the napkin dispenser" but misses the point. It doesn't matter whether there is one napkin or a thousand napkins

---

[2]C. F. Bond Jr. and B. M. DePaulo, "Accuracy of Deception Judgments," *Personality and Social Psychology Review* 10 (2006).

in a dispenser; what matters is whether customers can easily retrieve napkins when they need them.

Anyone who fills a dispenser could perform a simple, inexpensive test to see if the effort applied was valuable: pull out a napkin. Most napkin-filling failures will be revealed. As a hiring manager, you want to hire people who will decide for themselves to perform this test and adjust their behavior to pass that test every time. It takes empathy for customers and a will to innovate: two critical traits that every great employee will have.

Tough Calls: Hiring Stories

You meet all sorts of people when you interview. Some of them stand out and make useful (anonymized) case studies.

Kyle

An excellent recruiting sourcer located Kyle just as he was accepting an offer from a small firm in the Midwest. His résumé stood out because he had more than thirty years of experience in a variety of complex engineering domains. He knew half a dozen computer languages with expert proficiency, and he said he had built sophisticated algorithms to solve many difficult problems. I gave him a call.

At the time, the most difficult capability trait to recruit for was algorithms and coding, so my phone screen was concentrated on that domain. Because of his background, I decided to skip the introductory problem and start with a moderately difficult programming task. He solved it verbally, talking through the problem, and ended by telling me syntactically correct code without writing it down. Next I gave him a problem I was still calibrating (and eventually turned out to be generally too complex for phone screens), and he had no more trouble with it than he did the first. I spent a few minutes assessing his softer skills, and when I was satisfied that he had a good chance of meeting the position's requirements, I switched to answering questions and selling him on the job. He agreed to fly in and talk with us in a few days.

Whenever I bring someone on-site I am hopeful that he will test well—after all, I brought him in because I thought he had a shot. We gave Kyle a day-long slate of interviewers and I had a lunch interview with him. He was neat and friendly, and his answers were invariably well considered, but he was long-winded and a bit cocky. My overall impression was still strong, as he excelled in all the areas I specifically probed.

The rest of the day's interviews were quite technical, and he performed just as well in person as he had on the phone. Better, in fact. He was the only person we ever interviewed (before or after) who solved all of a particular series of increasingly complex coding tasks in forty-five minutes.

I didn't make him an offer. Despite his amazing technical capability—I'm confident he would rank highly among all programmers in the world—he managed to irritate almost everyone he met in one way or another. The most common complaint was arrogance. I needed to fill a position on a high-functioning collaborative team, and the likelihood was too high that Kyle would not form great working relationships.

Jacob

Jacob joined my team as a contractor. I rarely hire contractors, because they must be interviewed, too—effort that could be applied to hiring team members. Contractors have other obvious drawbacks as well: onboarding takes a large fraction of the time you get from them; they accumulate product knowledge and leave with it; and they tend to form less of an attachment with the team.

In this case I found it necessary to find a contractor and brought in Jacob after a brief interview where he demonstrated the ability to code and showed indications of the general ability to be productive quickly and with little direction.

He performed about as well as the full-time employees—more in some areas more and less in others. He loaned us a great deal of operationalized experience; he could see architectural and organizational problems coming a long way off and move to intercept or prevent them. That broad, long-term perspective was quite valuable to us, so I suggested he apply for an open position. Having seen him actually working with the team, essentially filling the role already, I was confident that he was the right person for the job, but company policy and prudence required that we give him a formal interview. After all, I might have developed biases clouding my judgment.

When we gave him an interview, he had been with us for six months and his contract period was up.

This particular company had something of a cultural bias against hiring contractors as full-time employees. There was no compelling reason for the bias, but it was a working reality. In that culture, I tried to make it obvious that I was hiring well, so I solicited an interviewing team from across the organization—mostly people who had never worked with Jacob.

I was surprised to find that the interviewers were generally unimpressed with Jacob's performance and most recommended not hiring. A key senior engineer was adamantly against it. To find out why this might have happened, I asked Jacob to whiteboard a coding problem for me. It was clear what had happened: his on-the-board coding style lacked aggression. He had tackled the minor coding problems we had given him at a relatively superficial level, belying his excellent performance on real-world problems in production systems. He was a poor interviewee.

Jacob was also a bit strange. He didn't fit the mold of an organization that had designed itself to hire inexperienced engineers. He liked powerful functional languages that many interviewers considered toys (for no compelling reason). He also considered the social context of his software architecture—how it had to fit the organizational model of the company as well as simply work. That was a foreign concept in the organization. It may be that the engineers who interviewed him, and the interviewing system itself, reacted like an immune system to his "foreign body invasion."

Aware that I might have developed a bias I could not see, I decided to see whether additional evidence could change the adamant interviewer's mind, vowing to pass on Jacob if I could not. I presented the interviewer with concrete samples of his actual work, and with those I got what amounted to a grudging agreement. I also knew the interviewer to be strongly biased against *all* interviewees, so this was sufficient for me to make the hire.

Jacob performed admirably. When he transferred to another team, his new manager came to me and asked, "So, how do I work with Jacob?" It took some getting used to his slightly alien approach to software development, but Jacob's net contribution was immensely valuable.

Christina

About two years out of a good college, Christina's résumé was short but had the right words on it and no red flags. I gave her a phone screen, and she did quite well with a design question—much better than average for her experience level. She solved a coding problem with a bit of difficulty, but she had notably good cheer, even exuberance. I asked an engineer to give her a follow-up phone screen, which produced the same results.

The ability to code well was a firm requirement for the position, so I carefully weighed the decision to proceed. Not everyone who codes with style and grace can do so on the phone. There were plenty of other positive indicators, so I brought her in.

Christina was certainly consistent: She did the same on site, struggling a bit with solving coding problems but managing to get through them cheerfully. My team did not need struggling coders, so I would normally pass on such a candidate, but there was another important factor.

We were able to include a company director on her interview loop, and his feedback was: "She had the most considered and challenging business and technical questions for me that I have ever received from a junior engineer. Actually, any engineer." Combined with the design question results, I had convincing evidence that she was a deep thinker. She was thorough.

Her background gave evidence that she was a quick learner, so I was certain she could rapidly bring her technical skills up to par and higher if she wished to. I made an offer.

She was unsure whether to accept, so I gave her the phone numbers of each person on the team (with their permission) and suggested she talk with any of them, asking whatever she would like to know that would make the decision easier. A few hours later we had a weekly team meeting, and we all found it hilarious as each person in the room excused him- or herself, one at a time, to take a call from Christina. She accepted our offer. She was indeed a thorough engineer and made a substantial difference to the success of the team over the next few years.

Sources of Error

Problems can occur in the interview process that can affect the usefulness of the outcome: environment, chance, poor interviewers, confirmation bias, halo and horn effects, and others.

Accidental Conditioning

Mood, health, and stress level all affect your judgment. If you're euphoric when you meet a candidate, you'll probably develop a favorable bias; if you're dysphoric, you'll probably bias against the candidate. It's a classical conditioning effect, used by marketers the world over, and the effect may be subtle or even unnoticeable to you. How you feel about a person you meet is measurably influenced by something as simple and subtle as the temperature of a cup of coffee in your hand.[3]

To prevent this bias from affecting your judgment, I suggest you postpone interviews, recap meetings, and evaluations until you are level-headed, or else delegate to someone in a stable state.

Bad Day

Everyone has off days. Family problems, illness, or even bad weather can upset, distract, or debilitate a person. Candidates may perform well below their peak or even below their average ability, so you may undervalue their true ability to contribute to your team. One way to combat this is to allow candidates to reschedule their interviews for a good time if they can't perform well.

---

[3]L. E. Williams and J. A. Bargh, "Experiencing Physical Warmth Promotes Interpersonal Warmth," *Science,* 24 (October 24, 2008): 606–7.

Bad Interviewers

Despite your best efforts, sometimes a person not qualified to interview or evaluate the candidate gets on the interview loop.

Salvage what you can from the interviewer's experience, even if this is just their personal interaction—establishment of rapport and so on. Then systematically ignore their interview feedback, excluding them from recap meetings if possible, so their unqualified perspective does not influence the hiring decision.

Confirmation Bias

Everyone has a tendency to make a decision and *then* find evidence to back it up.[4] That makes it quite difficult to change your mind even when there is contradicting evidence available. If you prevent yourself from making a decision *before* evaluating all the evidence, you will be better able to interpret each piece of evidence appropriately. If you start with an opinion, you will almost certainly collect, notice, and weigh more heavily any information that reinforces your initial determination, while unconsciously ignoring or inappropriately discounting evidence that contradicts it.

When interviewers succumb to confirmation bias, they may present and emphasize all their feedback on a candidate with either a positive or a negative aspect. No one is an angel or a demon, and interviewers should be able to find both positive and negative aspects of *every* candidate. When I am presented with one-sided feedback, I guide the interviewer into interpreting their information in another light, prompting for exceptions.

Confusing Domain Knowledge with Capability

In my experience, most people tend to conflate knowledge with capability. To a certain extent it is necessary and unavoidable to test for knowledge that successful engineers must have and perhaps for more specific domain knowledge you need for your team.

Some managers dismiss out of hand those candidates who don't have some particular knowledge or experience. They assume, for example, that a candidate who doesn't know how to design distributed systems *can't* learn to design them, or that a candidate without web application test experience isn't interested in the domain. Sometimes managers conclude that not knowing one thing or another means an engineer isn't interested in furthering his or

---

[4]This observation goes back at least to Sir Francis Bacon in the sixteenth century. For a comprehensive review, see Raymond S. Nickerson "Confirmation Bias: A Ubiquitous Phenomenon in Many Guises," *Review of General Psychology,* 2(2) (1998): 175–220.

her career. A conclusion like that sounds so irrational that you can't believe intelligent people would think that way, but I see it happen frequently.

Discounting the Ability to Learn

Technical hiring managers I have observed often devalue the ability to learn in favor of already acquired knowledge. Of course, we would like team members to perform optimally without effort or training, but it's unavoidable that engineers must learn on the job. Indeed, they learn continually so they can advance in their careers and push their performance forward.

On the basis of watching my colleague engineers, I observed that getting more done rarely seems to be the result of simply putting in more effort; it's the result of creating and accumulating more personal knowledge of effective practices—wisdom, if you will. That's everything from tagging releases in source code to when and how to use a new programming language or create one to solve a new problem.

Even average engineers have acquired a tremendous amount of academic and operational knowledge, which they build on every day. The great engineers—the ones you want to hire—regularly and naturally learn quickly and thoroughly. They will be up to speed and leading the charge with new ideas in less time than it takes to get used their presence in the team. Whatever their starting state in some domain knowledge past the utter basics, great engineers will be designing your new distributed systems before they find the candy dish on the second floor. My strong recommendation is to count on the learning process, hire engineers who can learn over those who already know, and move the candy dish from time to time.

Halo Effect

Beautiful people are not necessarily better programmers. It is obvious that there's no correlation between physical appearance and work capability, but if you ask many interviewers to evaluate the same coding performance by different candidates, on the whole view they will a beautiful person's performance more favorably than that of a less attractive candidate.[5] This is an instance of the halo effect: One positive trait creates an impression of *many* positive traits.

Physical attractiveness is obviously an unrelated domain for engineering capabilities. A more insidious form of the halo effect occurs when a candidate has a technical capability that stands out, maybe even a profound capability, and it

[5]K. K. Dion, E. Berscheid, and E. Walster, "What Is Beautiful Is Good," *Journal of Personality and Social Psychology*, 24(3) (1972): 285–90.

colors every other trait they appear to have in a positive way. For example, a masterful coder may not be any good at designing distributed data stores. But if you've seen a candidate create elegant code quickly and effortlessly, you are more likely to view stumbling on a design question in a forgiving and favorable manner. They seem *hesitant* rather than *incompetent.*

The net result of the halo effect is very destructive to the evaluation process. One way to reduce it is to have interviewers focus on a *single* capability as they interview. Their opinion on that dimension, good or bad, won't color opinions they don't form on other dimensions.

Horns Effect

A common saying is "Don't throw the baby out with the bathwater"—yet I have seen this happen in the hiring process. It is the simple inverse of the halo effect—letting one negative aspect overshadow all positive ones—but it's less widely considered and has a distinct impact on decision making that should be kept in mind whenever you evaluate evidence.

Personable Candidates

Being nice is necessary, but not sufficient.

Sometimes a candidate is so amicable and pleasant to talk to that it rather overwhelms performance evaluation. You can't help but like the person. There's an instant rapport, and maybe this is the kind of person who forms fast and easy relationships. That is a useful trait.

However, it's not enough to justify a hire. That extremely nice person is going to be harder for you to fire in six months when you realize that he or she can't actually perform the role you need filled.

Similarity Bias

I've seen a strong and unfortunate tendency in hiring managers to hire people who think, act, speak, and look like themselves. They are further encouraged in this by a team of interviewers with similar biases, and that team itself may have been selected as a result of a process with a similarity bias, perpetuating self-similarity over time.

It is hardly shocking news that diversity is immensely valuable to the creative process, or that engineering work is a creative process. Diversity helps create new and innovative approaches to problems, avoid known or foreseeable mistakes, and even finds new kinds of problems to solve. Teams with differences have more options, more opportunities, and more perspectives.

Combat this pervasive hiring bias by emphasizing locating and hiring qualified engineers who are *not like you*. They will have different genders, educational backgrounds, employment histories, mannerisms, accents, and thinking styles.

In particular, it can be hard to appreciate people who think differently: Their thought processes may seem scattered, even inverted; their speech may seem to meander; they focus on unusual areas of problems; and so on. These are not always bad signs. Sometimes it means you're talking with someone who has very different methods that are equally effective or better, and who can bring a new perspective to your team.

The Skill of Being Hired

Interviewing as a candidate requires some skills that are not exactly the same as the ones required to perform well on the job. Some people are especially good at getting hired, so you might hire them when you should not; others are particularly bad at getting hired, so you might pass over even exceptionally qualified candidates. The effect of this ability (or lack thereof) is to accentuate the basic difficulty of evaluating candidates.

The only good to come of candidates having this skill is that you can gain a competitive advantage by being a better hiring manager, sussing out the good and bad performers even when they make it difficult to do so by exercising great interviewing skills or lacking them altogether.

Engineers who are not good interviewees will fail when hiring managers are not perceptive enough to recognize their lack of interviewing skills. Focus on sorting out the good engineers despite any lack of interviewing skill, and it may pay off disproportionately well.

Using Nonevidence

People often unknowingly solve problems using the information they *have* instead of the information they *need*, even when what they have is essentially irrelevant. It is a manifestation of availability bias, a cognitive defect studied by Amos Tversky and Daniel Kahneman.[6]

If you don't have enough evidence, you cannot make a decision. You must take the default stance—no hire—or gather more data.

---

[6]Amos Tversky and Daniel Kahneman, "Availability: A Heuristic for Judging Frequency and Probability," *Cognitive Psychology*, 5(1) (1973): 207–32.

Hiring at the Right Level

The candidate who exceeds your expectations may be a better fit for a different job. For example, principal engineers are likely to sail through an interview for a more junior position, but they are not a good fit for a role that can only accommodate a junior engineer.

There is a highly productive work state called *flow* that people can efficiently enter when working on problems with a difficulty just below their maximum capability.[7] Flow is the feeling you get when you are totally "in the zone," focused and productive, and time seems to fly. Engineers love it, and if you can keep them in a flow state, you can probably keep them working for you indefinitely.

If the work you have available is not complex enough to occupy an engineer, they may grow bored and listless. That affects their work and the net result can be that a highly capable engineer is *less* effective overall when working on a long series of tasks that do not challenge them.

Still, if you have identified an engineer whose capabilities sufficiently exceed your available work and it's likely they will become bored, you have an opportunity. You might be able to rescope the role, create a new role, find a better fit in your department or company, or build a new team and new product around them.

Despite your best efforts, you may inadvertently hire low. Once you've hired them, you'll have to deal with poor performers as you would anyone else. Working with poor performers is beyond the scope of this book.

Compromise

Never hire below your standards. You set them high with purpose and vision. Every hire creates a ripple effect that is felt a long way away, affecting the business in myriad ways and leaving a legacy that may last longer than your own employment.

You probably feel pressure to hire so you can deliver to your goals, creating a strong incentive to get *anyone* working on those goals. But the trade-off is almost definitely not worthwhile.

Lower capability employees are not fun to work with. They will not attract strong talent. They will not compare favorably with other teammates, attenuating the team. They tend to take more of your management time. They are

---

[7]M. Csikszentmihalyi, *Flow: The Psychology of Optimal Experience* (New York: HarperCollins, 1991).

more likely to be terminated for low performance, a process that can take substantial management time as well as draining your energy and mood. Hiring low-capability developers sets them up for failure, hurts the team, hurts the business, and hurts you.

Hiring low is also not likely to save you time. Lower capability engineers will drag the team down and take longer to get up to speed and start being productive than a highly capable engineer.

Providing Feedback

A great interview experience keeps the candidate informed about the process and its results. If a candidate does not receive an offer, the natural question they ask is, "Why?" Questions beg answers, so it would be natural to give some useful feedback. This presents at least two problems: It opens the door to argument about an already finalized decision, and it may provide an additional opportunity for candidates to legally challenge the decision.

Many companies have specific policies about this, so check with HR.

In the absence of a policy and to avoid unproductive argument, I prefer not to answer a request for feedback directly. Instead, I give the candidate something meaningful to think about, on the lines of the following.

Me: "It was a pleasure interviewing you, but we're not a great match today. Gain some more experience, hone your skills—coding, design, and so on—and apply again in a year or two. We're likely to be here."

Candidate: "Will the position still be open?"

Me: "This position probably won't be, but it is possible we will have other positions open—businesses grow, people move on, and so forth. In any event, I wish you great success. Thanks for interviewing with us."

Record Keeping

Update your records whether or not you make a positive hire decision and whether or not the candidate accepts an offer. If you are maintaining a candidate book (there is an example in the Appendix), add the salient reasons that drove your decision. That information can guide you to better hiring practices over the long run. As you accumulate successful hires and unsuccessful hires, use the records you kept to form a clear historical view. It will also help you sidestep some memory-oriented biases, such as hindsight bias, rosy retrospection, and choice-supportive bias.

Offers

Through colossal effort or luck (probably both), you have identified a particular software engineer you want working for you. It's quite simple really: establish mutual interest, sell, negotiate, and bring on board. Simple to summarize, anyway. This chapter has advice on negotiating offers: what candidates may want and what compelling compensation you may be able to offer.

If you have been focusing on providing a great candidate experience, negotiating is easier than it might have been otherwise. Your competitors are probably not trying to impress and delight candidates before hiring managers are interested; like fair-weather friends, they are nice when they want something from you. Being mistreated during the hiring process is common in the industry, and candidates either don't notice it or expect it. You can stand out as an upright and interesting employer by simply treating candidates like people who matter whether or not you make them an offer.

To snag a great engineer, you must convince her to drop whatever else she is doing (or plans to do) and join your team. She needs to feel that doing so will to make her successful and the team successful. To create a situation she wants more than any alternative, look into what motivates her and make it happen.

At this point, your HR team or recruiter may step in and prepare, present, and negotiate the offer. If they are particularly effective at closing the deal, make sure they understand your compensation philosophy and let them run. Even if someone else now negotiates with the candidate, your involvement is far from over. You should at least expect to approve offers and do some selling.

Keep the candidate experience positive with plenty of communication and forthright dealing. Be transparent, obvious, honest, responsive, and quick.

What People Want

It is a simple truth that what people want and what they think they want are different. When you build and present an offer, you're selling a situation. The candidate who gets the offer has to imagine themselves in that situation, and it seems that people are generally not especially good at this. You've probably experienced this yourself: You thought something would make you happy, you got it, and there was no lasting change in your happiness. You may even have experienced buyer's remorse. A hiring manager must show developers what they think they want; then, when they are on the job, give them what they actually want. Be entirely truthful all along the way. You can accomplish it with appropriate emphasis: stress up front the parts candidates think they want and, later, deliver more on what will actually make them satisfied, motivated, and productive.[1]

What to Offer

"Total compensation" is a phrase used by some human resources departments to stand in for "everything we spend on behalf on an employee," including salary, annual bonuses, health care, investment plans, stock options, stock grants, education reimbursement, paid vacation, and all other perquisites. It is a useful concept even if your organization doesn't use the term, particularly when you can't offer gigantic cash salaries but you can offer tantalizing nonsalary benefits.

Thinking even more broadly, the total compensation you can offer is everything beneficial to the employee, including all aspects of the situation. There's some evidence that "more money does not mean more happiness"[2]—and, true or not, other perquisites *can* ensure happiness. A great developer's job offers many opportunities, and the more you can offer the better. For a software developer, that can include at least:

- Daily technical challenge.

- Opportunity to use expert skills.

---

[1] A full discourse on software developer motivation is out of the scope of this book, but this literature review is a good place to start reading: Sarah Beecham, Nathan Baddoo, Tracy Hall, Hugh Robinson, and Helen Sharp, "Motivation in Software Engineering: A Systematic Literature Review," *Information and Software Technology*, 50(9–10) (2008): 860–78, available at http://oro.open.ac.uk/20392/.

[2] Happiness economics (hedonics) is a field of active research. One study on the effect of wealth on happiness, which has useful references to many other papers on the topic, is Jordi Quoidbach, Elizabeth W. Dunn, K.V. Petrides, and Moïra Mikolajczak, "Money Giveth, Money Taketh Away: The Dual Effect of Wealth on Happiness," *Psychological Science* 21 (2010): 759–63, available at http://pss.sagepub.com/content/21/6/759.

- Opportunity to learn new expert skills.

- Opportunity to work with other experts.

- A fantastic manager.[3]

- Saving lives, entertaining people.

The last item is a placeholder for whatever your team does that positively affects the world that a candidate might care about. Most human endeavors do some sort of general good. Your team's positive effect may resonate with particular candidates more than others; game developers, for instance, tend to stick to and love game development.

If your team is doing no good at all or actively causing harm, consider finding a new team to lead. Life's too short.

A Fantastic Manager

This may be the most important part of a job offer.

As you may know from your own career, a manager can make or break a job. Candidates seek managers who think about and care about them, who think of themselves as servants more than bosses, and generally strive for self-improvement. They attract talent. In the opposite case, ineffective or tyrannical managers suppress or drive away talent. They say people take jobs because of the job, and then leave because of the manager.

It's tricky to tell candidates they should work for you because you're awesome. They won't take your word for it and may conclude you're an egomaniac they should avoid. How are they to know you're just stating the fact? You'll have to let someone else do the talking on this one. Get the candidates talking to people who do and used to work for you and, critically, ask these contacts to be candid. My practice is to ask candidates to speak with anyone they like about me and my management style. For internal recruitment, I suggest candidates simply ask anyone they want to about me—managers, peers, reports, or partners. When I'm negotiating with external candidates, I start them off with a list of names and contact info. In either case, I tell those contacts to never tell me what they talked about.

Of course I'm curious what they talk about, and I hope I could put the information to good use on self-improvement, but what I care about in recruiting is results. Candidates who reach out get the real story, good and bad, giving

---

[3]You are worth your weight in gold—on average, about $3.83 million at the time of this writing, according to Wolfram Alpha.

them a rare opportunity to find out what's great and not so great about the job, the people, and the manager before they take or decline an offer. Reaching out is an investment on their part as well, and by nature people value things more when they've put time into them, all else being equal.[4]

There's a downside to that level of openness, which is, frankly, that the candidate sees your downside. If you're an egomaniacal tyrant, they'll find that out and avoid you, and that does you little good in terms of recruiting. Look at the bigger picture: Egomaniacal tyrants don't deserve and should be kept away from reports. Tyrants cause stress and ill will, and it's unlikely to be a good bargain for any employee.

Vacation Time

Organizations typically have standard packages of nonsalary benefits that they offer to almost everyone: health insurance, investment plans, paid time off, and so on. Candidates may request compensation beyond whatever the standard is—for example, a candidate once asked me whether the company could extend health benefits to employees' parents. More commonly, people ask for additional paid time off.

More paid time off is the perk I have had the most difficulty providing. HR organizations sometimes set rigid rules that they won't change for anyone. Sometimes well-paid candidates are satisfied with essentially buying paid time off with unpaid leave, making up for the difference in take-home pay with a larger salary. The ones who can't be satisfied will move on.

Candidates frequently ask to keep vacation plans they have already made, "paying" for it with unpaid leave, borrowing against future accumulation of earned vacation, or taking paid extra days off for that purpose. I grant this request for cheap goodwill and employee satisfaction. Even tightly constrained managers can allow knowledge workers to take unreported time off if it's necessary to make a hire. (Don't tell anyone I told you so.)

Salary

The employment market varies substantially across regions, over time, and in niche parts of the industry. You must know the going rate for the role you're hiring for, so you don't aim too high or too low with your offers. Useful sources of information include other managers who are hiring, websites that specialize in salary surveys, the Bureau of Labor Statistics and other government publications, and

---

[4]The sunk costs fallacy. One should never provoke fallacious reasoning in another person, but in this case there's no avoiding it and it works in your favor.

perhaps most accurately, local recruiters who are placing developers. They will know what offers are going out and what offers are being accepted by developers right now. Great developers cost more than mediocre developers, so expect to pay near the top of the market, not at the median.

You'll know quickly if you are not offering high enough salaries, as developers will turn them down. Software developers tend to be sensitive to anything with a number attached, and the most obvious number in an offer letter is salary. When comparing offers, developers usually focus on differences between salary numbers before seriously considering other differences—even if they know perfectly well that they will be otherwise happier with one job than another.

There's a strong temptation to save money by offering the lowest salary a candidate may accept. However, a candidate who accepts your offer when it is lower than even one other offer may form a sense of loss associated with taking the job you offer. That may guide the candidate's behavior over a long time as she seeks (consciously or subconsciously) to get raises and bonuses to bring her income up to what it "should" be. Employees who focus on earning more money may not be focusing as much as they could be on the work.

Offering too much pay is another potential problem. Vastly disproportionate offers will override common sense, tempting candidates who should otherwise not take the job. When a candidate accepts a huge starting salary, the income can become a pair of golden handcuffs that will dissuade her from leaving later, even when it is time to move on.

Adapting to the Market

Compensation for software engineers has historically risen quickly and sometimes dramatically. As a curious by-product of this phenomenon, I have hired engineers with less experience than I have for more money than I make. The first time I did this, I was nonplussed—still, it makes sense. Engineers have a divergent skill set from engineering managers, and demand for each role changes almost independently.

Engineers are very clever—that's why you want them, after all—and they are likely to know what the market pays. The market fluctuates rapidly, so keep an open mind and stay up to date. If you are lucky, your company has compensation analysts that keep up with the times. Most companies do not react to market changes in less than annual intervals, so it may be worth planning a hiring spree to immediately follow compensation standards changes.

Signing Bonuses

Signing bonuses are enticing. They get a candidate excited to join and read to start quickly so they get the cash earlier. An especially important aspect of signing bonuses is that they help candidates get over the "hump" of acclimatization—the period of time after starting and before mastering the environment. The stress of proving oneself in a team of all-stars, personality conflicts, cultural quirks, and other normal events can discourage an otherwise happy and productive employee as they onboard and get through the first year or so. Employees sometimes walk away at that point, though with encouragement and perseverance they will thrive. To give them added incentive to barrel through initial frustrations, offer signing bonuses they must forfeit should they quit (sometimes called a claw-back provision).

When Short of Cash

On one occasion, I had to recruit when my budget per developer was too small. It had been set by an office in a faraway land that would not consider substantial market differences between locations. So it was as difficult as you would imagine to entice great developers. To compensate, I proceeded to emphasize everything else, not only in the offer but in the job. I started building an environment that would be more fun and more interesting to developers than the alternatives. Better vacation, better physical office layout, better policies—all friendlier and more suitable to great work and great fun.

In retrospect, I should have been doing that all along.

Selling

Engineers tend to be the sort of people who show up at a car dealership knowing more about each car model than the sales staff does. In my experience, most respond better to exposition than sales tactics, so I use straightforward explanations. When I need to sell to a candidate on the fence—which is unusual with great interview experiences and strong initial offers—I explain why it is to their advantage to join the team (and to my advantage, because knowing my motivation helps). I explain why I decided to make an offer. I tell them how the environment will encourage them to thrive and develop their skills further while enriching their lives and bank accounts.

A powerful aid in selling candidates is a sell sheet that lists the top reasons people enjoy working in the team and in the company—how they feel about it, what they get from it, and how they contribute to success. You can learn by asking peers and reports leading questions. Boil them down to bullet points and you have something to keep handy for quick reference, or you can email them to the candidate.

Always tell the straight truth about the company, team, work, and role. Candidates will appreciate it, make better decisions, and experience little surprise after starting.

There's a serious potential for downside, of course. If the work is largely maintaining a forty-year-old codebase riddled with bugs, the team is made of criminals and curmudgeons, and everyone huddles around the same dimly lit desk at the bottom of a well, you're going have difficulty finding someone who will jump at the chance to come on board. But be up front about it all, because it won't be long before the excited new employee gets hit by reality and falls down screaming.

In this circumstance, it may be possible to change the role into something more palatable and more productive at the same time. Perhaps you can define the role as not so much a software developer but as a turnaround specialist, who will not only pick up the work but change the way it's done.

Negotiation

I recommend not negotiating with candidates at all. Work out ahead of time what the best offer you can possibly afford is, and then simply present it to the candidate. In all likelihood, it's more than they would have asked for, and a hefty compensation package is both an easy sell and not really all that expensive in the grand scheme of things. Remember that a team of brilliant engineers on a well-run project creates business value so quickly that they are worth their weight in gold. Perhaps that is quite literally true, depending on the spot price of gold when you read this.

It's likely that you are more money-constrained than just paying employees as much cash as you can think of. Still, the easiest way to keep negotiation simple is to offer as much as you can up front and be clear about it. Tell them it's the most you can justify and leave it at that. Some people may be disappointed that they can't haggle—and may refuse to accept that you're telling the truth—but not everyone can be satisfied.

Time

Engineers are often quite cautious about accepting offers, so if negotiations stretch out for a few weeks, don't discount the candidate. I've seen managers write off candidates who spend time checking offers carefully, verifying the company's and team's strengths, pursuing all sorts of immediately available options such as other interviews, and negotiating. It seems like a sensible approach to me, revealing something of the candidate's cautious and thorough nature.

Negotiation time actually works in your favor, because when it takes a while, the sunk costs fallacy kicks in. Be careful not to fall victim to it yourself.

You have a choice when you're ready to extend an offer to a candidate—should you continue interviewing more candidates or wait? If you wait, your hiring process for that position is stalled and may have to pick up again after lost time. If you don't wait, you may find another great candidate and find yourself conflicted about the first offer, particularly if you have just one position available.

My practice is to continue interviewing until the moment a candidate accepts, and then cancel pending interviews. It keeps the machine in motion, and it applies some time pressure to the negotiations: when I find another suitable candidate, I ask for an immediate answer from the candidate already holding an offer. If declined, I start an offer for the second applicant. On the few occasions when I've had two candidates I could hire for one position on the line and the first accepted, I referred the second to another position in my organization. It's a win both ways.

Sell Calls

The power of manager and executive sell calls should not be underestimated. Always do some kind of sell. If someone besides you sends the offer, call each candidate immediately after it is presented to express how important she is and how much you are looking forward to working with her.

If you have any doubt about the candidate's enthusiasm for the job, arrange for the highest-ranking person you can get on the phone to call her. Start with the CEO and work your way down.

For a somewhat exaggerated illustration of the power of an executive sell call, imagine that you have two equally compelling job offers in front of you from major companies. Furthermore, the CEO or chairman of one of the two calls you directly to ask you to join that company. What would you do?

Aim for that effect and you may find that candidates give your offer a lot more weight, and new hires come in considerably more excited on day one.

Success

Once you have a signed offer letter, shaken hands, or whatever equivalent you're using, start the onboarding process. You don't need wait however long it takes for the candidate to walk in and sit down; you can establish rapport right away. Ask what they want to know and point them to learning resources (if they are interested in getting a head start, and many great developers are).

Not everyone who accepts an offer shows up to start work, so the hiring process isn't truly over until that happens. It's not even over until onboarding is finished. In fact, you should probably always be recruiting. In any case, update your candidate book and spread the good news, congratulate everyone involved, and start again.

Failing Negotiations

A heartbreaking reality is that negotiation does not always succeed.

If you were successful in communicating with the candidate, and they with you, then the incompatibility is fundamental and you should let the candidate go and wish her well. You might refer her to a different position, even to a different company—this costs nothing and earns you valuable goodwill.

Update your candidate book with reasons for any such loss and study it to discover what you need to change.

Candidates and recruiters won't always be up front about why they turned down an offer or fully understand it themselves. Some polite and careful questioning may reveal something useful. Failure may have been under your control or not. Anything you learn can help either change your behavior or let you recognize a looming problem when you see it again.

A Great Start

The test of a successful hiring process is whether the new employees thrive and contribute. Having put so much effort into finding a developer you have every reason to believe is highly capable, you should also do everything you can to set that person up for success. A supporting environment is critical for most developers to succeed and certainly to succeed and deliver right away.

Time is almost invariably the most critical resource dimension of any project. If you can save time by spending some money, you usually should do so. After all, your well-capitalized competitors will do the same and could beat you to market with innovative products. Ramping up a new developer to maximal productivity quickly is well worth the effort in at least two ways.

A less than fully productive employee is usually a net drain on the entire team's output. To deliver at the pace of the rest of the team, they need to do the core work and also gather domain knowledge by questioning teammates and reviewing their own work more carefully than usual. Any product that requires a team to build it is nontrivial, so team members invest a lot of time understanding the context of the work.

The fundamental practice of development is gathering and refining requirements, building and verifying designs, building software components, and delivering and maintaining that software. All of these stages go smoothly only when a team is engaged at the highest level.

Developers must understand the business context of their work, including the market, the customers, and their specific current and projected needs. They must understand and know how to work with the project management system in place, in terms of the planning and iteration process, ticket systems and management tools, contacts and social structure on and across teams, and so on. They need a detailed and nuanced understanding of the technical context: current and planned architecture and designs, patterns and idioms in use, existing tools and software, build systems, ticket and alert systems, and more.

Managers have many options for onboarding new employees. The key difference between one style and another is level of formality. Choosing the right level is important because it speeds the process and sets the tone for future work. Onboarding is the first process the developer will encounter, and the impression it makes lasts a long time.

Situations that demand increased formality include especially complex systems and specialized knowledge domains and products that demand special attention to detail, such as banking and life-critical systems. By contrast, informal teams tend to use and thrive on informal onboarding.

As usual, the best method requires extra work, and optimal onboarding is accomplished by tailoring the experience for each new hire. Different employees need differing levels of direct guidance. Onboarding is a bridge from what they did before to what they have to do now, so the more that process speaks to them individually, the better.

More senior developers, particularly those who have come through several stages in their careers, will have encountered a variety of organizational patterns they can recognize and quickly adapt to. Career contractors do the same; both of these groups are usually comfortable with less guidance. Green developers are eager to learn, which creates a level of adaptability that frequently counterbalances the learning curve, but they don't have a repertoire of work patterns to draw from and have to learn from the ground up.

I have observed that the developer's recent work history most drives their onboarding needs. When coming from a highly regimented and process-heavy company, a developer at any level may feel out of water in a more laissez-faire environment, and the inverse situation has the same outcome. Switching software domains can have a similar effect, as in going from shrinkwrapped to embedded software or from enterprise to gaming. In these cases, the developer won't know how to get things done, complicating their integration and distracting them from acquiring the other knowledge they need. They will need detailed instructions and some hand-holding for a while.

These factors weigh into the decision of how much guidance and personal energy you should plan to put into onboarding each new hire. A senior engineer with an adaptive personality coming from an organization with a similar level of organization, similar software domain, and similar technology suites can be more or less safely thrown into the fire. For everyone else, you should ramp up the heat a bit at a time.

Prestart

When I showed up excited and eager for the first day at my first development job, my first assignment was to spend a few hours constructing my desk from parts. This sort of irritated me until I realized how much I was getting paid to build furniture. As a manager, you always want your employees working on the highest value tasks available, and although it's your option to spend expensive developer time on office assembly and the like, you will probably be more successful if you do not allocate time this way.

Preparation will save time and send a message to the new hire about how much you care about them and their experience from the first moment. A new hire, showing up on day one to find no computer, no accounts, and no chair, leaves with a very distinct impression. Showing up to find your accounts prepared and everything on your desk cabled and orderly, with a map, business cards, a notepad with "Welcome aboard!" scrawled on it, plus a handful of sharpened pencils leaves quite another impression. Checklists are your friend here. What do you use every day that you should set up for the new hire?

Keep in mind that you may have to order equipment well in advance or be prepared to buy and expense/argue the point later. It's amazing what you can accomplish by spending money now and sorting it out later, but avoid it when you can and order in advance.

Relocation

New hires who move from far away to take a job face a huge number of challenges. Everyday knowledge like where to shop for groceries is suddenly obsolete and needs to be rediscovered, and it's hard to overstate the social impact of uprooting yourself and family. Stress will run high, but it may take only a couple of friendly gestures to make someone feel like they have found a new home they can settle into. You might present an inexpensive gift of a local coupon book, tickets to the movies or a sports game, or an invitation to a barbecue or poker night.

Why not do this for everyone you work with?

Start

Get people off to a great start by setting expectations and providing a starting guide. Tell them where to be, whom to talk to, and anything you wish you had known the first few weeks. After that, teamwork, participation, mentoring, and ad hoc questions should finish the integration so the new employee becomes a trusted team member.

Onboarding Plan

Even if you're comfortable that a new hire would love to be thrown into the workplace with no compass, map, or breathable atmosphere, there's an absolute minimum you have to do. It's up to you to map out the specifics, but the fundamental structure is pretty common. You can build and tailor it, type it up and present it on day one, or in the spirit of true informality just keep it in mind as you go. Here's an example.

First Week

- Schedule a recurring one-to-one meeting
- Business introduction
- Technical introduction
- Social integration (introductory email/announcement, morale event, or a team lunch)
- Administrivia: systems, permissions, passwords, mailing lists, ticket system, shared calendars, recurring meetings

First Month

- Clarify expectations and roles
- Schedule skip-level meetings
- Ask the new hire: how did the assumed role meet your expectations? Should the job description be updated? What should we tell the next person who starts? How can we improve the onboarding plan?

First Quarter

- Set annual goals
- Develop and execute on a career plan

First Year

- Introduce the employee to committees, boards, and positions of influence they can join
- Submit referrals for new candidates

Peer Mentor

New hires invariably benefit from having someone who is sure to have an answer (or direct them to someone who has an answer) for every random question—a first contact for whatever ails them. It must be clear that the peer mentor is not the *only* contact they should use, but someone who definitely *expects* to hear from the new hire frequently. Everyone on the team is a resource.

To find a mentor, you have options such as asking for volunteers, choosing at random, or choosing strategically. I usually ask a particular engineer to take this role, one who has expressed leadership capability or an earnest desire to grow those skills. It's usually someone on track to be a lead developer or principal engineer; sometimes it's a developer angling for a career change into management. Such a person is likely to do a decent job of peer mentoring, so everybody wins.

Questions

To fill their knowledge gaps, new hires will ask many questions, and the answers lead to new questions, and so on. Not only is it impossible to have enough documentation to preempt verbal querying, it would be mind-numbing to get all necessary information by reading. I set the expectation with new hires that they should ask incessantly. Shy or overly polite engineers will hesitate to ask repeatedly, particularly if asking the same question when they didn't have enough background to understand the previously given answer.

Commonly, people see asking as a sign of personal weakness: "They just don't have the mental horsepower or gumption or whatever it takes to figure everything out." If you're not used to asking questions a lot, it can be a bit of an ego hit to start doing so. You want to look and feel so smart that you don't need any help at all.

As the 1960s TV spy series *The Prisoner* put it, "Questions are a burden on others." This is technically true, and frequently they are also an interruption. No one wants to feel like he's placing undue burdens on others, especially on near strangers with whom he is still trying to establish working relationships.

To help people through this, I directly set the expectation with new hires that they should inundate their peers with requests. If they ask multitudes of questions, they will get up to speed more rapidly as well as create opportunities for communication and bonding—after all, getting someone to talk about their work is surest way to get them to talk at all, and most everyone seems to enjoy it. I tell new hires to keep stepping it up until I start to get complaints that no one can get any work done for all the asking. This is usually interpreted as a joke (it's not, really), but it gets the point across.

Introductory Documentation

An "onboarding wiki" of some sort is a must for any team, but all such documentation gets old and crusty and must be reviewed and corrected from time to time. The best person to review and update documentation is one who needs to use it to understand the system: the new hire herself. She has the most incentive and time to confirm, experiment, and integrate knowledge across different sources, so she is the most likely person to spot errors.

"Leave it much better than you found it, so the next onboard is easier and grateful." New hires will have a lot of empathy for the next person to come along, who will have to deal with whatever scanty and incorrect onboarding materials they started with, providing extra motive to be thorough. If you set a pattern of having the most recently onboarded team member mentor new hires, they have even greater incentive to upgrade the documents, scripts, and other materials so everyone's future work is easier.

Integration Plan

Working directly with the new employee will help with a great start, and you can do more to ensure success by also building and executing on a second plan: a plan for *integrating* the employee. This plan lays out how you will guide the team into a cohesive state or returning to a cohesive state, encourage camaraderie, bring this new person into the rhythm and pattern of the work, and otherwise set up a high probability of success.

Social Integration

Human social structures are in constant adaptation and negotiation, even when there's no particular outside force acting on them. A well-functioning team mostly settles into a pattern, but it's not static. The best case may be meta-stable, but—stable or chaotic—introducing new people into a team causes an upset. When there is a change, new opportunities open and old ones close. Everyone naturally and usually subconsciously reevaluates where they are in the social network and how they relate to the new person as well as to everyone else. The resettling process of the disturbed social web causes uncertainty, anxiety, and generalized stress across the entire team.

You can predict how a team will react to new members by how insular they are. If they have developed an us-versus-them attitude, newcomers are going to have to prove they aren't one of "them," and negative proofs are notoriously difficult. Teams with a noticeable openness toward working with others, that are new, or that have many new members will tend to welcome newcomers. They have developed an empathy response that quickens adaptation.

Preparing for the most likely scenario, practicing inclusiveness and egalitarianism, and arranging for teamwork and morale events will give the social network an opportunity to settle into a comfortable new dynamic. Sometimes it will start to settle into an unhealthy pattern, which you'll have to notice and disturb again on purpose.

Ostracism, attack, complaining, and resentment are clear signs of an unsuccessful social integration that you must take immediate action to correct. They can all be addressed with counseling, resetting expectations, and other standard approaches if you notice and treat the problem early. Failing to do so quickly can cost you a new hire with an early resignation or low productivity, or even kill the team. Most people are either unaware of their real attitudes toward others or are reluctant to discuss them, so it is critical to watch and listen carefully to how team members communicate with each other for the first few months.

Business Integration

Developers who understand the purpose of the products they create are substantially more likely to build useful products, interpret instructions and specifications favorably to customers and strategic plans, and select more effective options when dealing with the dozens of micro-decisions we all make every day.

Fully top-down management hasn't worked since the days of the big railroads. Knowledge workers like developers must understand the business milieu, including customers, products, competitors, market shifts, and—to the extent possible and known—the company's vision and roadmap.

New hires should use the product, meet customers, and talk with product management and marketing about how they see the products now and in the future. They should ask what forces inspired existing features and spawned the resulting technical structure, the next major customers the company wants to acquire and why, and who influences what happens next and where the product evolves. Tell new hires to do this and whom to talk to, and give them time to do it. It's possible that other team members could use a refresher as well. The business changes continuously and developers can maintain a narrow span of attention for a long time—a great asset while coding, but not as a permanent mode of engagement.

Technical Integration

Learning technologies and development environments is a core capability for engineers, so it's often not necessary to go into great detail and depth in planning a technical indoctrination. They will learn it all anyway, and since you hire fantastic engineers and great collaborators, they will be up to speed surprisingly quickly.

What you do need to provide to new developers is discussion and briefing time with current, well-informed team members. Engineers with broad or detailed knowledge and new hires need to spend many hours together at whiteboards and monitors to get the necessary information about tools, technologies, environments, architectures, patterns, historical perspective, and plans. Scheduling a few review sessions to get started—and get team members used to describing their work and collaborating—has worked marvelously for me.

Project Management Integration

Developers need to know how the team and organization plans and executes on projects. I've not found it necessary to focus on indoctrinating developers into a team's project management process. They will be swept along with everyone else, and my teams' processes are usually protean enough that it's better to just be in the middle of it all than try to grasp it from an outside or documentation perspective.

If your team uses a stable, consistent, documented, and formalized project management process, it's even less necessary to explicitly teach its operation to developers. If they can see all the parts (and you really should make sure they can), they will understand the process with little effort. All source code is just process description, after all.

Productivity Impact

Bringing new people onto a team has several effects: it upsets existing team balance, creates new communication paths, and obliges team members to train and mentor. This has the net effect of reducing total productivity for the short to medium term.

You should expect the productivity to dip and then slowly recover, then slowly exceed previous productivity levels. Introducing multiple new team members within a short time span will have a nonlinear, exaggerated effect. That's inevitable, and the best you can do is prepare for it, talk about it, and account for it. Make sure the team and your customers understand how the productivity will dip even as the total effort increases. No person should feel like an underperformer when they are not.

Communications Impact

It's a truism that larger groups require more total communications than smaller groups, so adding team members will definitely lower the team's ability to do things other than communicate.

If you treat the communication pattern of a group of coworkers as an abstract network, with team members as nodes, you could model it as a complete graph with all nodes connected to all others. For a small team working closely together, it's literally true that everyone can and does talk with everyone else. Adding a new node (team member) adds communication paths geometrically; for instance, a three-member team has three paths, a four-member team has six paths, and a five-member team has ten.

In larger teams, many potential lines of communication are used rarely and incidentally. Take out these weak links, and organization networks look a lot sparser than complete graphs. Adding a team member here does not cause a geometric increase in total communication paths, but neither should it be ignored. Smaller teams are accustomed to including everyone with everything; as the team grows, it will inevitably need to shift its communication pattern from a complete graph to a sparser one.

Exactly where this cultural shift is needed is up to you and your team, but every new team member brings your team closer to needing a new communications model—meetings with subteams instead of everyone, specialized mailing lists, multiple scrums, team leads, and so on. The transition can be tough for a team, and they will handle it better with your foresight and guidance.

Briefing Your Team

Because you cleverly involved as much of your team as possible in the hiring process, some or all of them have a basic familiarity with the candidate already. They will have shared some impressions with the folks who didn't get to participate deeply, but you probably still have to do some kind of introduction.

Any existing team will brace for impact and the resulting changes. That's stressful, so you might want to reassure them that the new hire was chosen for depth of technical capability (just like they were) and how likely they are to fit into the team and be productive (just like they were). Life will obviously be better now! Well, maybe not so obviously. You should at least say so, and you can back it up with the compelling reasons you decided to make an offer to the new hire in the first place.

This is a good opportunity to share your onboarding plan and ask for comment.

Check-In

It costs nothing and it's reassuring to ask candidates whether they have had any trouble for the first few times you meet privately. Is the work what she expected it to be? Does she have the tools, contacts, knowledge, and skills she needs to be successful? Is anything off-kilter, or are any subtle problems with the team developing? Is she glad she joined the team?

These are easy signals to gather with direct questions. I ask them regularly for at least three to six months, because it forces critical thought about the experience so far. If there's a need for change, detecting it up front and acting soon is cheaper and easier than finding out later.

Antipatterns and Pitfalls

Three key patterns of manager behavior will harm a new employee and set her up for failure: abandoning her, presenting her as a savior, and failing to account for her specific needs and circumstance.

Abandonment

Some developers fail to thrive because they do not receive deserved attention at onboarding time. Normally found in groups run by absentee managers, this also occurs when starting under difficult or unusual circumstances. It may be a team-wide or company-wide crunch time, many hires coming on board at once, or any other situation that spreads a manager's attention thinly. It can happen quietly, as when, owing to shyness or pride, new engineers fail to ask for help, even if they realize they need it.

If you are too busy to onboard someone properly, or you're not going to be around because of vacation or travel, don't start someone. Hurry it, delay, or—if you must (perhaps you fell ill unexpectedly)—arrange for another manager or helpful coworker to assist and monitor the onboarding process as best as can be done.

Golden Child Syndrome

Presenting or just treating a new hire as a savior will leave a sour taste in everyone's mouth. Maybe you're bringing on a new hire for just that purpose—to save a project or raise standards—but treating a new engineer this way will almost guarantee alienation, particularly if you have established a pattern of bringing in one "savior" after another. In any case, you end up sending the clear message that everyone else has failed you.

People should rightly be treated differently based on their needs and contributions, but obvious favoritism is poisonous.

They're All the Same

Repeating what worked last time is easy, natural, and prone to failure. Each engineer will respond to the strain and challenge of starting a new job in a different way and encounter unique problems, so they need careful monitoring and consideration.

Some engineers will look and act like founding team members a week into the job, and others will seem to be still getting their sea legs around the systems after six months. Neither may be exactly what they appear to be: Expressions of confidence are not the same as actual capabilities. Not only does each engineer need a different onboarding approach; each needs a different assessment of the results.

I keep a chart listing each engineer and my assessment of their familiarity with different parts of the technology and business. Thinking about each intersection forces me to evaluate the engineers in one area at a time, which makes them easier to profile, and I don't have to rely on a gut feeling of where they are or take their attitudes at face value.

Employee as Customer   A theme of this book is that you as a hiring manager need to treat candidates as customers, to see the world as if through their eyes so you can study and improve your hiring process. That perceptual mode doesn't have to end at hiring—and it shouldn't.

Your developer is still your customer. You have explicit and implicit responsibilities to make her work productive and her experience more than tolerable, and your payment for this service is the phenomenal output that only the best-managed developers can produce.

Keep providing effective management, protecting and assisting, and your developer-customer will keep producing. Go off track, or deliver a substandard service, and the developer will start shopping around.

Best of luck.

Sample Question Plan and Interviewer Book

Sample Question Plan

A question plan like the example in Table A-1 is the set of questions your interviewing team plans to ask to measure a candidate across the capabilities you care about. It's not necessary to have an explicit plan, to list every question or sort of evidence you want to gather, or to follow exactly the plan you make. Building a plan has value as an exercise, and a documented plan can be used in training or as a guide to set up a new interviewing process.

Table A-1. Example Question Plan for SDE Interview

Capability	Questions
Coding	Write a method to count the number of LED segments necessary to display an arbitrary integer number. (Moderately difficult)
Coding	Write a method to draw a line one pixel at a time given a starting point and ending point, and a method for drawing a pixel. `void drawLine(int x1, int y1, int x2, int y2)` (Hard)
Coding	Write a method that returns any terminal value from any path of maximum length through a binary tree. `int getDeepValue(Node node)` (Moderately difficult)
Collaborating	Think of the last specific incident in which you had a major disagreement with a colleague. Tell me the context and circumstance, what you disagreed about, and how it was ultimately resolved.
Designing	Design the API for a service that must negotiate throttling with a load balancer. (Calibrating difficulty)
Designing	Design a memory allocator that parcels out pieces of memory on request from a contiguous block and allows callers to return memory. (Hard)
Estimating	How long will it take to write unit tests for the method `double power(double x, double y)` which raises its x argument to the y power? (Easy)
Gathering requirements	I'd like a plug-in for my email client that warns me before I send a message with curses in it. What do you need to know before you can build it?
Learning	What was the most challenging technology you had to learn to use for your work? How did you go about mastering it?
Selecting tasks	Consider this scenario. You find yourself working alone one day, and three critical bugs are discovered almost simultaneously and sent to you. All of them affect live production systems. How do you decide which of them to work on first?

Interviewer Book

Keeping notes on your interviewing team, such as the example in Table A-2, gives you the ability to optimize their performance over time and select the best interviewers for any particular candidate—in the sense that they will provide the fairest interview and the most critical and insightful feedback. Using it as a guide, you won't accidentally stack an interview with all inexperienced interviewers, for example, or heavily load it with ones you know are incurably biased. As with any table of personal notes, you may want to keep some columns private and share others.

Table A-2. Example Interviewer Book

Name	Role	Experience	Specialization	Notes
Jillian	Sr SDE	90 interviews	SDE, SDET	Generous
Johann	Sr SDE	45 interviews	SDE	Fair
Joanna	SDE	55 interviews	SDE, SDET	Negative
Jules	SDET	8 interviews	SDET	Biased against junior SDETs

In the example provided, you may want to ensure that Jules has more opportunities to conduct interviews, and perhaps pair him up with Jillian so he is exposed to a more experienced and more generous viewpoint.

Sample Candidate Guide

A Guide to ExampleCorp's Interview Process

Dear Candidate,

This document briefly describes the experience you should expect during the application process.

First, thanks for your interest! We're glad to know of your interest in ExampleCorp in general and our team in particular. For skilled and ambitious people, this is a great place to work in many ways. Perhaps chief among those is our culture and its embodiment in us and our behaviors: customer focus, great engineering principles, delivering results, and so on. We have some seriously cool technology and technical challenges, too.

Here is an outline of the basic steps of the process and what you should see at each stage. This is a work in progress—this document as well as our evolving application process. It's possible we will make an error or two—please be patient with us and we hope you understand that we reach for the stars and sometimes don't quite make it (the first few times, anyway). *Ad astra per ardua!*

Your Résumé

Your résumé is an important document. You should and probably do put considerable thought and care into it. There are guides and books and professional services that help with creating a great résumé. We won't try to compress all that, but here are a couple of key points you may want to consider.

Tell us what you want to do. One sentence may do the trick, something like "I want a job as a software engineer." Succinct is fine; elaborate if you like or want to be more specific. It's not always obvious to a reader, and a modicum of clarity may save us all some time.

We care most about what you personally have done. Describe projects, to be sure—but when you do so, describe your actual involvement. What were your direct responsibilities? What actions did you take? A positive outcome is of course nice to see. A learning experience (failure) . . . well, you learned something! Especially, please help us understand why your work was valuable. Of course it was! We would like to know how or why.

Education takes many forms. Tell us what you've learned, whether through classical school curricula, postgraduate work or advanced degrees, or relevant professional development. Tell us what's relevant and helps us understand you and how it makes you likely to succeed here.

For software engineering, we tend to focus (but not exclusively) on core capability. We don't know what specific technologies, methods, or systems we'll need to employ later. Tell us what you've worked on and worked with, so we know you can develop deep skills and have essentially relevant exposure. But there's no need to list dozens of technologies and acronyms. Keep anything mentioned in the job descriptions you care about; otherwise, list the core stuff, and mention that there's much more if you like.

In engineering, technical accomplishments are important. Go ahead and list your patent numbers and published papers.

Also, keep up-to-date contact information right on your résumé. Multiple redundant means are fine; phone numbers, email addresses, and so on. Sometimes one or more will stop working—help us out by giving us options. If we can't find you, more's the pity.

What will we do with your résumé?

It is sent to one or more hiring managers for review. If it does not have basic qualifications, it may be passed on to a different manager—one with requisitions you may be a fit for. Your résumé may be rejected at this point and not proceed further.

If the résumé meets our qualifications, you are now a candidate and the hiring manager will ask for a screening call. This can happen directly or through a recruiter if your résumé was submitted through an agency.

The Phone Screen

The point of the phone screen is to avoid all of us spending time and energy on in-person interviews that are unlikely to succeed. It's not an exact science, but it's a relatively efficient way to qualify candidates without investing large amounts of time in every applicant.

We'll try to schedule the call. Give us multiple near-future options—the more we have, the quicker we can talk. Why not do it soon? The future waits for no one! You may get one or two screens, depending on the outcome of the first and the team's policy. We're trying new things all the time. Indeed, your experience may well vary from this or any other description as we reengineer the recruiting process.

At the agreed-on date and time, we will call you. It's an interview. You will need a quiet place to talk and something to write with. For some teams and positions we'll ask you to have an Internet-ready computer so we can ask you to do some online coding. In this case you'll get a link to the web tools from us ahead of time.

If you haven't had technical screens before, you can learn about them online, where people talk about technical screens with many companies such as Amazon and Microsoft. Probably most of it is accurate. No guarantees, though. Here's what we can tell you.

It's going to take an hour or less—sometimes as short as a few minutes.

Your interviewer is an ExampleCorp employee who conducts phone screens. This is a person in a related role or position: the hiring manager or a hiring manager nearby in the organization. The interviewer has had training and practice, sometimes a lot of practice. We have a high hiring bar and take recruiting seriously. You want to work with the best, too, so we are sure we're in agreement that this is important.

There is a chance you will be talking with someone on a different team, maybe a very different team. It means we're trying to get you an interview more quickly than we could schedule a team member. Don't worry about this, because we generally do our phone screens against a sort of platonic ideal: a candidate and skills in isolation, so to speak, of the actual day-to-day job on the actual team. Once we hire a great employee, we hold onto them as long as is appropriate and mutually beneficial. This may span many projects, many technologies, and several teams over time. We're hiring for the long haul.

The interviewer has several questions for you. The goal is to learn about you and your capabilities. This will be as objective and fair as possible, and there are a variety of "correct" answers to most questions. Some will be specific, some are vague. All are designed to learn about your approach to problem solving as well as fundamental knowledge in your field. For engineering positions, the topics include but are not limited to object-oriented design, data structures, algorithms, computer science fundamentals, and coding.

We will definitely ask you to write code for us. It's a bit unnatural to code "over the phone"; we know that, and we make allowances for it. But we must ask you to code. The problems won't be extremely hard, but expect moderate difficulty. Be prepared to develop and reason about algorithms as well.

General phone screen tips may be available online.

The interviewer will take notes, either quietly on paper or typing on a computer. After the interview, you'll get another call from a recruiter.

At this point, you may be politely thanked for your time. Unfortunately, we might not have much to tell you about why. For reasons you can probably imagine, many companies are reticent to give extensive feedback about interviews (though you can be assured we considered everything carefully). If this happens, consider the interview carefully yourself. Learn what you can from the experience, build your skills, and apply again in several months. We will be here.

If you have a second phone screen, much the same thing will happen as the first time, but with a different interviewer. This interviewer will have different questions and will try to cover approximately the same topics, particularly any that were not adequately covered the first time for any reason.

Three things can happen now. You may be politely thanked for your time, as after the first screen. You may be invited to come in to interview in person. Or you may be asked to do a third phone screen. We try not to keep you doing phone screens forever. It's rare and probably our fault. Alternately, we may want to evaluate you for a different role, which may have competencies we haven't explored yet.

At this point you may be invited to interview in person. Congratulations! Many people do not get an interview due to fit and capability. A recruiter will extend this invitation and work out a date with you. Sooner is better, of course!

The In-Person

If you need to arrange long-distance travel, your recruiter will work this out with you. (Welcome to Seattle!) You'll get a time and place to show up.

Your interview will consist of a series of meeting people, usually two at a time, who will ask you questions. Again, we're doing this to learn about you. By observing and talking with us, you'll have a chance to learn about us as well. (Consider that most of our interviewers will have an hour with you; you'll have several hours with us.)

Keep calm and carry on. We're likely to ask you difficult technical and behavioral questions. You don't have to ace every question to do well overall.

You will have the chance to ask questions. Prepare a few that probe topics you care about and that will help you make a decision about a potential offer. If you don't get this opportunity, tell your recruiter. We'll set up a call or follow-up visit with a hiring manager.

There is a substantial chance we will send you home early. This is not necessarily a failure on your part. We make a judgment call after each interview about whether to continue. Sometimes it is simply obvious that we will not make an offer and no upcoming interview will change that. In this case, we try to save both of us some time and energy for other projects.

General in-person interview tips can be found online.

Be sure to get a validation if you parked. It's on us. Thank you very much for coming, and we hope you had a great experience while you were here! If you did not have a great experience, we implore you to provide us feedback about this. As wage earners we interview, too—that's how we got here. You're a customer and every customer deserves excellent attention.

Next you'll hear from a recruiter, who may thank you politely for your time, suggest an alternate position to apply for, or offer you a job. If it didn't work out, then consider the experience carefully, build your skills, and try again later. On the other hand, you may find us not to your liking.

We make offers conservatively, erring on the side of no offer—so we sometimes fail to hire otherwise qualified people. The upside is that we rarely accidentally hire people who are not qualified and not fun to work with. That's not a lot of consolation for those caught in a conservative no-offer situation, but it is reality.

The Offer

You might get an offer. Consider any offer you get (from anyone) carefully. Look at compensation, opportunity, and all the factors that matter to you. And, you know, take it. ☺

Sample Phone Screen Transcript

[Dial number: 1-800-DRUIDIA[1]]

Patrick: Hello, this is Patrick calling from ExampleCompany for Roxanne.

Roxanne: Yes, this is Roxanne. Pleased to meet you!

▨ **Comment**   Make sure you're talking to the right person.

Patrick: Wonderful. You were expecting my call today?

Roxanne: Yes, at this time.

Patrick: I am a software development manager at ExampleCompany and I'm calling to do a technical phone screen for a software development engineer position. Is that what you were expecting?

Roxanne: Yes, that and the Spanish Inquisition. You never know.

---

[1] *Spaceballs* (dir. Mel Brooks; MGM, 1987), act I, ccene iv.

> ▦ **Comment**   This introduces you and sets up the context for the call. If you get a "no" in response, find out what you can, apologize for the confusion, and get off the phone. Then tell someone about the problem.

Patrick: Let me start by telling you something about ExampleCompany. We rock. We're hiring a bunch of rocket scientist software engineers so we rock harder. We're building out and building up!

Roxanne: Yes, that's what I expected.

Patrick: Great. This is going to take up to forty-five minutes. Still a good time to talk? We can reschedule if it's not.

Roxanne: Sure, I have this time set aside, I can go up to an hour today.

> ▦ **Comment**   Candidates sometimes complain later that they were under some sort of duress— worrying about a personal or work issue, ill, or something like that. This may be a legitimate concern, but they should also feel free to ask for a reschedule. I would rather reschedule a few times than misread a candidate. It's hard enough to evaluate them as it is, and candidates will appreciate the flexibility.

Patrick: Okay! So here's how we'll do this. I'm going to ask you several technical questions to gauge your overall proficiency, including a couple of coding problems, and spend a few minutes answering any general questions you have toward the end. Ready?

Roxanne: I was born ready.

Patrick: You won't need to use a computer or access the Internet for this interview. Do you have something to write with?

Roxanne: I shall improvise with this 1975 lead "goblin archer" figurine and some fast-food receipts.

> ▦ **Comment**   They may need to find something to write with. Now they know they are going to need to write something.

Patrick: Good. We'll start with a coding question. There's no set way to do this and no strict time limit; you can listen to the question, do it quietly and tell me the answer, or talk out loud as you go, whatever you're comfortable with.

Also, don't hesitate to ask for clarification or help. None of my questions are meant to be tricks. What I'm looking to get, at the end, is for you to read me essentially working code.

▦ **Comment** Coding on the phone is unnatural enough. This preface seems to disarm most of the nervousness candidates bring in to the interview.

Patrick: Write a method in C, C++, C#, or Java that takes four separate integer parameters and returns the value of the largest one.

▦ **Comment** This is the Trivial Coding Question. Its purpose is to warm up good candidates and weed out bad ones. Yes, not everyone with ten years of development experience can solve this. Yes, I know that's really sad.

Roxanne: That's not so difficult. I'll assume you pass the integers in as an array.

▦ **Comment** Candidates make this assumption all the time, no matter how clearly you pronounce "separate integer parameters." Chalk it up to phone entropy.

[Two minutes pass]

Alright, here's my solution.

```
public int max(int ints[])
{
   int max = -1;
   foreach(int i in ints)
     if (i > max)
       i = max;
   return max;
}
```

▦ **Comment** There are several ways to write the function correctly. Here's how to evaluate the answer you get: it must *work*. It must *not use collections*. It must *not use an array*. It's no problem if the candidate reaches for an ArrayList or something, throws in the parameters, calls .Sort() and returns the last one. Just say, "That works, but pretend you don't have access to collections," and make them solve it like civilized people.

If the candidate does *not* solve this problem in *less than six minutes*, get off the phone. Say something like this: "This position is going to require substantial fluency with coding. At this point I don't think you have that fluency, so I'm going to save us some time and end our conversation here. I have enjoyed speaking with you, however, and very much appreciate your time." Then draw a big X through the résumé.

Patrick: I believe I see a problem in your code. Would you find and fix it for me?

[In a moment]

Roxanne: Yes, sorry, my assignment statement had *i* and *max* reversed.

Patrick: All right, that's logically correct. There is a small problem, though. I expect to pass the integer arguments in as separate parameters, not in an array.

Roxanne: Okay. Then what I'll do is create an array up front, *ints*, and populate the array with the parameters.

Patrick: Yes, that will work. However, it does just sort of patch the original solution rather than rethink it, and there's a fair amount of unnecessary work going on. Can you refactor this method for efficiency?

[One minute passes]

Roxanne: Very well. I don't know if this is the most efficient possible solution, but it's straightforward.

```
public int max(int a, int b, int c, int d)
{
    int max = a;
    if (b > max)
      max = b;
    if (c > max)
      max = c;
    if (d > max)
      max = d;
    return max;
}
```

Patrick: Sounds good. Okay, let's move to a slightly more complex coding problem. I'd like you to write a method that computes a discrete Fourier transform over an arbitrary sequence.

Roxanne: What??

Patrick: Just kidding. Write a method that finds the maximum depth of a binary tree, given a root node. The signature is int getDepth(Node node) where Node is a data structure that contains a Node `left` and a Node `right`, either or both of which could be null. If this is not a perfectly straightforward question, I am happy to clarify and explain what I mean.

Comment   This is the Moderate Difficulty question. Its purpose is to test the candidate's ability to reason with data structures and build algorithms using recursion. You can solve this with iteration. If the candidate gives you an iterative solution in less than ten minutes, call me!

Roxanne: Is this a binary search tree? Is it balanced?

Patrick: Maybe and maybe.

Roxanne: Can I assume the existence of a massless elephant?

Patrick: If it helps you solve the problem.

Roxanne: I've always wanted to assume that. Tree problems often lend themselves to recursion, so I'll look at that first. Let's see ... each node only knows that it exists, that it has children, and whatever its children tell it. If we start with the opening method signature, then the children report the maximal depth at their own level. Hmm. I'm going to draw a tree to help me think.

Comment   In reality this question frequently trips up candidates, particularly very senior ones, who haven't thought about trees in a long time. They may spend a little more time on this problem, but they still need to solve it. If the candidate doesn't make progress, offer a couple of hints such as these:

Suggest drawing an example tree.

Suggest a recursive approach.

Suggest looking at the stopping condition of the recursion: what the last function will return.

Suggest not using a static variable. It's really not needed and it's just tripping you up.

[Time passes]

Roxanne: I have a working approach. A method is called with the root node. If there is no root node, there is no tree, it has no depth, and it returns 0. If the root node has no children, its depth is 1 and it returns that. However, if it has children, what we care about is the maximal depth—whichever child reports greater depth. The node then includes itself and passes that maximum value + 1 upwards. Here, let me express it in code.

```
public int depth(Node node)
{
   if (node == null)
     Return 0;
   Return max(depth(node.left),
     depth(node.right)) + 1;
}
```

▨ **Comment**   Usually candidates give a messier answer, with temporary variables and what not. Sometimes a candidate will make a helper function that takes a second parameter such as "int maxlevel." It's possible to make that work.

Here's how to evaluate their answer: it must *work*.

Patrick: Okay, I think that algorithm will work. I'd like you to reason about the time and space complexity of your algorithm. Let's start with time complexity, in Big O notation.

Roxanne: Well, it's clearly in the complexity class "quasi-polynomial time," at $O(\log^2 n)$.

▨ **Comment**   This question is used to probe the candidate's understanding of the algorithm they just used as well as the ability to reason about the efficiency of the code they write.

Sometimes candidates already know the answer to the maxDepth question (or any other question you just asked), and this follow-up question sometimes reveals that prior knowledge; a total failure to answer means their answer to the previous question is, unfortunately, useless.

Patrick: What??

Roxanne: Just kidding. We need to examine each node of the tree exactly once; so we're going to run in $O(n)$ time.

▨ **Comment**   A common failure path is to say it's $O(\log n)$ time. This is because they are stuck thinking of a binary tree as a binary search tree even though you just told them it isn't. It's okay. Take a deep breath. Your brain malfunctions under stress, too. Ask them to explain why and you will have the opportunity to correct that assumption.

Patrick: That sounds like good reasoning. How about space complexity? It's not a common concept, shall I elaborate?

Roxanne: Lay on, MacDuff.[2]

🔳 **Comment** This tests the candidate's application of familiar concepts in novel situations. She will also need to understand stack and memory allocation, of course.

Patrick: I shall. Space complexity is like time complexity. With time, we want to know about the worst-case scenario of time consumed by the algorithm in relation to the size of the input *n*. With space, we want to know the worst-case scenario of space consumed (maximally, at any time) by the algorithm in relation to input size *n*.

Roxanne: Um … we only allocate space during our recursion, so what we really need to understand is how deep our recursion can get based on the size of the tree. A tree can degenerate to one node per level, so, in the worst case, we recurse *n* times. Space complexity is O(n) just like time.

Also, I'm going to go ahead and take the opportunity to word-drop "tail recursion" because it makes me sound sophisticated.

Patrick: You are correct, sir.

Roxanne: Madam.

Patrick: Er, sorry.

Roxanne: No problem. Please go on.

🔳 **Comment** Politeness goes a long way. There's a power imbalance between interviewer and interviewee; there is no need to further exaggerate the effect on the interview.

Patrick: So what is tail recursion?

Roxanne: I'm sorry, it's actually beyond my experience. Something to do with not accumulating stack frames for some kinds of recursions, in languages that support it.

Patrick: I see. It's time to ask you a design question. Please design the API for a spell checker. It will be a shared component for two products, including a word processor and a spreadsheet program. As much fun as it is to design the

---

[2]*Hamlet*, act V, scene viii.

implementation for a spell checker, what I need from you is just an API. The engineers who will use it expect an object-oriented interface, so in the end what I need from you is the classes and methods that you'll present to them.

Roxanne: Let me make sure I understand. This is a spell checker that will be a library or part of a library that both products will include—it's not a service? And should I assume a particular language for the API, or IDL, or . . . ?

Patrick: Pick an object-oriented language you're familiar with, as you did with the previous questions. Yes, assume a statically linked component, or the equivalent for the language.

Roxanne: Huh. Well, let me think about spell checkers I have known and loved. . . . They have come a long way. These days they tend to detect errors immediately, automatically correct common mistakes, and suggest corrections when it's not totally obvious what word is meant. And, speaking of meaning, sometimes they worry about grammar, too. Which of these are in scope for this spell checker?

Patrick: Glad you asked. You've probably noticed that there's a distinct shortage of grammar checking in the world, but for this question, consider both suggestions and grammar out of scope.

Roxanne: Right. Let me draw on my paper for a minute.

[Time passes]

Roxanne: Wait, you said there were two different products using this API. Do they have different requirements? Different usage patterns?

Patrick: They certainly do! The spreadsheet team expects to have lots of small nonwords, like you find on Twitter, and the word processing team wants to check large documents at load time, say 50,000 words at once. Both of them do want to check for errors "as they go."

Roxanne: Ah, interesting. And now that I think about it, there's more than one language. I'm going to assume that the callers will want to specify which language to check against. Stop me if I'm wrong about that. So, here's my preliminary sketch of a design. Callers send in either one or many words and the library says yes or no to all of them. There should be a batch interface to support many words without round-trip method calls. I'll keep it really simple and make it just as complex as I need.

```
Class Spellcheck
{
    Spellcheck(Language l);
    Bool checkword(String word);
    Bool[] checkwords(String[] words);
}
```

The single word check is obvious, but let me explain the batch interface. First, the caller has to decide what words to send. Who knows what internal representation they use for their documents? So I'm going to ask for a string, which is a simple, baseline data structure to represent each word. The service returns an array of yes/no Boolean answers for each word: yes, it's spelled correctly; or no, it's not. As an aside, I'll go philosophical—or call it linguistic—and say that the spell checker doesn't really check spelling. It doesn't even know if you're giving it words or just garbage characters. It just checks to see whether it recognizes the string as one in a dictionary specific to the language.

Patrick: A sensible distinction, though the caller probably doesn't care about that. You mentioned a dictionary but not how that's related, and you referenced a class or structure called "Language." Tell me more about those.

Roxanne: I guess I really mean "culture" more than language, because that's not specific enough. What counts as a word depends on where you live and who you talk to, right? So that should be a "culture" object passed into the constructor, and I'm going to lean on a standard native library to provide that infrastructure rather than creating my own. I don't want callers to have to worry about making or loading dictionaries, so I'll make that an implementation detail internal to the library.

Patrick: Some library users might care. One other question about this: Do you expect callers to keep one of these Spellcheck objects "on file," or build new ones when they need to check words?

Roxanne: On file. It could take time to load dictionaries, and this is an implementation detail, but I'd want to cache results so it was more efficient over time for callers like word processors. It would work either way, but keeping one around would work better for callers. I'm not sure how I could indicate that in my API, though.

Patrick: Perhaps through a factory pattern of some sort. Anyway, those were all the questions I had for you today, so thanks for putting up with the barrage. Do you have any questions about the job, the company, the team, me, the weather? I'll answer whatever we have time for and that is not actually confidential.

■ **Comment**   Never write a check . . .

Roxanne: Why is it so cold?

Patrick: Arctic air from the central continent is entering the region through the Columbia River Valley and the Fraser Gap.

■ **Comment**   . . . that you can't cash.

Roxanne: Why should I work for your company? Google and other great employers are hiring!

Patrick: We have substantial engineering challenges, solid funding, brilliant coworkers, and free ice cream.

Comment If you have time, gush! If the candidate throws you a doozy ("what do you like least about your job?") then improvise but be *honest*. People know when you're not. Especially your mom. You may want to call her up and apologize.

Patrick: I enjoyed our conversation today! I know your time is not free, so thank you for spending some of it with us. I'll share my notes with our recruiters and you should expect to hear back from us shortly. I hope you have a great rest of your day!

Roxanne: All righty!

Comment End the call on a positive note even if—especially if—it did not go well. The candidate is a customer, a fellow professional, and a human being. Be even more awesome than you would hope for if you were on the other end.

Your goal: The candidate hangs up smiling and feeling good about you and about us. Even if we don't move forward, the candidate refers her friends.

Sample Feedback for This Interview

Coding mixed. The candidate stumbled through the warm-up method. Didn't ask for clarification and had trivial initial bug. Patched it inefficiently rather than refactoring it. When prompted, she refactored quickly and effectively; the final solution was fine. Produced an elegant solution to the more complex method pretty quickly. Perhaps she anticipated the question beforehand and studied it explicitly?

The design was average to above average. Thought through the requirements, produced a simple solution that met major needs. The answer she gave was in the uppermost quartile.

[Copies of the candidate's code included in the feedback.]

Index

CPSIA information can be obtained at www.ICGtesting.com
Printed in the USA
LVOW090507171112

307759LV00004B/2/P